KNIFE EDGE

Malorie Blackman

First published 2004 by
Doubleday, a division of
Random House Children's Books
This Large Print edition published 2011 by
AudioGO Ltd
by arrangement with
Random House Children's Books

ISBN: 978 1405 664332

British Library Cataloguing in Publication Data available

Printed and bound in Great Britain by
CPI Antony Rowe, Chippenham and Eastbourne

*This book is dedicated with love
to Neil and Elizabeth
Who bring every colour of the rainbow
And more besides.*

*And a big thank-you to everyone
who asked,
'What happened next?'*

He who binds himself to a joy
Does the wingèd life destroy;
But he who kisses the joy as it flies
Lives in eternity's sun rise.

WILLIAM BLAKE

THE DAILY SHOUTER

www.dailyshouter.news.id   Wednesday 12th May

Nought Terrorist

Shot Dead

BY JON GRESHAM

Yesterday evening, a nought suicide bomber was shot dead as he entered Ackton Palace train station. He was found to be wearing a money belt packed with explosives. A police spokesman told the *Daily Shouter*, 'We had a tip-off that this terrorist planned to board the next commuter train and detonate his bomb once the train was underway. As it was rush hour, the consequences would've been devastating. This is typical of the cowardly acts we've come to expect from the Liberation Militia.'

A nought eyewitness stated, 'Four plain-clothed police officers opened fire the moment the man stepped onto the station concourse. He didn't stand a chance. People were screaming and running. It was terrifying—like something out of a film.' But as a police spokesman was quick to point out, 'Make no mistake, had we shouted a warning or alerted the terrorist to our presence, he would've immediately detonated his bomb, maiming and killing goodness only knows how many people. Better one dead nought terrorist than the deaths of dozens of innocent people including children.'

The Liberation Militia sent out a press release condemning the death of one of their members. 'This was nothing less than state-sanctioned murder. Our member wasn't even given the chance to surrender. Whilst these state atrocities continue, the war between Noughts and Crosses will never be over.'

Kamal Hadley, the Deputy Prime Minister gave his reaction to the outrage. 'These sub-human nought terrorists will never win. Their blatant disregard for life, be it nought or Cross, will ultimately be their undoing.'

Given the fact that Kamal Hadley's daughter, Persephone was kidnapped last year by the Liberation Militia and held for ransom, the Deputy Prime Minister's reaction showed remarkable restraint. Whilst a prisoner, Persephone Hadley was made pregnant by Callum McGregor, one of the nought terrorists who abducted her.

When Callum McGregor was hanged last year for kidnap and political terrorism, there was a

(continued on page 5)

RED

Pain

Anger

Rage

Blood

Tempests /Storms

Bullets

Uproar

Screams/Shouts

Loud

Fireworks/Bangs/Explosions

Birth

Whirling/Thrashing

Fire

Scarlet/Burgundy/Crimson/Pink

Betrayal

War

Hatred

one. Jude

'Oh, come on, Jude. My feet are killing me,' Morgan moaned.

'Tough!' I said from one of the two single beds in our hotel room. 'And keep watching out the window. We don't want any surprises.'

'I've been watching the traffic for the last three hours.'

'And you've got an hour to go, so shut up complaining,' I ordered. He was getting on my nerves and no mistake.

Morgan sighed and moved the dark-brown curtain slightly so he could continue to look past it to the street below. He took another swig from his can of lager, which had to be lukewarm by now—he'd been holding it for the last hour at least. I scowled at his back before turning my attention to the remote control in my hand and the telly in front of me. Five minutes of flicking later, I hadn't found a single thing worth watching. So much for that then. There was bugger all of any use on, so I plumped for some inane soap which required minimum brain power to follow. Which was just as well, because my mind, as always, was on other things.

Like Andrew Dorn.

He was my immediate priority now. He was the General's second-in-command, but if the information we'd been given was correct—and

each passing hour convinced me that it was—
he was also a traitor. It was thanks to him that
our kidnap of Sephy Hadley had gone so
spectacularly wrong. Thanks to his betrayal of
us, every member of my assigned Liberation
Militia cell had been killed or captured—all
except Morgan and me. The General didn't
know it but Andrew Dorn was working hand-
in-hand with the Cross authorities, particularly
with Kamal Hadley, the Cross MP who loathed
us noughts and everything we stood for. That's
why we'd decided to kidnap his daughter,
Sephy. Not just as a political statement, but to
hit Kamal Hadley where it'd really hurt. But
the whole operation had gone pear-shaped.

Thanks to Andrew Dorn.

And I had no idea where he was or how to
get to him.

The thought of a man like that so high up on
the Liberation Militia ladder—well, it made
my stomach turn over. How many others had
he betrayed? How many other men and
women had worn a tie of rope all thanks to
him? How I yearned to get hold of him. I
wouldn't need long. Three seconds with Mr
Dorn would be more than enough for what I
had in mind. We in the L.M. needed to do
something, anything to put the heart back into
our organization. Since my brother Callum's
death nothing had gone right. The police had
cracked down on us hard and offered huge
cash rewards to anyone giving them
information which would lead to the capture

and conviction of any one of us. The media called us ruthless terrorists. We're not. We're just fighting for what's right. Being born a nought shouldn't automatically slam shut myriad doors before you've even drawn your first breath. Being a nought shouldn't automatically make you a second-class citizen. What was it about our lighter skins that made the darker Crosses so afraid of us? So we're fighting for what's right. But that's not how the authorities saw it. It was open season on the Liberation Militia. No reasonable betrayal declined. And no doubt there was a nice little bonus to be had if they could hang us into the bargain.

We in the L.M. officially became the hunted whilst still trying to do a little hunting of our own. But the Cross authorities had made a big mistake killing my brother. Now Callum was a martyr and martyrs were far more dangerous. So many noughts had demanded reprisals for what they had done to Callum—and not just members of the Liberation Militia either. Not that I cared anything about that. Every night before I went to sleep, and every morning as soon as I woke up, I promised my brother that I'd make sure those responsible for his death would suffer. Every one of them.

But with all the Liberation Militia cells nationwide scattered to the four winds and desperately fighting for survival, it was hard to rest long enough to come up with some kind of long-term strategy. Long-term living had taken a back seat to short-term survival. Take that business with the so-called nought terrorist being shot dead at the station. A prime example of how the police were cracking down—hard. Our L.M. fighter didn't stand a chance. The police obviously had a new policy—shoot first and have a cup of tea afterwards. So here we were—Morgan and me—cooling our heels in a cheapish, three-storey hotel in a semi-dodgy area, but an area at least where we had friends. Morgan stirred his just-add-hot-water dinner in a plastic pot, still muttering under his breath. I ignored him. Sometimes he was hard work. More than once since our aborted kidnap attempt of Persephone Hadley, I had to remind myself that we were supposed to be friends. Mind you, living from shabby room to room, always on the move, always on the run, was enough to make anyone edgy.

But we'd finally been given another assignment. After months of almost total silence, we were being let back in from the cold. And our orders were to book into room fourteen and wait. So here we were, booked in for two days now and still waiting. I turned to pick up my newspaper from the bedside table, even though I'd already read it.

'We've got company,' Morgan said from his position beside the window.

He didn't need to say it twice.

'How many?'

'Two . . . no, three cars.'

If they could muster three police cars at the front of the hotel, no doubt there'd be more than one round the back.

'How did they know we were here?' Morgan asked, running to grab his holdall.

'Let's worry about that later when we're out of here,' I told him. *If* we got out of here . . . I grabbed my rucksack off my single bed and headed out behind Morgan.

We ran along the corridor to the fire exit. When I stayed in hotels and B&Bs, I always made sure that I was only a few rooms away from a fire exit for exactly this reason. Although we'd been told which room to occupy, luckily it was only three rooms away from the fire exit. Had we been set up? If so, why weren't we put further along the corridor where it'd be harder to escape? And why wait till we'd been in the hotel for two days to tell the police? Unless it'd been hoped that we'd relax and get careless. More of Andrew Dorn's handiwork? Morgan yanked open the fire exit door and leapt down the first set of concrete stairs, with me right behind him.

I pulled at Morgan's shirt and put a finger over my lips. Morgan froze. Beneath us came the unmistakable sound of footsteps, more than one pair, charging up to meet us. Every contingency covered. One of my questions was answered. I pointed upwards. Morgan and I turned and ran up the fire exit stairs instead of down, fast but silent. We raced up the stairs to the second floor.

Now what? Morgan was responsible for ensuring we had a contingency plan for every place we went. Time to see if he could plan worth a damn.

'Follow me,' Morgan hissed.

I had nothing else planned for the evening so I legged it after him. We sprinted along the corridor. Morgan came to a halt before room twenty-five. He banged on the door whilst I watched up and down the corridor, my hand already on the gun in my jacket pocket. It felt like ice beneath my fingertips, cold and hard. And reassuring. Whatever else happened, the hangman's noose would never kiss my throat.

The door opened almost immediately. Morgan raced inside, followed only a moment later by me. I shut the door and immediately stood to one side of it with my back against the wall. It wasn't unknown for the police to gun down an innocent door without warning, and tough luck if you were standing behind it. A muscled, middle-aged Cross man, with a moustache and short-cut hair, stood in the middle of the room watching us. He'd had sense enough to move out of the way when Morgan burst into his room. I put my ear to the door and listened. I couldn't hear anyone running, or walking for that matter, but I knew better than to let my guard down.

'They've gone to our room on the first floor,' I turned to whisper to Morgan. He nodded, but I was surprised to see that he didn't have his gun out. The Cross man was still watching us, but he didn't look scared. His expression didn't even make it to anxious.

'We've got to get out of here,' I said.

'Chauffeur and secretary?' asked the Cross.

'That OK with you, Chief?' Morgan asked me.

Scrutinizing the Cross in the room with us, I nodded. So this Cross was here to help us, was he? I didn't know his name and I didn't want to know it—but it was just as well Morgan had set up a backup plan. Chauffeur and secretary was one of the standards. The only trouble was, with the hotel being surrounded, I wasn't sure if it'd even work.

'I'm Dylan Hoyle,' said the Cross. He held out his hand. I didn't take it. Morgan started to until I glared at him, then his hand fell to his side. Dylan looked from Morgan to me and shrugged.

'I just thought—' Dylan began.

'You thought wrong,' I interrupted harshly.

'Fair enough,' Dylan shrugged again. 'You've both worked for me for the last eighteen months. Your false papers are in my jacket pocket.' He took out the papers and handed them to us. 'You'd both better get a move on. We've got less than five minutes before they start checking every room in the hotel. Try to make yourselves look as much like the photos on the fake IDs as possible.'

'Do we stand a chance?' asked Morgan.

'Only if you do what I say,' said Dylan, adding as he turned to me, '*Exactly* what I say.

9

There are clothes in the wardrobe. You'd better get them on. Wigs and glasses are in the bathroom.'

Morgan and I were in a Cross's hands. Not a place I wanted to be, but we had no choice. Dylan Hoyle was a Cross. I didn't trust him, or any of them. And if he so much as twitched out of place, he wouldn't get the chance to do it twice.

two. Sephy

I held you in my arms, waiting to feel something. Anything. And I waited. And I waited. And nothing came. No pleasure. No pain. No joy. No anguish. No love. No hate. Nothing. I looked down into your dark-blue eyes, blue as an evening ocean and your eyes swallowed me up, as if you were waiting for me to . . . recognize you. I can't explain it any other way. But I didn't know you. I looked at you and you were a stranger. And I felt so guilty, because I still felt the same way about you as I did when you were inside me. I'd still trade all my tomorrows with you for one slice of yesterday with Callum. And that's not the way I'm supposed to feel. So that's what I'm made of now. Regrets and pure, unadulterated guilt.

'Why don't you see if she'll feed?' asked

Nurse Fashoda with a smile.

I didn't want to but she was watching me. And I didn't want her to guess what I was really feeling. New mothers aren't supposed to feel *nothing*.

'Do you have any bottles?' I asked doubtfully.

'That's not this hospital's policy. We don't provide bottles for babies unless there's a good medical reason and even then it has to be OK'd by a doctor,' Nurse Fashoda informed me, adding with slight disdain, 'Besides, bottles are for rich women so that they can hand their babies over to a nanny before they've had their first poo.'

The nurse regarded me pointedly as she spoke. Well, apart from the bit about being a woman and being rich, she'd got it absolutely right. At eighteen I felt nothing like a woman. Just the opposite. I was a frightened girl running barefoot on a knife edge.

'So how am I meant to feed her then?' I asked.

'Use what women fed their babies with long before bottles were invented,' said Nurse Fashoda, pointing to my breasts.

She wasn't joking either. I looked back down into your eyes, Callie, and you were still watching me. I wondered why you weren't crying. Babies cry all the time, don't they? So why didn't you? After a deep breath, I pulled down one side of my nightgown, too tired now to be embarrassed by Nurse Fashoda's

11

presence and too heartsick to care anyway. I tried to raise you up in my arms so that you'd be at the right level to feed. But you wouldn't latch on. I tried to turn your head towards my breast. 'Sephy, you're not screwing in a light bulb,' admonished Nurse Fashoda. 'Don't swivel her head like that. She's not a plastic doll. Turn her gently.'

'If I'm doing such a bad job, why don't you do it instead?' I said with belligerence.

'Because it doesn't work that way,' the nurse answered.

And as I looked at Nurse Fashoda, I realized in that moment just how much I didn't know about you, Callie, or any baby. You weren't some nameless, faceless abstract *thing* any more. You weren't a romantic ideal or some stick to beat my dad with. You're a real person. Someone who had to rely on me for everything.

And God, I've never felt so scared.

I looked down at you again and it hit me. Hard. And kept coming. Into my heart and straight out the other side. Callie Rose. You were . . . you are my daughter. My own flesh and blood. Half me, half Callum and one hundred per cent yourself. Not a doll or a symbol or an idea, but a real, new person with a new life.

And totally my responsibility.

Tears trickled down my cheeks. I tentatively smiled at you and even though my vision was a bit blurred, I'd swear you smiled back at me.

12

Just a little smile, but that was all it took. I tried again, turning you gently in my arms until your face was towards my breast. You latched on to me this time and immediately began to feed. It's just as well you knew what you were doing because I didn't have a clue. I watched you then because I couldn't tear my gaze away. I watched you feed with your eyes closed and one fist balled up and resting against my skin. I could smell you, smell us. I felt you take more from me than just milk. And with each breath we both took, the last nine months faded away into long ago and far away. But you didn't feed for very long. A couple of minutes, that's all.

'Try switching her to your other breast,' said Nurse Fashoda.

So I did, moving you round awkwardly like you were made of bone china. But you didn't want to feed any more. You lay on my chest, your eyes still closed, and just like that you went to sleep. And I closed my eyes and leaned back against the pillows behind me and tried to follow your lead. I felt rather than saw Nurse Fashoda try to pick you up. My eyes opened immediately, my arms wrapped around you instinctively.

'What're you doing?'

'I'm just going to put your baby in the cot at the foot of your bed. You've had a long labour and it's time for you to rest. You'll be no good to your daughter if you're dog-tired,' said Nurse Fashoda.

'Can't she sleep on my chest?'

13

'Our beds are too narrow. If she fell off, she'd hit the floor,' said Nurse Fashoda. 'You'll have to wait till you're at home in your emperor-sized bed before you can do that.'

I studied Nurse Fashoda, wondering at the antagonism in her voice.

'I wasn't criticizing,' I said.

'Look around,' Nurse Fashoda said. 'This is meant to be a community hospital but we don't get half the equipment or staff that a Cross hospital gets. Not too many Cross patients want to set foot in Mercy Hospital.'

'I'm here, aren't I?'

'Yes, but you're the only Cross in the maternity ward. And when you leave, you'll move back into your fancy house in your fancy neighbourhood and after a long, hot shower we'll all be forgotten.'

And just like that, I'd been assessed and judged. Nurse Fashoda didn't know the first thing about me but she'd taken one look at my face and now she reckoned she knew my whole life history—what had gone before and what was yet to come. I didn't tell her that the bed in my flat was narrower than the one I was now lying on. I didn't explain that my bedroom, bathroom and kitchen combined were about the size of this labour room I was in. No matter how much talking I did, Nurse Fashoda would never hear me. She'd only ever hear what she wanted to hear, what she already 'knew' to be true. I knew her type.

Besides, I was too weary to argue with her. I

14

watched her settle you down in your cot and the moment you were covered with the white, cotton blanket, I closed my eyes. But the instant Nurse Fashoda left the room, my eyes opened. I scrambled up onto my knees to look at you. I touched your cheek. I stroked your short, dark-brown hair. I couldn't take my eyes off you. Even when tears blurred my vision, I didn't take my eyes off you.

three. Jude

My wig was blond and long, down past my shoulders. Morgan had on glasses with black frames. I took the sunglasses and put them on, then pushed them up onto the top of my head until if and when needed. We changed out of our usual uniform of jeans and shirts and I now had on a cheap but effective dark-blue suit. Morgan wore dark grey trousers, a dark blue shirt and a long raincoat. Our old clothes were packed up in one of the medium-sized suitcases by the door. I didn't have time to check out the other suitcase.

'Tie your hair back in a pony-tail,' Dylan told me, handing me an elastic band.

Biting my tongue, I did as he said.

'I'd better take back the IDs,' said Dylan.

Morgan gave his back immediately. I was more reluctant.

15

'Each of you take a suitcase and walk behind me. Neither of you is to speak without looking at me for permission first. Is that clear?' asked Dylan.

Morgan nodded, already acquiescent. Subservience didn't come so easily to me. I was used to giving orders, not taking them. And as for doing what a dagger told me to, that stuck in my craw.

'You want to live, you'll do what I say,' Dylan said directly to me. 'You lose sight of the fact that I'm here to help you and we're all dead.'

'OK. Fine,' I spat out. 'Let's do this. But Dylan, you try to betray us, and you won't live to regret it.'

'Why would I betray you?' Dylan asked.

I didn't answer.

'Oh, I see. If I could work against my own kind then I can't be trusted by anyone—is that it?'

Jude's rule number two: *Never trust a Cross. Ever.*

'I suppose it doesn't occur to you that I can think the system just as unjust as you do,' Dylan continued.

'Is the system a bit unfair?' I mocked. 'You see that then, do you? How's the view from your warm, comfortable position on the inside?'

'I hate to interrupt the philosophical debate, but can we get the hell out of here?' Morgan hissed.

Dylan and I glared at each other. But each of

16

us backed off—for now. Dylan looked at each of us critically.

'Morgan, take that suitcase. Jude, take the other one. We've got one shot at this, so no foul-ups.'

Dylan went to the door first. He took a deep breath, then opened it. He sauntered out of the room and headed for the one lift in the middle of the corridor, with Morgan and me only a couple of steps behind him. As he pressed the button to call the lift, he began to whistle tunelessly to himself. I'll say one thing for him, he faked nonchalance really well. The lift arrived after a few seconds. We all stepped in. Dylan pressed the button for the basement, which led straight out to the small car park at the back of the hotel.

As the lift sped downwards, my heart began to beat a little louder, a little faster. My free hand snaked into my jacket pocket, reassured by the feel of my automatic gun inside. My gun had fourteen bullets in the magazine and one in the chamber and I had four loaded clips on me, one in each sock, one in my other jacket pocket and one tucked into my belt at the back. Meggie McGregor didn't raise any stupid children—just damned unlucky ones.

'Take your hands out of your pockets,' Dylan told me without turning his head.

I reluctantly did as I was told. The lift opened. We walked through the hotel delivery and storage area. On one side of us were metal and wooden crates and boxes, some stacked on

17

top of each other. On the other side were laundry bins full of dirty sheets and towels and wooden boxes, some filled with eggs and others with row upon row of sausages, covered only with cellophane. A mixture of smells assaulted my nose, most of them unpleasant. We made our way across the room to the double doors on the other side. Dylan pushed against one of the doors which led out to the car park. We walked out after Dylan, with no idea what we were getting ourselves into. A familiar feeling crept over me. A sense of suppressed panic and misplaced excitement. My adrenaline was definitely pumping. I decided that now was a good time to don my sunglasses. I pushed them down from the top of my head to cover my eyes.

'Excuse me, sir.' An armed dagger cop immediately came running up to us. Another one stood his ground, just a few metres behind him, his gun already in his hand.

Only by a supreme act of will did I stop my hand from flying into my jacket pocket.

'Yes, officer?' Dylan stepped in front of me and Morgan. 'Can I help you?'

'We're looking for two nought terrorists who're believed to be staying at this hotel,' said the officer. 'Have you seen anyone suspicious in the hotel?'

'Good God—no!' Dylan replied, shocked.

What acting! Next stop—the Academy awards.

The officer side-stepped Dylan to look

18

directly at Morgan and me, then down at the sheet he had in his hand. Even from where I was standing, I could see a photo of both Morgan and myself. Suddenly our disguises seemed anorexic to say the least. There was no doubt about it—Morgan and I had been set up. I'd thought we were being let back into the Liberation Militia. Big mistake. Andrew Dorn was just letting the Cross authorities do his dirty work for him.

Dylan looked around, alarmed. 'You don't think the terrorists are in this car park, do you?'

'No sir, at least . . .' The officer scrutinized us like we'd just run over his dog or something.

'And you are . . .' he asked me directly.

I remembered my part and looked at Dylan as if for guidance.

'This is Ben, my chauffeur, and that's John Halliwell, my secretary,' Dylan said. 'These two I can vouch for.'

'I see,' said the officer. He turned back to me. 'Can I see your ID card please? Yours as well,' he said to Morgan.

'When they're with me, I keep their ID cards, officer,' said Dylan.

'Why?' the cop asked, with a curiosity that verged on suspicion.

I held my breath.

'It's been my experience that if you grab a blanker by his ID card, his heart and mind will surely follow,' smiled Dylan. 'I'm not taking any chances on my nought staff skipping out

19

on me with my car or my important documents. You understand?'

'I see.' The officer returned the smile as Dylan dipped his hand into his jacket pocket for our cards.

He handed them over to the cop, who looked at them, then handed them back.

'OK, officer?' asked Dylan.

'Yes. One last question. Why d'you have two suitcases?'

Nosy bugger. This cop would find curiosity killed more than the cat if he didn't let up.

'I've been away on business—at least that's what my wife thinks,' winked Dylan.

'I see. And if I asked to look in your suitcases, you'd be fine with that?'

'Of course—if you're really that keen to see my dirty laundry. John, open my suitcase please.'

Morgan unzipped the suitcase and threw open the lid, all without saying a single word. It was full of socks, shirts, trousers and underpants. A couple of financial magazines sat in one corner and a fat crime thriller book sat in another.

'Ben, open the other case.'

I bent down and slowly began to unzip it. My suitcase contained Morgan's and my original clothes.

'That's OK, sir,' said the cop. 'You can go.'

I zipped up the case, just as slowly. No haste, no speed, no suspicion.

'So you're on your way home, sir?' asked the

cop.

'Yes, officer. Arriving without my secretary and chauffeur might get me into trouble. And these blankers know how to keep their mouths shut.'

'That makes a change.'

Dylan laughed at the funny, funny joke and the dagger cop joined in.

'Thank you, officer,' Dylan smiled, one Cross to another. Perfect understanding and, of course, much too subtle for us lowly blankers.

Dylan made his unhurried way to the mid-sized, black luxury car closest to the road. He took out his car key and pressed the button on the key to open the doors. Then he threw the key at me and waited, looking pointedly at me.

What the hell is he looking at me like that for? I wondered.

And then it hit me. Biting down hard on the intense antagonism I felt, I opened the back door of the car for him. He slid in like it was only natural. Taking the suitcase from Morgan, I deposited the luggage in the boot. It took all my self-control not to turn round and look at the cops behind me. What were they doing? Watching me? Could they smell the adrenaline pumping through my body? Could they hear my heart thumping like a relentless boxer? Or had they already left to help their colleagues search the hotel? I got behind the wheel of the car. Morgan sat next to me. I started the engine and we were away.

'Drive like you haven't got a damned place to go,' Dylan hissed at me.

And that's what I did. I drove like I had nowhere else to go—which was easy, because it was true.

four. Sephy

Dear Callie,

We've been together for a few hours now. I'm out of the labour room and back on the ward and it's just after dinner-time on the first day of the rest of your life. You're in a transparent, plastic cot at the bottom of my bed and I keep stealing glances at you 'cause I still can't quite believe you're mine. I'm writing this in between watching all the other mums on this ward welcome their loved ones— husbands, partners, other children, parents. Every bed has at least one visitor—except mine.

I can't stop thinking about Callum—your dad—and wishing he was here to see us, to be with us. But at least I've got you, Callie. You and me against the world, eh? How do I feel? I'm not even sure. It feels like my mind is still numb—or maybe just stuck in neutral.

But I take another glance at you and tell myself that we're still here. We're alive. We're together. Is this what Callum wanted? I think so. I hope so.

You and me against the world, my darling.

You and me against the world.

five. Jude

We drove past a number of police cars on either side of us. I kept my gaze on the road ahead. The last thing I wanted was to catch a dagger cop's eye. At the end of the road I turned left, heading into town. After I'd been driving for at least five minutes, Dylan piped up.

'Take the next left,' he ordered.

I turned into the indicated road and carried on driving at a steady speed, well within the limits.

Dylan now took over, telling me when and where to turn until after about fifteen minutes, we turned into the car park of a hypermarket. The car park was about half full. Most of the cars were parked as close to the hypermarket entrance as they could get. I cruised to the emptiest part of the car park, which was the area furthest away from the shop entrance. The odd trolley sat conspicuously in various bays where no one could be bothered to put them back where they belonged.

'This is where we part company,' said Dylan once I'd stopped the car.

'Thanks, Dylan,' Morgan said gratefully. 'I

23

owe you one.'

'You owe me several,' Dylan told him. He turned to look at me. I kept my mouth tight shut.

'You can take the suitcase with your stuff in it out of the boot,' said Dylan. 'Could I have the wigs and glasses, though. I might need them again.'

'Are you telling me what to do?' I asked.

'No. Merely suggesting,' said Dylan.

We pulled off the disguises, then all got out of the car. The early evening sun shone warm and welcoming but I felt uncomfortably hot. I dismissed it as nerves. Being outside the L.M. fold had made me jumpy. Nervous. I looked around. I didn't fancy hidden police springing out from behind a load of cars and ambushing me. Morgan and Dylan shook hands.

'Till next time,' said Morgan.

'Till next time,' Dylan said seriously. He nodded in my direction. I ignored him. No way was I going to get chatty with a dagger. Dylan got back into the car, this time in the driver's seat, as I took out the suitcase which contained our luggage. I'd barely slammed the boot shut before he was off, the wheels slipping slightly on the gravel beneath them. I turned to Morgan.

'Since when have you been so matey with a Cross?' I said.

'Are you accusing me of something, Jude?' Morgan asked mildly.

'No. Should I be?'

24

Morgan shook his head. 'Dylan is a contact I made a few years ago, before you'd even joined the L.M. You left me in charge of contingency planning and that's what I did. I installed him or other Crosses who're on our side at all the dubious hotels we've stayed in over the last few months—just in case.'

'I see,' I replied.

And I did see. I'd left all our backup plans to Morgan, relying on him to make sure that we always had a way out in case the cops came knocking. And I'd never questioned him about his plans or procedures before now. What he did and how he did it was his business. And deep down, I had to admit that without the dagger, it would've been much harder to get away from the hotel. But that thought burned through my gut like excess acid.

'I don't like relying on daggers,' I admitted. 'There's not one of them that can be trusted.'

'Jude, sometimes we have to work with sympathetic Crosses,' said Morgan.

' "Sympathetic" and "Crosses" are two words that're mutually exclusive. They've been in power for centuries. They're not going to give it up now. Not to us—our skin is too light.'

'The Liberation Militia aren't asking Crosses to give up power. I don't know what you're fighting for, but I'm in the L.M. to fight for equality. All we want is a level playing field.'

'You need to wake up and smell the coffee,' I scoffed. 'Level playing field, my left ass cheek. I've got news for you. We're not on the playing

25

field. We're not even in the game.'

'Yes, we are. Thanks to people like Dylan, we are,' Morgan told me. 'And your kind of negative thinking holds us back.'

At my snort of derision, Morgan continued, 'I've worked with Dylan and other Crosses before.'

'And you're OK with that?' I asked.

'I'm OK with whatever will further our cause.'

'And you don't care who we have to crawl into bed with to do that?'

'I'm not . . . blinkered enough to think that every Cross on the planet is against us—no,' said Morgan.

'Then more fool you,' I said with scorn.

Morgan regarded me steadily. 'You'd better be careful, Jude.'

'What's that supposed to mean?'

'I joined the L.M. to fight for equal rights for noughts,' said Morgan. 'What's your reason?'

'The same,' I shrugged.

'You sure? Or is the L.M. just a way for you to carry out your vendetta against every Cross who crosses your path. 'Cause that's how it looks from where I'm standing.'

'You need to look again then, or stand somewhere else,' I told him.

'Which is it, Jude? What d'you care about most? The cause or vengeance?' said Morgan.

How dare he ask me that? 'I'm not even going to bother answering that,' I said with all the disdain I could dredge up. 'We have more

26

pressing matters to discuss—like who tipped off the cops that we'd be at the hotel.'

Pause. Then Morgan nodded, prepared to go along with my blatant change of subject.

'Yes, I've been thinking about that too. It has to be Andrew's handiwork. He must be getting desperate.'

'Which makes him even more dangerous,' I pointed out.

'Yes, I know.'

'The police know we're together, so we need to split up,' I said reluctantly. 'We'll use our mobile phones to stay in touch and meet at least once a month. That way we can co-ordinate our efforts to bring down Andrew Dorn.'

'I'm not going to rest until he's paid for what he did to us,' Morgan said stonily. 'What he did to all of us. Pete's dead, Leila's rotting in prison and your brother was hanged because of him . . .'

'Callum's death wasn't down to Dorn—or at least only in part. My brother died because of Persephone Hadley,' I said harshly.

'I'm not even going to go there,' said Morgan, refusing to discuss it. 'We both lost a lot—let's leave it at that.'

We stood in silence as we both thought about just that—what each of us had had taken away from us. Morgan had lost the stability and sense of belonging that came from being at the heart of the L.M. I'd lost all that and a lot more. Morgan didn't understand, but then how

27

could he? No one could begin to guess at the depth of the hatred I held for Sephy Hadley and all daggers. But mainly Sephy Hadley. Everything began with her and my brother. And that's how it would end. Callum was gone. Sephy would pay. Destroying her would be my life's mission. My over-riding, overwhelming ambition.

'We're agreed then? We'll lay low until we can bring down Andrew Dorn?' said Morgan. I nodded. 'And we'll keep in contact?'

'Yes,' I said, my tone clipped. 'You'll be OK?'

Morgan nodded. 'So where should we meet?'

'The second of next month at Jo-Jo's in the Dundale Shopping Centre,' I decided. 'And we mustn't phone each other unless it's an emergency. If the police get hold of our phone IDs, they can trace and even listen in on every call we make.'

'Should we still change our phones regularly?'

'We'll play it by ear—OK? But whatever else happens, we mustn't lose touch.'

'OK,' Morgan agreed. 'Well, until we meet again, keep your head down.'

'You too.' And with that I turned and walked away, my footsteps crunching on the gravel beneath my feet.

And even though I wanted to, I didn't look back. I could sense that Morgan was still watching me but I didn't turn round. Jude's rule number five: *Never get so close to anyone or anything that you can't walk away at a*

28

moment's notice if you have to.
When you have to.

six. Sephy

Darling Callie,
There's so much I want to say to you. So much I need to explain. So much I want to share. It frightens me how much I'm beginning to care about you. You're just two days old and I feel like . . . like your heart and mine are somehow knitting together. Does that make sense? Probably not. When you read this you'll probably think your mum is talking fanciful nonsense. Words about personal things, words that tell the truth, they're so hard to say. If I used words that meant nothing to me at all, then they wouldn't tear off pieces of me as I wrote them. I read once that when a bee stings, it tears its body apart trying to get away from its victim. That's what the truth has done to my life.

And here's some more truth.

Callie, I want to be honest with you—always—but this isn't easy to say. When I was pregnant with you inside me, I hated you. You were alive and Callum, your dad, wasn't. I hated you and me and the whole world for that. But now that I have you here, against my heart, I feel the beginning of peace. Like this was meant to be. Strange that I should feel

29

such strange calm. Maybe it's just an 'eye of the storm' calm. After all, I'm about to be chucked out of my flat, my money is almost gone and I don't have a pot to pee in. I should be panicking. But I'm not. We're going to be all right, I think. I hope. I pray.

I sit on my hospital bed with you in my arms and I watch you. Just watch you, absorbing every line, every curve of your face. You have your dad's eyes, the same shape, the same quizzical expression, but your eyes are dark, dark blue, whilst his were stormy grey. You have my nose, strong and proud. You have your dad's forehead, broad and intelligent, and you have my ears—and yet you don't look like either of us. You're new and unique and original. You're a lighter brown than me. Much lighter. But you're not a Nought, not white like your dad. You're a trailblazer. Setting your own colour, your own look. Maybe you're the hope for the future. Something new and different and special. Something to live on whilst the rest of us die out, obsolete in our ignorance and hatred. We'll be like the dinosaurs, dying out—and not before time either. And yet I can't help worrying. You have to live in a world divided into Noughts and Crosses. A world where you will be biologically both and socially neither. Mixed race. Dual heritage. Labels to be attached. Tags to be discarded. Don't let the world stick markers and brands and other nonsense on you. Find your own identity. I hope and pray you find

30

your own place and space and time.

But I can't help worrying.

I watch you and I can't stop tears rolling down my face. But I don't want you to see me cry. I don't want anything bad or negative in your life. I want to surround you with love and warmth and understanding. I want to make up for the fact that you'll never know your dad. His name was Callum Ryan McGregor. He had straight brown hair and solemn grey eyes and a dry sense of humour and a mountainous sense of justice. He was very special. I'm going to tell you about him every day. Every single day. I'll sit you on my lap and tell you how the corners of his eyes crinkled up when he laughed. How a muscle in his jaw twitched when he was angry. How he made me laugh like no one else. How he made me cry like no one else. I loved him so much. I still do. I always will. He's not here any more. But you are. I want to hold you tight and never let you go. I'll never let anything or anyone hurt you. Ever. I promise.

How strange, but before I had you, I always thought of myself as a pacifist, as someone who'd never be able to deliberately physically hurt anyone. But I look at you and my feelings have already changed so much, it frightens me. For you I would die. But more scary than that, for you I would kill. In a second. I know it as surely as I know my own name. I won't let anyone hurt you.

Not anyone.

31

My feelings terrify me. Loving you so much terrifies me. I've only ever loved one other person the way I love you and that was your dad, Callum. And my love for him brought him nothing but misery. Love is bad luck. At least, mine is. And now I'm lying here feeling so sorry for myself because Callum's not with me. And I know that you're here with me, Callie Rose, but I miss your father.

I miss him.

With every breath and every heartbeat, I miss him.

seven. Jude

I sat opposite her house in my newly acquired car for I don't know how long, just watching and waiting. Though if you'd asked me what I was watching and waiting for, I wouldn't've been able to tell you. A glimpse of her. Just a sight to see she if was all right. This, my most recent car, was around five years old—a black, four-door saloon. I'd gone into a car park across town, barrelled the lock and hot-wired it. I never stole new cars, they were too conspicuous. A five-year-old car wouldn't get too much attention. I needed to blend into the scenery, especially sitting outside her house. Did she know how much I missed her? Could she sense me watching her front door?

I tilted back my head, still watching Mum's

house, willing her to look through a window or open the door and see me. This whole situation was bizarre. I'd thought that more and more often over the last few months. I was a boat with no oars and no sails, drifting where the currents swept me. I even missed Morgan's regular company. But we were both better off this way. I had no friends, I had no home, I didn't even feel safe belonging to the Liberation Militia any more—not whilst Andrew Dorn was the General's right-hand man. My life had moved past unreal into surreal. At least that's how it felt a lot of the time. Most of the time. But then I'd remember the sight of my brother swinging on the gallows, and painful reality whipped back at me with enough force to knock me off my feet.

Callum McGregor, my brother. Callum, who was like my good reflection. He was the one in the family who was meant to make it. Get out. Get on. Get ahead. But he hadn't. And if he couldn't make it, what hope did the rest of us have? If it's possible to truly loathe and love someone at the same time, then that's how I felt about my brother. He had it all.

And it killed him.

Mum, I'm still here. I haven't abandoned you. I hope there's some way you can feel my thoughts and know that I'm thinking of you. Does she get my money? I don't send it every week and the amount varies according to how much I can afford but at least I try. Mum, I wish I could step out of the shadows and knock on your door like any other person would, but I can't. I'm wanted—by all the wrong people. The government, the police—and some within the Liberation Militia. But I'm still here, Mum. I still think about you—in spite of Jude's fourth law: *Caring equals vulnerability. Never show either.* But you're all I have left in the world, Mum. And that means something to me. I wish it didn't, but it does. So here I am, sitting in a stolen car outside your house, watching and waiting and wishing all our lives had turned out differently.

I'd better go before someone spots me. It wouldn't surprise me if they're still watching your house, hoping I'll turn up. Hang in there, Mum. And don't worry. I only have one desire, one ambition left. I'm going to make them all suffer.

I'm going to make them all pay.

Wait. Her door's opening. She's bringing out a rubbish bag.

Oh my God! She looks so old. When did she get so old? Head bent, shoulders drooping, shuffling like an old woman. But it's only been a few months. A few years. A lifetime. Look what they've done to you, Mum. Look at the state of you. She's looking up—straight at me. Can she see me? Of course she can. What am I thinking? I have to get out of here. I must've been mad to come here in the first place.

She's calling my name. For God's sake, Mum, don't do that. You don't know who's watching or listening. What was I thinking?

34

She's dropped her bag and is running towards me now.

Move the car, Jude. NOW!

Get going.

Go.

Mum, don't cry. Please don't cry.

Sorry.

It was a mistake.

I'm so sorry.

I'd broken Jude's first cardinal rule.

Never, ever allow yourself to feel. Feelings kill.

eight. Sephy

Darling Callie,

Whilst you were sleeping:

I thought of Callum.

I phoned three quality newspapers and used my credit card to put a birth announcement in each of them. If Dad thinks I'm going to disappear into the woodwork now that I've had you, he's got another think coming. I hate his guts.

But I thought of Callum.

And I kissed your forehead. And breathed you in.

I thought of Callum.

I chatted to Meena in the bed next to mine. She's had a girl too and she's going to call her Jorja. That's a pretty name, isn't it? Jorja.

I thought of Callum.

I had a quick shower because I didn't want to be away from you too long. Not that I could linger, even if I wanted to. The queue to use the showers is always horrendous, so you have to be fast on your feet and slip in and out before some irate woman bangs on the shower cubicle door, hurling abuse because the hot water is in danger of running out.

And I thought of Callum.

In that order.

nine. Jude

I sat in the Golden Eye bar, tucked away off the High Street, sipping at my lager. This wasn't the kind of place I usually frequented— a bit too consciously cool-chic for my taste— but it was off the beaten track and I needed a drink and an hour or two to myself. The Golden Eye was almost three quarters full of revellers enjoying a drink after work. Mostly noughts but quite a few daggers. It was one of those places where daggers could come for an hour or so once a week and try to fool themselves into thinking they were liberal and not prejudiced because they actually drank in a place where noughts were drinking next to them and not just serving. I took another sip of my drink and looked around. The bar sure was busy. But then they did serve the best beer I'd had in months.

The place should've been called the Wooden Eye. People stood on the beer-stained wooden floor, propped up the wine-stained wooden bar, sat on barely-upholstered wooden benches, stools and chairs. And I was one of them. I sat at a table, opposite a canoodling nought couple who had eyes for no one but each other. I could've sprouted another head and I'd've still been invisible to them. So I sat and sipped, and sipped and sat. But I was tired of my inactivity. I was tired of running and hiding and living from day to day. Slamming my bottle of lager down on the table before me, I decided I'd sat on my backside for long enough. It was time to get some purpose back into my life. I couldn't rely on the L.M. for support—not when someone, probably Andrew Dorn, was out to get me. And my mum could do nothing for me. The only person I could rely on was myself.

The first thing I had to do was get money. Lots of it and quickly. And if I could stick it to the Crosses at the same time, then so much the better. There were plenty of banks and building societies and jewellery shops that needed someone like me to help keep their profits on a more manageable level. So really, I'd be providing a public service. I smiled, imagining that defence in court. Who knows! If they ever caught me, I just might try it.

'Hi. A seat! A seat! My kingdom for a seat! Is this seat taken?'

I looked up, then scowled up at the Cross

woman standing before me. She wore her hair in thin braids tied up with an orange ribbon. Her silk shirt was also flame orange and her wraparound skirt was dark, either black or blue—it was hard to tell in this light. Couldn't she find somewhere else to sit? I glanced around but it did indeed look like every seat was taken. Tough! I didn't want one of them sitting next to me. But then, out of the corner of my eye, I saw two coppers enter the bar— one a nought, the other a Cross.

'If you'd rather I didn't,' the woman shrugged. And already she was turning away.

'No! No, that's OK. It's all yours,' I said quickly. I even managed to squeeze out a smile.

The Cross gave me another hard look before deciding I wasn't an axe murderer. 'Thanks,' she smiled as she sat down. 'I'm Cara.'

Jeez! What made her think that the invitation to sit down meant I wanted to talk to her? But the coppers were still in the bar and I couldn't afford to take any chances.

'Steve,' I replied without even blinking.

'Hi, Steve,' Cara the Cross continued. 'This place is jammed tonight. It's not usually this busy during the week.'

'I don't really come here that often,' I said.

'I thought I hadn't seen you in here before.'

Shut the bloody hell up! I don't want to talk to you. I don't want to sit next to you. I don't want anything to do with you. But I smiled and was careful to keep my true feelings off my

38

face. I'm good at that. Years of practice around Crosses. I've lost count of the number of times a dagger has told me what he thought of me and 'my kind', usually followed by 'But I don't mean you! You're all right!' And what did I do when daggers spouted their nonsense? I smiled and said nothing. Or at least I used to, when I was younger. No-one's tried to talk to me like that for a while. Now I choose not to hide my feelings unless absolutely necessary— and maybe it shows.

'Those two are enjoying themselves, aren't they?' Cara nodded at the two in front of us, who were still kissing like there was only a minute left before the world ended.

'D'you think if I shouted fire, they'd stop?' I asked wryly.

'I doubt if they'd even hear you. So d'you live around here then?' asked Cara the Curious Cross.

'No. I'm just visiting my sister. She lives a couple of streets away from here.'

'What's her name?'

'Why?'

'Maybe I know her, if she comes in here a lot,' said Cara.

'Lynette,' I replied without hesitation. 'My sister's name is Lynette.'

Cara frowned. 'Doesn't ring a bell.'

I shrugged. Cara smiled. I glanced around the room. The cops each had a couple of sheets of paper in their hands and they were looking around.

'So, Cara,' I smiled, moving closer to her. 'D'you work around here then?'

'Yeah, in Delany's Salon, the hairdresser around the corner,' said Cara.

'Who's Delany?' I asked.

'That's the name of the shop,' Cara explained. 'Delany was the woman who used to own the shop but she packed up and moved on ages ago. It's had two or three different owners since then.'

'Who owns it now then?'

'I do,' Cara smiled. 'In fact . . . I own a chain of Delany's Salons nationwide.'

'How many?' I asked lightly.

Cara sipped at her drink and looked at me almost apologetically. 'Seven at last count. Not many yet, but I'm planning to expand in the future.'

Who did she think she was fooling with the false modesty act? Not me, that was for damned sure. But she owned shops. Going concerns. Money-making propositions. That could be useful.

'That's unusual.' I pointed at the necklace she was wearing. The cops were getting closer and closer.

'It was my mum's,' said Cara.

It was a silver or platinum fine-link chain with two overlapping circles inside an oval.

'Does it mean anything?' I asked.

'Love and peace,' Cara told me. 'They flow into each other and renew each other. Anyway, that's the idea.'

'Sounds deep!' I said sceptically.

Cara smiled. 'It isn't. It just means love and peace—that's all.'

'I'll drink to that,' I said raising my bottle of lager.

The cops were only a table or two away now. They were flashing photos at everyone they passed. Could they be the photos of Morgan and me that the cops in the car park had shown?

'You're very beautiful,' I whispered to Cara.

And I kissed her, feeling sick to my stomach. The cops walked past me. It took every gram of strength I had to stop myself from pulling away until the cops had well and truly gone. Across the bar someone shouted out, 'Oi, you lot! What's with that table? Get a room! Get two!'

I pulled away slowly. Girls like that. It makes it seem like you're reluctant to stop.

'Is this where I get my face slapped?' I asked.

'I dunno. Tell me what that was all about and then I'll decide.' Cara's eyebrows were raised but she had an amused smile on her face.

'I couldn't resist,' I said. 'I hope you don't mind.'

'I should, but I don't,' said Cara, adding melodramatically, 'I'll just tell myself that once again a man found me *irresistible*!'

I smiled, then took a swig of my lager to wash the taste of her lips off my mouth. 'Can I get you a drink?'

'OK,' Cara smiled. 'I'll have what you're

having.'

You wouldn't last five seconds if you had to have what I've got, I thought scornfully. But I smiled and stood up. I knew that she was just being friendly when she chatted to me, but then she'd let me kiss her. She could've pulled back, she could've protested, but she hadn't. Stupid Cross slapper. I turned and headed to the bar. Once my back was towards her, I surreptitiously wiped the back of my hand across my mouth. Two more lagers bought and paid for, I headed back to my table.

'Thanks,' Cara replied, reaching out for it.

'Any time,' I replied. 'After your drink, d'you wanna get out of here?'

'I don't think so . . .'

'Fair enough. It was just an idea . . .'

We both took a sip of our respective drinks.

'Where would we go?' Cara asked at last.

'Anywhere you want,' I said. 'To see a film, for a walk or maybe you could show me your salon—you name it.'

Cara scrutinized me. It was quick but thorough.

'OK,' she said after a moment's hesitation.

'Which of the above d'you fancy then?'

'All of them,' Cara laughed.

I sipped at my lager. Cara finished hers in double quick time. 'Ready?' she smiled.

'Willing and able,' I added, standing up.

Cara might've been a stupid Cross slapper, but she'd fallen into my lap. And I was never one to pass up an opportunity. I needed money

42

and fast, and Cara was going to provide it for me—whether she wanted to or not.

ten. Sephy

Darling Callie,
    Please, *please* don't go. I don't know what I'll do if I lose you too. They've taken you away from me and put you in SCBU, the Special Care Baby Unit. I'm so frightened. But you're having trouble breathing and you're losing too much weight so they've put you in an incubator. I sit in the chair beside your incubator and will you to get well. I have to put my hands through two arm-sized holes in the incubator to touch you and stroke you. I try to pour all the love and hope I can muster out through my fingertips, so that it washes over your skin and through you and around you constantly. I can't even hold you to me and it's killing me.
    It's so hard here, tougher than I ever thought it would be. Mercy Community Hospital only has four incubators. Just four. But I don't have the money to take you to a private hospital with better facilities and more resources. The bulk of the money my grandma left me is all tied up until I'm twenty-one and, when I moved out after Callum's death, Dad froze my allowance. I can't ask Dad for help and I won't ask Mother.

I'm being selfish, aren't I?

Callie, I won't sacrifice you on the altar of my pride. I'll give you a few hours more but if you don't improve, if it looks like you're actually getting worse, I'll call whoever I have to, to make sure you survive. I'll even phone Dad if I have to.

If I absolutely have to.

I feel so helpless, so exactly like the day Callum was killed. No . . . this is worse because although I can't help but hope for the best, I fear the worst.

It's all my fault. After all my fine sentiments, I tried to use you to get back at my family, my so-called friends, at everyone who allowed your dad to die and never said a word, never lifted a finger. Never even phoned me to show they gave a damn. So I put an announcement in the personal ads of all the quality newspapers—because you're quality, you see. I thought by the time the announcement was run, you and I would be back in my flat—but then you got ill and we're still in the hospital. Nurse Fashoda told me that the hospital has already had loads of phone calls, condemning me and the hospital's part in all this. She told me with great relish how there are some people out there who think Callum got off easy by being hanged. They think he should've been boiled in oil and tortured on a rack first. And there are some people who think Callum was a traitor for taking up with me, 'his oppressor'. When did Callum and I become emblems and symbols and all that other rubbish? When did we stop being people, being human? All those people phoning the hospital, full of poison, full of hate—Noughts and Crosses alike. I shouldn't call them people. I should call them *coins*—people who hold extreme opposite views but who are basically saying the same venomous thing. Noughts and Crosses shouldn't mix. Noughts should go back to where they came from—wherever that is.

I'm not quite sure what I meant to happen with the birth announcements. I guess, I just wanted the notice to be a kick in the teeth for Dad. It hasn't happened that way. Even if Dad does know about you by now, why would he care? He's the one responsible for the death of your father and I mean less than nothing to him now. So why was I stupid enough to think he'd give a damn?

Is all of this happening to you, Callie, because I put that ad in the paper? I can't bear the thought that it might be. Is it because I wanted to use you to stick two fingers up to my dad? It wasn't only that, I swear. I wanted the whole world to know about you and how much Callum loved you and, oh, lots of reasons. It wasn't just to get back at my dad.
Get well, Callie.
Get well and I promise I'll never, ever use you or your birth in that way again.
Just get well.
I couldn't bear to lose both you and Callum. If you die, you'll take me with you. Please,

please don't die.

Oh Callum, I wish you were here. I need you so much.

eleven. Jude

On our way to the cinema, we passed a small park with a children's playground. Cara smiled as she watched the kids run around, screaming with laughter. There were brightly painted climbing frames on one side of the playground. One was a huge star shape made up of thick ropes attached to a steel framework, another was a blue and yellow helicopter shape, another was a red rocket shape. There were three swings, a roundabout and a see-saw. Four children were picking sides for an obstacle race around the climbing frames. One was a nought, the other three were Crosses. And they were choosing who would be paired with who for the race. But they couldn't decide.

'I know,' said the nought girl. 'Eenie, meenie, minie, mo. Catch a blanker by the toe. If he squeals, let him go. Eenie, meenie, minie, mo. You're on my side, Michael. Ready, steady, go!'

And the girl and Michael held hands and raced off together, as did the other two. I watched as they all tried to negotiate their way up to the top of the star and back down again, each team still holding hands. And the girl's rhyme kept ringing in my ears. How did she feel saying that rhyme? Did she even know what she was saying? I glanced at Cara. She was looking at the children, a strange expression on her face. She turned to me and gave a tentative smile. I didn't smile back.

'We'd better get going,' Cara told me. 'Or we'll miss the start of the film.'

Cara chose some drippy romance film. I had to fight to keep my eyes open through most of it, then Cara's sniffing and sobbing during the last ten minutes kept me awake. It was bloody awful. This man and woman sighing and yearning and suffering through most of the film before they finally and inevitably got together and they all lived happily ever after. I mean, give me a break! Cara tried to disguise the fact that she was crying but she wasn't doing a very good job. I thought about her seven salons up and down the country, I thought about the money I didn't have but soon could if I got close to her and reluctantly put my arm around her shoulders. She instantly put her head on my shoulder. It really shouldn't've been this easy, but getting every penny from Cara was going to be like taking sweets from a toddler. On our way out of the cinema, Cara kept going on about Daley Mercer, the latest Cross heartthrob.

'I don't think I've seen a single film of his that I haven't liked,' Cara sighed. 'And he's so gorgeous, don't you think?'

47

'He doesn't do much for me,' I told her honestly.

She laughed. 'I'd be disappointed if he did!'

'He's got another film coming out soon, hasn't he?'

'*Destruction*,' Cara informed me. 'It's out next week. I can't wait to see it.'

'What's it about?'

'It's a historical ghost story. Daley's character is a wealthy landowner in the eighteenth century who has a secret which will ruin him if it's revealed. And then this rich woman played by Dessi Cherada comes to his mansion to . . .'

I switched off at that point. It sounded even worse than the neck-high drivel we'd just waded through. A few minutes passed before Cara finished telling me the plot.

'Apparently the tickets are selling like patties, so I'll have to wait a while before I see that one,' she sighed.

Personally, I'd rather have had my toenails extracted than watch that dagger rubbish. Yet another film where there wouldn't be a single nought in sight—except possibly as slaves. I hated historical films in particular for that reason. Even in so-called contemporary films, noughts were few and far between.

The meal we had afterwards was curried lamb and rice flavoured with coconut. She wanted to pay, but I insisted. In the end we decided to split the bill in half. I knew when I took her home that she wanted to see me again. She didn't invite me in but I could tell

48

that she was debating with herself whether or not she should. I made up her mind for her by bidding her goodnight.

'Maybe we can meet up again—for another drink or something?' said Careful Cara.

'I'd like that,' I told her.

We stood in silence outside her medium-sized house, with its medium-sized front garden and the medium-sized silver or grey car in the driveway—it was hard to tell in the street-lit night.

'I'll give you my phone number,' said Cara, caving in.

'I'd like that too,' I smiled. Success! She was giving me her phone number. I didn't have to ask for it. The running in this relationship had to be done by her if I was to get a single penny out of her. I watched her dig into her jacket pockets, taking out a pen from one and a napkin from the other. She quickly wrote down her name and number, never once looking at me. I could feel her radiating embarrassment. She handed it to me, then almost ran for her front door.

'Cara?' I called after her.

She slowed, then stopped. Turning slowly she looked directly at me for the first time since we'd arrived at her house.

'I'll see you soon,' I said.

She nodded and I'm sure I saw hope and something more on her face. I watched her go into her house before I turned and walked back the way I'd come. I was aware of a face at

49

the window in the next house along. Pretending that I didn't know I was being watched, I carried on walking at an unhurried pace, my face slightly averted from the voyeur's gaze. I still had to be careful. I couldn't help wondering why Cara didn't seem the least bit self-conscious about being seen with me. I mean, even when paying for the cinema tickets, I'd been aware of the looks we were getting. But I'd looked at Cara, and she'd smiled at me like, at that precise moment, I was the only thing that mattered. So I swallowed my embarrassment and smiled back because Cash Cow Cara was going to help me get back on top. I just had to play my cards right. But I wasn't worried.

Playing cards has always been one of my favourite pastimes.

And as Jude's law number six says: *Do unto others as they would do unto you—only do it first.*

twelve. Sephy

Darling Callie,

The doctors tell me that you're holding your own. They try to suggest that I'm not doing myself any good by not resting and eating properly, but I hardly hear them.

You've been in the incubator for almost three days now. I sat down next to your bed this morning, my arms through the holes in the incubator. I was so exhausted, I dozed off in my chair. The next thing I knew, I was being gently shaken awake.

'Miss Hadley? Miss Hadley?' The gentle but insistent voice finally got through to me.

I opened my eyes and gazed up at a male nurse and two female doctors, one a Nought, the other a Cross. I was instantly awake.

'What is it? What's happened?'

'It's OK, Miss Hadley,' said Dr Aldener, the Cross doctor. She gave what was obviously meant to be a reassuring smile, but it only served to make me feel that she was hiding something. 'We have good news. Your daughter is getting stronger. We'll keep her in the incubator for today and if she continues to breathe on her own without any problems, she can go back to the ward with you either later this evening or some time tomorrow.'

The bubble burst of joy inside me quickly subsided and doubt took over. 'Shouldn't Callie try breathing by herself for longer than a day before she's moved?' I asked.

Did they really believe you were fit to be moved, Callie, or was it that at the first sign of recovery they were going to move you so some other baby could have the incubator?

'We won't move her until we're sure it's absolutely safe to do so,' the other doctor soothed. 'But we all feel that she's out of the woods.'

'You're sure?' I asked, only slightly mollified.

'Absolutely,' smiled the Nought doctor.

51

Yes, I was being selfish, but no way was I going to let them move you before you were completely better. So I watched and waited. But mainly waited. All day and into the night. You breathed by yourself without that awful tube up your nose but you were still a bit snuffly. I fed you every time you woke up, holding you against my heart, my finger on your palm as your tiny fingers grasped it like a life line. It was the first time I'd been able to feed you since you'd been put in SCBU.

I tell myself that being allowed to hold you and feed you myself must surely be a good sign. We'll be out of here soon, Callie. I've got it all planned. We'll go back to my home and I'll make a good life for both of us, I swear I will. I don't have any money but I'll get a job and work hard. School will have to wait for a few years. I'm only eighteen. I've got all the time in the world to go back to school and then on to university to maybe study law. I'd still like to do something useful like Kelani Adams—she's the lawyer who defended Callum and his dad Ryan when they were both dragged to court on spurious charges. I still live in hope that one day I'll be able to be a lawyer like her, or maybe I can get training to provide legal aid for those who need it. Maybe one day. So don't worry, Callie. We have all the time in the world and then some. But you come first now. So I'll get a job. Callie, you and I are going to be so happy together—you just see if we aren't.

I've got it all planned.

thirteen. Jude

I had trouble sleeping last night. Three o'clock in the morning came and went and I was still wide awake. And it was so cold and still in my room. It's cold and still in my world. Where did my childhood go? What happened to all the things I wanted to do and wanted to be? I can't even remember. The way I live now is the only life I know.

But last night was one of the bad ones.

Some nights I sleep just as soon as my head touches the pillow. Some nights, sleep and me are strangers. Those are the nights when I can't get my brother out of my head. Maybe Cara had something to do with it. Me and a dagger—who would've thought it? But she's just a means to an end. And don't we all do what we have to, to survive? Callum, I don't understand why I'm still here and yet you couldn't make it. Maybe I never will. You were always so much brighter and bolder than I was. But thinking of you through the night brought me no joy, no comfort. My body tensed. My fists clenched. My eyes burned into the darkness around me. Not just my body but my whole soul was swallowed by rage. Rage enough to consume the whole world. Just thinking of you, Callum, made all the hatred

53

inside me swell and explode like napalm fireworks. A feeling so intense that I scared even myself. So I lay on my bed and stared into the darkness and plotted and schemed until I fell asleep, exhausted.

My room was cold.

But my heart was colder.

I phoned my girlfriend, Gina, in the evening. She didn't sound too pleased to hear from me. Or maybe what I mean is, she didn't sound happy to hear from me. Not impatient or indifferent, but not happy either. I don't know what I was expecting. Our on-again, off-again relationship had been off for quite some time now. But I was alone and thought she'd be as good as anyone to talk to.

'Jude, I'm a bit busy at the moment,' she said, less than two minutes into the conversation.

In the background I could hear music softly playing. A love song. I had no doubt it was from the Gibson Dell CD she always played when we were together.

'I haven't seen you in a long time, Gina. I thought we could have a chat,' I said.

'I really haven't got time at the moment,' Gina said again, her tone more clipped, her voice getting higher. A definite sign of stress. I'd phoned her at home. She obviously wasn't alone.

'Who's there with you?' I asked silkily.

'No one,' Gina replied quickly. Too quickly.

So I'd been right.

'Who's there with you?' I repeated.

54

'Jude, I don't own you and you certainly don't own me. I haven't seen or heard from you in months. I'm not some kind of machine that only comes to life when you can be bothered to get off your backside and call me.' Gina's words were spilling out now, tripping over each other in their haste to be heard. And her tone was getting more shrill. She was with someone and she was feeling guilty about it.

'I thought we were together—an item,' I told her. 'My mistake.'

'Don't you dare!' she shouted at me. 'Don't you dare blame me. You don't talk to me for weeks at a time and when you are with me, you make me feel like you could quite happily be somewhere else.'

Gina's words didn't shock me and, truth to tell, I was a bit surprised to find that I wasn't the least bit upset that she was seeing someone else. But her total over-reaction to what I'd said told me that there was more to this than met the eye. And then it clicked. Took me a couple of seconds but it was late and I was tired.

'Let me speak to Morgan,' I told her.

There was a deathly hush which spoke more than volumes.

'Gina, put Morgan on the phone,' I ordered. I sensed that the slightest hesitation on my part would result in her shrieking her denial at me. A dull ache was beginning to form behind my eyes. I closed my eyes and groaned inwardly. I had the beginnings of a killer migraine.

'Hello, Jude.'

Even though I was expecting his voice, it still made me start. Suspecting something, no matter how strongly, is never the same as having your suspicions confirmed.

'Hello, old friend,' I said deliberately.

'You weren't interested, I was,' said Morgan at once.

There was no apology, no remorse in his voice. Just a belligerent challenge.

I was too tired and my head was throbbing too much to care. 'You can have her, Morgan—but believe me, you can do better.'

'Is that all you wanted to say to me?' asked Morgan, icily.

'No, but I can't talk to you now. We'll talk tomorrow. Call me from a phone box on my mobile.' And I slammed the phone down.

Alone again.

Naturally.

I flung myself down on my bed, groaning as my headache kicked in with a vengeance.

fourteen. Sephy

Darling Callie,

You did it! You made it! We've both survived the last few days. I never want to go through that again. But you're out of SCBU and back on the ward with me now and you're breathing

56

fine and your weight has stopped dropping. They won't let me out of here until you weigh at least ten per cent more than your birth weight though, just to be on the safe side. I don't mind that. To be honest, I'm not in a rush to get back to my flat. I didn't go home when Callum died. I never will either. That's my old life. You are my new, the future. But Callum is my ever-present. It's like where he's concerned, time is just standing still. And I can't believe I'll ever feel any different.

I tell myself to grieve and let it go, but with each breath I just seem to hold onto him tighter. I don't want to let him go. He was more me than I am. I know that doesn't make sense, but that's how I feel.

But you're safe now and getting better and I'll focus on that.

fifteen. Jude

I stood at the side of my window, watching the world pass by. The sky was a blanket of grey, tarmac-coloured clouds with no hint of the blue beyond them. The air hung heavy and still, even managing to muffle the sound of the traffic outside my window.

Monday morning.

A man and a woman walked by below me, hand in hand. The man stopped abruptly before turning to his partner, a smile on his face. He said a few words to her. I couldn't see her face as her back was towards me, but I could see his. And he only had eyes for the woman before him. He smiled at her then, cupping her face with his hands, he kissed her. I watched, the seconds ticking by, and still neither of them came up for air. I wanted to open the window and shout out, but I didn't. I wanted to walk away from the window and leave them to it—but I couldn't. I watched as they pressed their bodies closer together. I watched as the man finally, reluctantly, let go of his woman, only to stroke her face before taking her hand. And then they started walking again. I stared at the couple, willing them, daring them to look up at my window. But they didn't. The woman was a skank. She had to be to go with a Cross man like that. She wasn't even trying to hide the fact that they were together. But I knew what she was. The only nought women who went with daggers were skanks.

Unbidden, the image of Sephy's face came into my head. Sephy and my brother, Callum. What were they like when they were together? Well, that was easy. Callum was . . . misguided—to say the least. And as for her? She was his nemesis, dressed up in a mantle of wealth and false friendship. I watched as the nought woman and the dagger man turned the corner, playing at being lovers in an unloving world.

Time to do a little playing of my own.

Wasp Sting 'Full of Hate'

Yesterday it was announced that the Wasp Sting's invitation to sing at the Party in the Park has been withdrawn. A Spokeswoman for the Heritage Charitable Trust, who stage the concert each year, told the *Daily Shouter*, 'Since announcing that Wasp Sting were due to appear, we've been inundated with complaints. Although they are a very popular nought rock band, many have protested at the type of lyrics this group expound. Their song, *Behind the Flag*, has been called a blatant incitement to violence against the police. Others have called them a group full of hate. We have therefore taken the difficult decision not to include them in this year's programme of events.'

When Aidan Doyle of Wasp Sting was told of the news, he is reported to have said. 'The *!£%*@# Heritage Charitable Trust can kiss my a***. If they're afraid of us, then we'll play to those who *!£%*@# aren't.' One woman who regularly attends the Party in the Park told us, 'No way would I ever take my family to a concert where Wasp Sting are playing. They are a foul-mouthed so-called rock group who shout obscenities and stir up trouble. Not the sort of thing I want my children listening to, thank you very much.'

sixteen. Sephy

Darling Callie,

Guess who visited me today? My sister Minerva. I was reading a newspaper and didn't even realize she'd arrived until her shadow fell across my bed. I haven't had any visitors since you were born, you see. Wasn't expecting any either. Don't need any. But here was my sister, standing over me, her face as solemn as a church engraving.

'Hello, Sephy.'

'Hello, Minerva.' I put down my paper.

Several seconds passed as we regarded each other.

'How's your arm?' I asked at last.

I guess I should let you know that your Aunt Minerva was shot in the arm when I was six months pregnant with you. Should I tell you who did it? I guess by the time I'm ready to give you this journal and you're old enough to understand what's in it, you'll be old enough to know—so here goes. Your Uncle Jude shot her. Jude is your dad's brother—and he hates my entire family, but especially me. Waiting in the hospital after my sister had been shot was awful. I didn't know whether she was going to lose the use of her arm, or lose her arm altogether—or her life. It's one of those memories you squash down and try and sit on to hide it away like one of those squishy,

60

foamy cushions. But it just explodes and bounces you off it and refuses to stay hidden. When Minerva woke up, I begged her not to report Jude to the police. I asked her to say that an unknown, hooded intruder had burst his way into my flat and when I refused to give him any money, had shot Minerva before running away. Minerva didn't want to. She wanted Jude to pay for what he did. So did I.

But I knew it wouldn't happen that way.

I was being selfish—I admit it. But I was desperate not to drag up the whole business of the McGregors and the Hadleys again. I didn't want the press camped on my doorstep and hounding me everywhere I went for an interview. I didn't want photographers' flashbulbs stinging my eyes at all hours. I didn't want to reopen old wounds for Jude's mum or for myself. But mainly for myself. I was almost hysterically selfish. I begged and pleaded with Minerva until I wore her down and she promised me she'd do as I asked. But after that, our relationship shifted again— irrevocably, I think.

Stay away from Jude, Callie. He'll stop at nothing and use anyone to get what he wants. And what he wants more than anything else is my heart on a platter and my head on a pike. I'm not the least bit scared of him. If it were just me and him then I'd stand before him and tell him to Bring It On. Do his worst. But that's not the way it'll happen. Whatever else Jude may be, he's not a fool. He wants me to suffer.

And he knows the only way to do that is through you.

'My arm's fine now.' Minerva flexed her fingers to show me. 'It aches occasionally when it rains but at least it still works.'

'Minerva, I'm sorry about . . . what happened to you,' I said, for probably the thousandth time.

'Could you please stop apologizing?' Minerva said wearily. 'And stop calling me Minerva.'

'What am I supposed to call you then? You hate it when I call you Minnie.'

'Minnie is fine.'

'You've spent years telling me the exact opposite,' I reminded her.

'Yeah, but Minnie is what my sister calls me,' said Minerva pointedly.

I knew what she was saying, but she wasn't Minnie any more and probably never would be again. Plus it was hard to get past the fact that because of me, my own sister had been shot.

'Can I sit down?' she asked at last.

I waved at the visitor's chair next to my bed. Its upholstery had faded away to a sorrowful, stained, pale blue and the seat of the chair was lumpy and uneven. Minerva sat down, her bum sinking into it like a toddler sitting on an empty potty. Hoisting herself up, she sat at the edge of the chair where it was firmer.

I waited for the snide comment or the whining complaint, but none came. Minerva looked around the ward. I did the same. A quick glance told me we had the attention of most of the people—visitors and patients alike. I suppose they were wondering why I hadn't had you in a private hospital, Callie, but the truth is I wanted to have you at the Mercy Community Hospital. It was important to me. I think Callum would've wanted it that way. But I was very aware that I was only one of two Cross patients in the maternity unit and I was certainly the most . . . shall we say—known. Known is the polite way to put it. Notorious is closer to the mark. The other Cross woman, who had only come in yesterday as an emergency, lay in the bed directly opposite mine. She was watching us too. She was only here—as she'd been at great pains to tell me— because her baby had been in the breech position when she'd gone into labour and Mercy was her nearest hospital. Now that her baby has been delivered, she's getting transferred to County General Hospital later on this evening or first thing tomorrow morning at the latest. I turned to my sister.

'How did you find me?' I couldn't help asking. Then I realized. 'The ad in the paper.'

Minerva nodded. 'We saw it. *All* of us.'

'It wasn't an invitation for any of you to come and visit me,' I told her. 'I pre-paid for the ad and told them to run it when I thought we were about to leave this place, but Callie got ill. If I'd known we'd be in hospital this long, I would've delayed the announcement until we were out of here.'

63

'Serves you right then,' said Minerva evenly.

My lips fused together at that. It didn't take her long to get mean—but then again, I'd started it.

'I'm sorry. I didn't mean to be bitchy and I didn't come here to start a fight,' sighed Minerva. 'Do you have everything you need? Can I get you anything?'

'Yes to the first question, no to the second,' I said.

I waited.

'So can I have a look at my niece then?'

'She's down there.' I pointed to the transparent, plastic cot at the bottom of the bed.

Minerva stood up and went to have a look at you. She gazed down at you without saying a word. She neither moved nor spoke. Then at last she slowly stroked your cheek with one finger.

'Are you really going to call her Callie?'

'Callie Rose,' I told her. 'Like it said in the newspaper ad.'

'Hello, baby,' said Minerva.

'She has a name. Why're you here, Minerva?'

'I wanted to see you.'

I let that one slide.

'How long have you been in this place then?' asked my sister.

'Just under two weeks.'

'Why so long?'

'Callie had respiratory problems. She only came up from the special care baby unit

64

yesterday.'

'Oh, I see. Is she all right now?'

Holding myself on a tight rein, I answered, 'Yes, though she's still a bit underweight so they're going to keep her in until she starts to put more weight on.'

Minerva regarded me. 'You look tired, Sephy.'

'I *am* tired,' I replied. 'I've just had a baby.'

Minerva nodded—like she'd know anything about it. 'So who's feeding her?'

I frowned. 'I am.'

'Aren't you afraid of your boobs drooping?'

I gave her a look which apparently spoke volumes because she smiled and said, 'You don't really give a damn, do you?'

'Minerva, if you can work "rat's arse" into that sentence, you'll just about have it,' I added.

'Fair enough,' Minerva laughed, but her smile quickly faded. 'Not Minnie any more, eh?'

'I think we've both grown out of that,' I said at last.

Minerva regarded me but, as I stared right back at her, she dropped her gaze. The days when she could intimidate me with just one look were long gone.

'Why're you here?' I asked again. 'I mean, why now?'

'I wanted to see you,' Minerva told me, her tone defensive.

'You've already said that. But you didn't

65

want to see me after you'd been shot, so why now?'

'I was angry and blamed you for what happened to me—especially after you persuaded me to let Jude off the hook,' Minerva explained. 'And I'm really sorry about that. It was unfair.'

I shrugged. 'I understood.'

'Once I'd come out of the hospital, I did want to see you,' Minerva said. 'You're the one who disappeared. You moved out of your flat and no one knew where you were. It was like you'd vanished in a puff of smoke.'

'I was around.'

'Where?'

I shrugged, unwilling to say more. What was there to say? Well, actually, Minerva, if you think my old flat was bad, wait until you see this one. I'm now living in a poky, icy box of a bedsit, with not even a separate bedroom. Just a two-ring, countertop cooker, a sofa bed and a tiny, freezer-like bathroom.

And it's not funny how quickly money disappears when you have to pay bills and rent and buy essentials, like food and a baby carry-cot and nappies and a buggy and all the other stuff that babies need. I had about a month's money left and then I was going to be stony broke.

'Why didn't you come home after . . . after what happened with Jude?' Minerva asked.

'It isn't my home any more,' I told her.

'Yes, it is. We all want you to come back.'

'Minerva, after you were shot, you hardly spoke to me, so don't pretend I would've been welcomed home by you with open arms.'

'I told you, I was angry, but I soon got over it.'

I didn't.

'Mother and I miss you,' Minerva continued.

There wasn't much I could say to that, so I kept silent.

'I mean that,' Minerva said earnestly.

'How is Mother?' I asked.

'Fine. At least, she pretends to be.'

'Is she still drinking?'

'No,' Minerva surprised me by saying. 'Now that Dad has packed up and gone for good, I was more than worried that she might start again. But I doubt if she's even missing him. She's too busy regretting all the things that went wrong between the two of you.'

'I doubt it.'

'She is.'

'Have you left home yet?' I asked.

'No. I don't want to leave Mother all alone but she wouldn't be too cut up if I did. You were always her favourite,' said Minerva evenly.

I narrowed my eyes. 'What're you talking about? My entire life, all Mother ever did was wish I could be more like you.'

'Just talk,' Minerva dismissed. 'You answered back. You never did as you were told. Mother loved that. I'm the boring, obedient one. You're the free spirit.'

67

'You're talking crap,' I snapped. I had enough journeys of my own to make, without Minerva trying to take me on a guilt trip.

'Sephy, I'd been asking Mother if I could go to Chivers boarding school since I was at primary school. I never made it past Heathcroft High.'

'And it didn't occur to you that Mother was just happy to be rid of me?'

'Didn't it occur to *you* that Mother just can't say no to you? You wore her down after a few weeks. I couldn't do it even after five years.'

I wasn't about to jump onto the 'who had it the toughest' bandwagon. I lowered my gaze. Minerva sighed again, then smiled. 'What is it about you and me that means we always end up arguing?'

'Just lucky, I guess!'

Minerva started to laugh but it didn't last long. I so wanted her to be Minnie again, I really did. My sister glanced down at her watch.

'I have to go now,' she said. 'Sephy, is it . . . is it OK for Mother to visit?'

Ah! Now we had it.

'And no, before you ask—I'm not here just to ask if Mother can come and see you,' Minerva leapt in. 'I wanted to see you and meet my niece.'

'Fair enough,' I shrugged.

'So is it OK?'

I shrugged again. 'If she wants to visit, I can't stop her.'

'She won't come if it's going to upset you.'

'Tell her not to say a word against Callum and then I won't get upset,' I told my sister.

'Fair enough.' Minerva glanced down at her watch again.

'Where're you rushing off to then?' I asked.

'Job interview,' said Minerva.

'Where?'

'The *Daily Shouter*.'

'To do what?'

'Journalism,' said Minerva. 'I'm going to be a star reporter.'

'Well, excuse me all over the place!' There was no denying that I was impressed.

'I haven't got the job yet,' Minerva pointed out. 'But if I don't make it on to the *Daily Shouter*, I'll get on another national newspaper. It's just a matter of time. I'm very ambitious.'

'I didn't know you were interested in that kind of thing.'

'I was editor of the Heathcroft newsletter for two years—remember?'

'No,' I frowned. 'I don't actually.'

'That's because all you had eyes for back then was Callum. If he wasn't involved, you weren't interested.'

Which stung. But was nothing less than the truth.

'So you really want to be a journalist?' I asked.

'Yeah, I've been thinking about it more and more recently,' said Minerva.

'Print the truth or be damned, eh?'

'It's "print the truth *and* be damned",' Minerva corrected.

'But the truth will get a look in?'

'Another typical Sephy statement,' said Minerva.

'Sorry. That was snide,' I replied.

'Yes, it was.' Minerva smiled. 'But I'm a bitch to you and you're snide to me and that's the way we'll always be.'

I didn't deny it, but now that she'd said it out loud, it didn't seem so relentlessly awful any more. It was just the way we were with each other. But I did care about her. And in spite of everything, I think she cared about me.

'Well, good luck at your interview,' I ventured.

'Thanks.'

Minerva headed off down the ward before turning back after a couple of steps.

'By the way, Sephy,' said Minerva. 'You have a beautiful daughter.'

'I know,' I replied.

seventeen. Jude

I was going to phone her but I decided against it. I had a shower, put on some of my more expensive aftershave, a clean pair of black jeans, a matching black polo shirt and a black leather jacket and headed out the door. It was

70

already on the hot side of warm outside. Another couple of hours and it'd be baking. I looked up at the blue sky and sighed. Maybe I should go back in and dump the leather jacket, but I couldn't be bothered. Besides, I knew I looked good in it.

Half an hour later I was standing outside Cara's hairdressing shop. It was mid-morning and already the place was full. I could see a number of women having their hair cut or braided or corn-rowed or whatever it is women do in these places. Three women and a man stood above the various clients, chatting and smiling. The women hairdressers were Crosses, the male hairdresser was a nought—which surprised me no end. I watched through the window as they all got on with it.

And there was Cara, smiling via a wall mirror at one of her customers. A nought customer who was having her blonde hair braided. Cara must've said something hilarious because the woman creased up laughing. I debated whether or not to go in. But I needed money. And possibly a place to stay. And Cara could give me both. I walked into the shop.

'Can I help you, sir?' The woman on the reception desk pounced before I'd even closed the door.

'I'm here to see Cara,' I said.

'D'you have an appointment?'

'No, I don't.'

'I'm afraid we're really busy today.' The receptionist rushed into her apology. 'She won't be able to—'

'It's OK. This is my friend Steve.' Cara was already coming over to me, a big smile on her face. When she smiled it was like she lit up from within. She didn't just turn up her lips like some women I knew, she lifted her head and smiled with her eyes and her cheeks and her lips. And why shouldn't she? She was a Cross who had it easy. 'How are you?'

'Fine,' I replied. 'I hope you don't mind me dropping in.'

'No, of course not. I'm glad to see you,' said Cara.

And she really did look like she meant it. I didn't understand her at all. We were being bombarded by curious glances. I took a step forward, as well as a deep breath, before I could say the next thing. It didn't come easily asking a dagger for anything, and certainly not a date.

'I managed to get hold of two tickets for *Destruction*, that Daley Mercer film you wanted to see. I just wondered if you wanted to come with me?'

'When?'

'Tonight.'

'Oh, I'd love to, but we have late-night closing tonight,' said Cara regretfully. 'What time does the film start?'

I looked around. We were the floor show. All eyes were trained on us. I moved in closer to Cara so no one else would hear what I was saying. This was embarrassing enough as it was.

'Not until eight-fifteen.'

'I don't finish till after nine,' Cara said unhappily. 'I have to lock up after everyone else has gone.'

'Never mind. It was just an idea,' I said.

So much for that then. Maybe this wasn't going to be as easy as I'd first thought.

'Tell you what, why don't I cook a late dinner for us back at my place to make up for it?' said Cara. 'I have to warn you though, I'm not a very good cook.'

'I am,' I said truthfully. 'If you provide the ingredients, I'll do the cooking.'

'It's a deal.' Cara grinned enthusiastically. 'D'you want to meet me at my house?'

'No. I'll come here at nine,' I decided. 'Then I'll walk you home.'

'Thanks, Steve. I'll see you later then. And I'm sorry about the film.'

'Don't worry about it,' I said. 'See you later.'

And I headed out the door. I made sure to turn back and give her one last wave though. Girls like that sort of thing. How easy was this? Stupid, stupid cow. She called me her friend, but her saying it didn't make it so. She didn't know me from a bar of soap and already I was being invited back to her house. Tonight, she'd be the last one left in the shop to lock up. It'd be just me and her. I was looking forward to it. I was going to be teacher.

And Cara was going to learn that it really didn't pay to be quite so trusting.

eighteen. Sephy

Dearest Callie,

I got talking to the woman in the next bed to mine today. She only came in yesterday. She's really lovely. Her name is Roxie and I'd put her somewhere in her mid to late twenties—although I'm useless at judging people's ages. She had a son a couple of hours ago and she's leaving tomorrow. Lucky cow! I wish I could get out of here. But then I think about what I've got waiting for me, a horrible flat with a view of a brick wall out of the one and only window, and wonder why I'm in such a hurry to leave? I don't want to take you back there, Callie, but I've got no choice. I promise you this though, it'll only be for a little while. Once I get on my feet again, I'll get you the kind of place you deserve.

I thought Roxie was like me—no family. But I got that very wrong.

It was seven o'clock at night and I'd just finished feeding you. As I put you back in your cot, I looked up and Roxie caught my eye and smiled.

'Your daughter is very beautiful,' she said.

'I think so,' I replied. 'But then I'm biased!'

Swarms of people were beginning to flood down the ward.

'Are you expecting company?' I asked.

'I'm not sure. My partner's working in

Sheeley up North and he can't get back until tomorrow afternoon.'

'What does he do?'

'He works for National Rail as a track layer so he's up and down the country, going where the work is,' Roxie replied. 'My brother and sisters might visit though.'

'How many sisters have you got?'

'Three.' Roxie smiled. 'And one brother, Jaxon. Oh, there he is.'

I looked down the ward and watched as a tall, blond man with shoulder-length hair marched down the middle of the ward like he owned it, a guitar slung across his back. The man didn't look much older than me. As he got closer, I saw he had blond eyebrows and, more strangely, blond eyelashes which made his eyes the first thing you noticed. His ice-blue eyes were oddly hypnotic, like a snake's eyes. They stood out because there seemed to be nothing for them to hide behind—or under.

'Hi, Sis!' Jaxon bent to kiss his sister's cheek before scooping his nephew out of her arms.

'Jaxon, this is Sephy. Sephy, this is Jaxon Robbins, my brother.'

'Hi, Jaxon,' I smiled.

He barely nodded in my direction, his attention on his family.

'So what's the sprog's name then?'

'My son's name is Sam,' Roxie said loftily, before giving me a long-suffering look. 'And he's not a sprog.'

'Sprog? What's that?' I asked.

'An ankle-biter, a little 'un, a rug rat, a—'

'Thank you, Jaxon. I think Sephy gets the idea,' Roxie interrupted.

'I've never heard any of those phrases before,' I smiled.

'That's because they're nought words. Not everything in our lives has been dictated by Crosses. We noughts have our own language, you know. We need to keep something that's just for ourselves,' said Jaxon, looking directly at me for the first time.

'Fair enough,' I told him after a pause.

'Is it? Is that what you really think?' Jaxon challenged. 'We use our own words, our own phrases, our own accents and we're told we're not talking properly, that we're inarticulate or illiterate.'

'I'd never say that,' I said.

'But you feel threatened, I bet. The words sound so similar, yet the meaning is so different,' said Jaxon. 'Our language is something you Crosses can't understand and can't control.'

'Jaxon, leave her alone,' Roxie rounded on him. 'Sephy, I'm sorry about him.'

'Don't worry about it,' I shrugged. 'Besides, I prefer plain speaking. Then everyone knows where they stand.'

I moved down to the cot because I could hear you gearing up for a cry.

'It's OK. Mummy's here,' I soothed, hugging you to me.

Out of the corner of my eye, I could see

Roxie whispering something to her brother—and all the time he was listening, he kept looking at me. Ignoring him, I checked your nappy—which was loaded! Jaxon walked over as I was cleaning you up.

'If you want to rub that dirty nappy in my face, I wouldn't blame you,' he told me.

'Why on earth would I want to do that?' I laughed.

'Roxie's just told me who you are,' Jaxon admitted. 'I didn't recognize you. I didn't realize you were one of us.'

My smile wavered momentarily.

Us and them. Them and us.

Always the same. Never changing.

Jaxon looked down at my daughter and gave a start, the way most people did when they first saw her. She was too light to be all Cross and too dark to be all Nought.

'What's her name?'

'Callie Rose.'

'That's pretty. It suits her,' he said.

I just smiled. 'She's my rainbow child—like in the song.'

'What d'you mean?' Jaxon leaned forward for a closer look.

'I'm talking about all the colours she brings, not the colour she is,' I said.

'Oh, I see.'

'So where d'you play that thing?' I asked, pointing at his guitar.

'This?' Jaxon pulled the guitar round so that it was under his arm. 'I play any time, any place, any where.'

After a quick glance up and down the ward, I said, 'How about a tune then, to cheer us all up?'

I was only joking but Jaxon leapt on the suggestion immediately. 'Only if you join in!' he said.

'Suppose I can't sing?' I asked him.

'Even better,' Jaxon grinned.

Roxie shook her head. 'Sephy, please don't encourage him, because he really will do it.'

I looked up at Jaxon, who was smiling at me, and decided that Roxie was right. Jaxon looked like the kind of guy who went full-steam ahead one hundred per cent of the time.

'Well? You gonna chicken out?'

'What song?' I asked, placing an already dozing Callie back in her plastic cot. I guess she wasn't hungry after all, just uncomfortable.

'You two aren't serious,' Roxie asked, aghast.

'Which song?' I smiled again.

'Suggest something,' said Jaxon.

'*Rainbow Child*? For all the new-borns in here.'

'Go for it,' said Jaxon. He began to strum his guitar.

Jaxon started singing, a challenge in his eyes as he looked at me.

'You bring a sweet embrace
And with the smile upon your face
You bring me grace, my rainbow child.
You bring me Autumn days,

78

Turn my face to golden rays,
You bring me bliss, my rainbow child.'

I took a deep breath and after the first couple of lines I joined in, quietly at first but picking up volume with each word. I saw Jaxon look at me in surprise when I started to sing. I knew he thought I'd lose my nerve. But then he smiled and we carried on singing together, getting louder.

'And what was life before you?
And do you know how I adore you?
And it scares me how I feel,
All my past scars fade and heal
When I hold my rainbow child.

'You bring a quiet time,
Life has meaning, thoughts have rhyme,
You bring me peace, my rainbow child.
You bring down all my fences,
You invade my heart and senses,
You bring me hope, my rainbow child.'

Jaxon had a good voice. Me? At first I just worried about keeping up and not forgetting the words. But then I kind of got into it. And by the end of the second verse, I was actually enjoying myself. And I wasn't even nervous any more. I mean, our singing wasn't raucous, it was just . . . heartfelt. Of course, by the time Jaxon and I hit the chorus for the first time, we had the full attention of everyone on the ward.

And d'you know something? We didn't sound too bad. In fact I was amazed at how tuneful I sounded! I'd been in the choir at school but I was never one of the ones picked out for solos in school plays or concerts. I was always one of the chorus and happy enough with that. But here I was doing a duet and no one was throwing up. The others in the ward were actually smiling and clapping along. And even though Jaxon carried on singing, he was regarding me with the strangest expression on his face. But then I saw Nurse Solomon marching up the ward towards us.

'*There is no singing in the ward,*' she tried to shout over our voices. We completely ignored her. If anything, we sang louder.

'And what was life before you?
And do you know how I adore you?
And it scares me how I feel,
All my past scars fade and heal
When I hold my rainbow child.'

'THERE'S NO SINGING IN THIS WARD.' Nurse Solomon was more screaming than shouting now.

It was just a lark, a bit of fun. But Nurse Solomon was getting really wound up. And then she grabbed for Jaxon's guitar. Big mistake. The sudden change in his demeanour was like a switch being flicked on.

'Listen, you dagger bitch—don't you ever, as long as you live, touch my guitar again,' Jaxon

80

said with quiet menace.

Nurse Solomon certainly got the message. She drew back her hand as if scalded, then turned to look meaningfully at me. Apart from the odd baby's cry, the ward was silent. Nurse Solomon walked back to the nurses' station. Jaxon's words had been like a slap round my face. And then I remembered something— something unbidden and unwelcome. Callum's first day at Heathcroft, my old school. There'd been a mob outside the school entrance protesting against Noughts being allowed into the same schools as us Crosses. And I remembered what I'd shouted out to stop the Noughts trying to get into school from being abused, how I'd accused my friends of behaving like animals. Worse than animals, like *blankers*. And the look of Callum's face when I said that was something I'd never, ever forget. I'd come so close to losing him that day. Callum made me promise to never say that word again. Callum was right, words did hurt. Like now. I was just as wounded as Nurse Solomon and, worse still, I felt like I was the one who'd caused the verbal attack in the first place. I glanced at Jaxon before moving down the bed to check on my daughter.

'Sephy, I'm sorry about that,' said Jaxon with an easy smile. 'But she shouldn't've touched my guitar. I didn't mean you.'

'Yes, you did mean me. I'm a Cross too,' I pointed out.

'The words were for that nurse,' said Jaxon.

81

'Yeah, but they apply to me too,' I told him.

'No, they—'

I raised a hand as if to deflect his words.

'Jaxon, they apply to me too. Now if you don't mind . . .' I picked you up, Callie, and stood in front of him, waiting for him to move so that I could get back into bed to feed you. You didn't really need feeding as you were more than half asleep but I had to do something to mask my humiliation.

Jaxon walked back to his sister's bed. I completely ignored him and settled down with you, Callie. But I couldn't ignore his words.

One of us . . .

One of them . . .

One of us . . .

One of them . . .

A rhythm playing like train wheels on a circular track—never ending but going absolutely nowhere.

nineteen. Jude

I stood outside the darkened shop and checked my watch. Five minutes past nine. I peered through the glass window of the shop but there was no one there. The place was empty. The bitch had stood me up. She probably had no intention of ever going out with me in the first place. No doubt she'd had a good giggle with all her friends when I'd

82

gone, chuckling at the way I'd be left outside the shop like a lemon whilst she was out with her mates enjoying a drink and a good laugh at my expense. My hands slowly curled at my side.

'Steve? STEVE!'

I turned to see Cara running up the road towards me.

'Thank goodness. I thought I was going to miss you,' Cara gasped as she got closer to me.

Forcing a smile on my face, I said, 'I thought you'd still be working.'

'The last customer left about twenty minutes ago, so I popped to the night bank to deposit the day's takings. I don't like leaving all that money in the shop,' Cara explained.

'We could've done it on our way to your house,' I said easily.

'Yes, but I live in the opposite direction to the bank,' said Cara. 'I didn't want to put you out.'

I shrugged. There was no point in arguing about it, no matter how disappointed I was. So much for my idea of picking up some easy money without too much work. I'd just have to be patient a while longer.

'So what am I cooking for us?' I asked.

'If you still want to do the cooking, I've got some pasta in the house. And some mince, I think. And fish.'

'What kind of fish?'

Cara frowned as she tried to remember. 'Haddock, and I think I've got some sea bass

83

that has to be used by tomorrow.'

'Sea bass it is then,' I smiled. 'Let's go.'

I let her do most of the talking as I walked her home. I asked her about her day in the salon and then let her blather on about her clients and her colleagues. Apparently Delany's was one of the few hairdressing salons which catered for both noughts and Crosses. Apparently seeing nought women and Cross women in the same hairdresser's was as rare as rocking-horse droppings. Cara had a vision . . . blah blah blah. I tuned out after about the first forty-odd seconds, only dropping in the occasional 'Is that right?' and 'Really?' and 'I didn't know that!' as and when her monologue seemed to require it.

'God! I've been going on and on and probably boring you rigid,' Cara exclaimed as we reached her house.

Yes, you have actually.

'Of course not,' I replied. 'You love your work and it shows. There's nothing wrong with that.'

'You're really nice, Steve.' Cara smiled at me gratefully. 'Most men's eyes would've glazed over long before now.'

And the warmth of the smile she gave me made me feel . . . uncomfortable. Which I didn't expect. Which made me feel worse. Cara let us into her house. What was I going to do now? Of course, I could get rid of her, but what was the point? I didn't have her money. I wouldn't be able to stay in her house as her

84

friends would soon come knocking on the door asking questions. So why bother? I'd cook and put up with this dagger's company until I had what I wanted—and then what would be, would be. I just had to bide my time.

'D'you know, I don't even know your name,' Cara told me.

'Steve,' I frowned.

'No. I mean your last name.'

'Winner. Steven Winner,' I told her.

'Shall I take your jacket, Steven Winner?' Cara asked once the front door had closed behind us.

I took it off and gave it to her without arguing. We stood for a moment in awkward silence. We were in her house and alone. As the silence stretched on, I wondered if she was beginning to think better of inviting me in. I looked around the hall. Sunshine yellow with poster prints on the wall. And a maple wood floor. A small telephone table to my right held a telephone and a small bowl of lavender pot pourri which made the whole hall reek. What was it about Crosses and their potpourris?

'Very nice,' I said inanely.

And then a thought occurred to me. This was the first time I'd been invited into a dagger's house since I was a kid. It was strange. I couldn't get over the feeling that I really shouldn't be here. It didn't feel right. It didn't feel completely *safe*.

'The kitchen's just through here,' said Cara, leading the way.

I followed her into a small but functional kitchen, with cream walls and oak cupboards. The floor was of light-coloured stone.

'You have a lovely house,' I told her. 'Delany's must be doing very well.'

'We do OK,' Cara shrugged. 'Although I have to admit, I bought this house with some money that was left to me.'

'A rich relative?' I smiled to take the sting out of my words.

'No. My dad died of a heart attack four years ago. I bought this place with the money I received from his life insurance policy.'

'Oh, I see. I'm sorry.'

Cara faked a nonchalant shrug. 'He'd been ill for some time.'

'Must've been hard though,' I said, remembering my own dad. I didn't think of him every day, but when I did, it still hurt. A lot.

Cara opened the fridge door and took out a bottle of wine. 'Help yourself,' she said, leaving the fridge door open for me.

I looked into one of the best-stocked fridges I'd ever seen in my life and I said as much.

'I must admit, I rushed round the supermarket at lunch-time so you'd have a choice of things to cook,' Cara admitted.

I turned to look at her, wondering why on earth she'd bother. She looked so embarrassed when she smiled at me that I couldn't help smiling back. And then I remembered why I was there—and who she was. And even though my smile continued on the outside, I stopped smiling on the inside.

I hacked off the heads and washed and seasoned two sea bass, then stuck them in the oven.

'Why did you cut off the heads?' asked Cara.

'I can't eat fish if the head is on it,' I told her truthfully. 'The eyes look up at me like they're saying, "How could you?"!'

Cara smiled as she shook her head. 'Strange man!'

And we exchanged a genuine smile of amusement. I turned away first. I bunged some new potatoes into some boiling water whilst Cara made a salad. We both sipped at our glasses of Pinot Grigio as we cooked. Cara put on some rock music from one of my favourite singers. Was the nought music for my benefit or did she really like it?

'Do you really like Wasp Sting then?' I couldn't help asking.

'Yes, I do. I love rock and white metal.'

'I'd've thought you'd be into Jam and Sync and classical and music like that,' I said.

Cara tilted her head as she regarded me. 'You mean, Cross music as opposed to Nought music?'

'I suppose I do.'

'You're not one of those who thinks that only Crosses can appreciate Cross music and only Noughts should listen to Nought music, are you?'

'No, I'm not,' I said. 'But I think it's unfair

that a nought can bring out a single and a Cross can cover the same single and yet the one that makes the charts and the one that gets played on the radio is the Cross version.'

'I agree,' said Cara instantly. 'The best version should be the one that gets played, regardless of who's singing it.'

'That's not the way it works though, is it?' I said, warming to my theme. 'Look at white metal. That's a music form created and sung by noughts. Yet who's the best-known—and richest—white metal singer? DeCosta Bafenweh—a Cross.'

Cara nodded. 'You're right. And I do have a DeCosta Bafenweh CD. But I have three Wasp Sting CDs.'

'That's all right then.' I forced a smile. I took a few sips of my white wine, swirling each small mouthful across my tongue before swallowing.

'How's the wine?' Cara asked.

'Fine,' I told her.

Taking a small but very sharp vegetable knife out of the cutlery drawer, I checked on the new potatoes. Halfway through prodding the second or third spud, some sixth sense told me that I was being watched. I swung round to see Cara studying me. But this time she didn't look away when I caught her scrutinizing me.

'Is something wrong?' I asked.

'I'm just wondering about you,' Cara admitted.

'Wondering what?'

'If I was right about you,' said Cara.

'Right about what?'

'That you're as lonely as I am,' Cara said at last.

My whole body froze. My grip on the knife in my hand tightened so much that my knuckles were beginning to ache. And still I didn't reply. Cara looked straight at me.

'That's why I thought we'd get on,' she carried on. 'Lonely birds of a feather and all that.'

Lonely birds of a feather . . .

I may be lonely but I'm not desperate enough to go out with a Cross, I thought bitterly. And yet here I was in a dagger's house, listening to her try to psychoanalyse me. I needed to put down the knife before I did something stupid. I slowly placed the knife on the work surface. And still I didn't answer.

'Is this where you tell me you've got a wife and two kids?' Cara smiled uncertainly.

I shook my head.

'Am I right about you?' Cara asked. 'I mean, if I'm not, I'm sorry.'

Silence.

'Yes, you're right about me,' I said at last. 'I've got no one.'

Which was the first time I'd ever had to say that out loud. And who was the first person to hear it? A dagger. I hated it. I hated myself. Some things shouldn't be said. Saying them out loud made them all the more real, even more true. I closed my eyes and looked away from her. I didn't want her to see at that moment

89

just how much I despised her for making me articulate my loneliness.

When the time was right, she'd pay for that as well.

But then she did something that took me completely by surprise. She came over to me and kissed me on the cheek. Startled, I turned to her, staring at her. She smiled at me and then went back to making her salad. I stood there, a strange longing eating away at me. I stood there, drowning in self-pity and misery.

But drowning just the same.

We both continued doing what we were doing in silence for a while. I think we were both embarrassed. I know I was.

'Fruit salad and vanilla ice-cream OK for our pudding?' asked Cara.

I nodded, not trusting myself to speak.

'OK. You can help me prepare it,' said Cara.

We worked in a companionable silence, washing and slicing strawberries, grapes, a couple of mangoes, peaches, lychees and every other soft fruit she had in the house. The music on the CD finally faded as the last track came to an end.

'I'll go and put some more music on,' said Cara, and she headed off towards the living room.

I frowned as I watched her retreating back. Where was she going? We wouldn't hear music played from the living room in the kitchen unless she really cranked up the volume. And Cara didn't strike me as the kind of girl who played her music loud. Unexpectedly, soft, soulful music gently filled the room, originating from somewhere above me. I looked up at the two ceiling speakers I hadn't noticed before. I should've guessed.

As Cara came back into the room, I asked, 'How many rooms does the music get piped into then?'

'In here, the living room, the dining room, the bathroom and my bedroom.'

'That's . . . nice,' I said inanely. 'So what's this you've put on then?'

The intro of the music was still playing so I didn't immediately recognize the artist. Cara opened her mouth to tell me, but before she could say a word, the lead singer of Jet Stone started up. I'd've known his falsetto voice anywhere.

'Ah,' I said. 'Mystery solved.'

'D'you like Jet Stone?' Cara asked.

'They're all right,' I said, trying to tune out the lead singer's sickly sweet voice which filled every corner of the room.

'You don't like them, do you?' said Cara. 'I can take them off if you'd rather listen to something else.'

Oh, for heaven's sake! I walked over to Cara and held out my hand. Even though there was a questioning look on her face, she still put her hand in mine without hesitation. I moved closer to her and slipped my arm around her waist. Cara smiled up at me as we started dancing. I only did it because girls like that sort of thing. Cara wrapped her arms around my waist, resting her head on my shoulder. I glanced down at her and could see that she'd closed her eyes. We swayed in time to the love song, whilst I stared off into the middle distance.

She has money. You need money, I told myself.

Jet Stone didn't even play my kind of music. But how easy it'd be to forget everything I held true. How easy it'd be to just close my eyes.

'Come on, Steve. Be honest. You hate Jet Stone!'

I didn't realize Cara was looking up at me until she said that.

'Well, I must admit,' I said, 'the lead singer always sounds to me like a crab has got hold of his gonads!'

Cara burst out laughing. After a moment's surprise that she found that funny, I started to grin too.

'You just don't know great music when you hear it,' said Cara.

'Must be my upbringing!'

'You do make me laugh, Steve,' said Cara. 'I guess that's why I like you so much.'

And she really meant it. And for that at least, I was unexpectedly grateful.

twenty. Sephy

Darling Callie,

This is definitely my week for visitors. Guess who turned up this morning? Mother. I watched her glide up the ward looking neither right nor left like some kind of imperious empress. And shall I tell you the strangest thing. I was so glad to see her. She approached my bed without a smile, her eyes clear, her expression alert. I realized with a start that she wasn't drunk or in any of her usually drunken stages—no hangover, no hunted, haunted, anticipatory gleam in her eyes as she contemplated her next drink—nothing. She was clean. I'd seen her once at the hospital when Minerva was shot. She'd said hello to me. I walked past her without saying a word. I didn't want to speak to her then. I wasn't sure what I wanted now.

'Hello, Persephone.'

'Hello . . . Mother.'

Mother headed straight for the cot. The moment she saw you, Callie, she stopped still. A slow smile curved her lips and lit her face from within. I've never seen an expression on her face like it—before or since. It was a look of complete, unconditional love. As she bent to pick you up, my hand went out to stop her, only to fall back to my side. Mother held you up high, never taking her eyes off you before she cradled you in her arms.

'Hello, Callie Rose—and welcome,' Mother whispered.

A single tear escaped down my cheek at that. I turned my head so that Mother wouldn't see and surreptitiously wiped my cheek. Not that I needed to hide my face. Mother only had eyes for her grandchild.

'Sephy, she's so beautiful,' Mother said, almost awe-struck.

'Yeah. She looks just like her dad,' I said quietly.

Mother looked from me to you, Callie. I found myself holding my breath, waiting to hear what she'd say to that. I thought she'd put you down and change the subject at the very least.

But she didn't.

'Yes, she does,' Mother agreed at last. 'I assume you called her Callie after Callum.'

'It was the closest girl's name to his that I could think of.'

'Callie Rose . . . It's a beautiful name,' said Mother. 'It suits her.'

I wanted to scream at her to stop. Her condemnation and contempt I could handle. But this being kind to me, the approval and the love in her voice as she looked at you slipped under my guard and was hurting. Very much. Her indifference was much easier to fight against than her understanding.

'Why're you here, Mum?' I asked, deliberately calling her Mum because I knew

94

she preferred Mother. But she didn't have a go. She just smiled.

'I wanted to see you and my granddaughter,' she said. 'And if I'd known where you were living, I'd've been round to see you a lot sooner.'

'You saw the newspaper announcement?'

'Knowing you, wasn't that the whole idea?' asked Mother.

'As I told Minerva, Callie and I were meant to be out of here by the time they ran it.'

'Then I thank the heavens that you weren't,' smiled Mother.

I looked at her then, really looked at her. 'So how come you didn't come to visit before now.'

'I wasn't sure of my welcome. But Minerva seemed to think you wouldn't have me thrown out,' said Mother.

'I'd never do that,' I said.

'I wouldn't blame you if you did,' Mother shrugged. 'So when d'you come out?'

'It was meant to be today but they're keeping us in for one more night.'

'And what're your plans?' asked Mother.

'To live each day minute by minute. I don't have any other plans,' I told her.

Not any more.

'Minute by minute doesn't work with a baby. You need to plan ahead, for your daughter's sake.'

'And how old can she be before I stop caring like you did?' I asked with venom.

'Sephy, I know I wasn't there for you when

95

you needed me most, but I want to make up for it now—if you'll let me.'

I didn't reply.

Mother sighed. 'I was a politician's wife, Sephy. Public duties often had to come before everything else—including you and Minerva. And including my own wants and needs. Your father expected nothing less.'

I shrugged. Mother wasn't telling me anything I didn't already know.

Silence. 'D'you still blame me for Callum's death?' Mother asked.

I looked away from Mother when she asked that. Her repeated sigh told me that she thought I'd answered her question. But the truthful answer was . . . no.

'Sephy, the past is over and it's time for all of us to let it go. We have to do what's right for your daughter now,' said Mother.

We . . .

'And that is?' I tensed up, waiting to hear her talk about adoption or fostering or farming out my baby to anyone who'd take her.

'I think it would be best for you and Callie Rose if you both came back home with me,' said Mother carefully.

I started to laugh—I couldn't help it. 'You must be joking, Mother.'

'Why not?' Mother asked quietly.

'Because we can't turn the clock back. We've both said too much and been through too much . . .'

'I'm not suggesting we turn the clock back,'

96

said Mother. 'What I want is for the three of us to move forward from here and now.'

'Just like that?'

'Just like that,' said Mother.

'It's that simple?'

'It is if you let it be. Sephy, you've always been one to do things the hard way. This is easy,' said Mother. 'Come home. You and Callie Rose will be more than welcome.'

'Really?'

'Yes. I want you home with me more than anything else in the world. I want us to be friends again. And I want to help with Callie.' When I tried to interrupt, Mother rushed on. 'I won't try to take over—and I'll respect the fact that you're Callie's mother, not me. But I want to be a part of your life again, Sephy. And I want to be part of my granddaughter's life as well.'

Mother and I regarded each other. How I longed to be welcome—anywhere. And I could see that Mother meant every word. We'd both said some hateful, hurtful things over the last few months but I was tired. Was I too tired to even hate her any more? *What should I do, Callum?* Moving in with Mother would be so easy. And Callie and I would be safe in Mother's house. Jude wouldn't be able to get near us. But more importantly than that, I wouldn't be alone with a new baby. I wouldn't have to cope on my own and Mother would be there to back me up. To draw a line under the past and move forward . . . I longed to be able

97

to do just that. Maybe moving back in with Mother was the first step. With a start, I realized I was already trying to talk myself into it.

'I still think about Callum a lot,' I warned her.

'I wouldn't expect anything less,' said Mother. 'He was your first love and the father of your child. That counts for an awful lot.'

'It's a shame you didn't see it that way a few months ago when you were trying to force me to have an abortion.' I couldn't hide the bitterness that crept into my voice.

'Yes, it is,' Mother surprised me by agreeing sombrely. 'And I'll regret that to my dying day. But please let me make it up to you, both of you.'

It was so much to forgive and forget. Maybe too much?

'Can I think about it?' I asked at last.

'That means no,' said Mother sadly.

'No. It means I'd like us to be friends again but I've rushed into so many bad decisions recently, I just need to think about it a bit more,' I said.

'Sephy, your daughter needs a stable, steady home,' said Mother, using my daughter against me.

'Are you still drinking—even a little bit?' I asked.

Mother stiffened at the question, but no way was I going to trust her with my daughter if she was still drinking.

'I haven't drunk anything stronger than orange juice since the day Callum was . . . killed,' Mother informed me.

'How come?'

At first I thought Mother wasn't going to answer, but at last she said, 'Because I didn't just lose the son of one of my best friends that day. I lost my daughter as well.'

No denials. No arguments. No words.

'Come home, Sephy. Please,' Mother said softly. 'I promise you things will be different.'

'OK,' I nodded.

'What?'

For the first time in living memory, Mother forgot her manners! No 'Pardon?', no 'Excuse me?'—just 'What?'! I laughed.

'I said, OK!' I repeated. 'I'll come home with you.'

'You will?' Mother's face lit up like a lighthouse. She looked so happy. Joyously happy. And I'd done that. Seeing her so happy made my mood lighter as well. I'd be lying if I said I was entirely convinced about the wisdom of what I was doing. Was I just taking the easy way out? What about all my big talk about standing on my own two feet and never asking anyone in my family for anything again? But I had someone else to consider now as well as myself. And at least, good or bad, I'd made a decision. Maybe the future didn't have to be quite so daunting after all.

'I'll go home now and get your room ready. And I'll have the study converted into a nursery. D'you want Callie Rose to sleep in the same room as you for the time being? I don't mind having her in my room and feeding her through the night if you want a good night's sleep. Goodness, I have so much to do . . .'

'Mother, slow down,' I told her. 'I don't want any fuss. And please don't do anything to the study. Callie will sleep in my room until she's a lot older and then maybe we can decorate one of the spare bedrooms for her.'

'Fair enough. I guess I am getting a little ahead of myself,' Mother laughed.

'Just a bit,' I agreed.

Mother placed my daughter very carefully into my outstretched arms.

'Sephy, it'll be so good to have you home.' Mother kissed me on the cheek, something she hadn't done in years.

'It'll be good to be home, Mother,' I replied.

But somewhere inside, a flicker of lingering doubt still remained. Was this the right decision? Or just another of my hasty, bad ones?

I'd know soon enough.

twenty-one. Jude

I lay in bed this morning going over and over in my mind the events of the night before with Cara. I was still trying to understand what had happened. By which I mean, nothing

100

happened. We ate dinner, we listened to music, and we talked. And laughed. And talked some more. And that was it. And through it all, I tried not to look into her eyes for too long. I tried not to laugh too hard at her awful jokes. I tried not to relax or smile too long at the good music playing. I tried not to touch her any more than I had to.

But I failed.

We ate and chatted and I told myself I'd wait half an hour before making my excuses to leave. Almost three hours later, Cara walked me to the door and then we stood in an awkward silence as she waited for me to make the next move.

An offer of another date? A kiss? What?

I turned to her and said, 'Thank you for a lovely evening. I've really enjoyed myself.'

'So have I,' said Cara.

Pause.

'I hope we can do it again some time,' Cara continued.

'I hope so too,' I replied. 'Well, I'd better get going.'

I opened the front door and stepped out into the night. Truth be told, I couldn't wait to get out of there. The whole evening had been an uncomfortable mistake—because I'd enjoyed it too much. There I was chatting and eating and laughing with a Cross. As I walked away from her front door, I had to remind myself exactly why I was with her. I told myself that the end would justify the means. If I had to make love to a dagger to get the money I needed to further our cause, then I'd have to bite the bullet and do it. She was just a dagger woman—and all daggers deserved what they got. I'd get money and anything else I could from her and then cut her loose. And I needed to do it fast.

How ironic then that my evening with Cara had been the best I'd spent in a long, long time. It'd been relaxing and pleasant and only served to reinforce all the things I'd missed—not just for months but for years. There was a stillness about Cara that allowed me to be still too. A calmness around her that forced me to relax. But I wasn't going to let my guard down. Not for Cara. Not for anyone.

That would be fatal. Not just physically but mentally—which would be worse.

All of Jude's laws from one to six applied in this case—but especially number one.

Never ever *allow yourself to feel. Feelings kill.*

twenty-two. Sephy

Darling Callie,
We're going home. Tomorrow morning. A firm date at last. Yesterday they said I could go home today but it now looks like it'll definitely be tomorrow. *We're going home.* At last we're getting out of here. And whilst part of me is looking forward to getting away from this

hospital, another part of me is so terrified I'm going to mess up. I know Mother will be there but ultimately it'll be down to me. My daughter, my responsibility. Callie, I look down at you, asleep in my arms, and I still can't believe you're mine.

My daughter.

I'm still so young and I have a daughter. I look at you and it scares me how little I know. About anything. I raise my arms slowly, the better to smell you. You smell so fresh and new. I never get tired of the way you smell. I stroke your cheek and it's as soft as a whisper. That's how I spent my time today, Callie. Gazing at you for countless minutes, drinking you in, until I realized that I was being watched. I looked up and jumped when I saw who was standing at the foot of my bed.

Meggie McGregor. Callum's mum.

I couldn't've been more shocked if she'd marched up to me and slapped me round the face with a frozen kipper. My mouth gaped open as I continued to stare at her.

'Hello, Sephy,' Meggie said quietly.

'Hello . . . Mrs McGregor,' I said.

I used to call her Meggie, but that was before I realized I had absolutely no right to do so.

'How are you?'

'Fine.'

What was she doing here? I hadn't seen her since before Callum died. What did she want? Had she come to spit in my eye over the death of her son? I wouldn't blame her if she hated

103

me as much as Jude did. That bloody ad in the paper. Another one of my so-called brilliant ideas that'd turned round and bitten me on the bum. My rear end was blood-raw from my so-called brilliant ideas rebounding on me. I glanced down the ward to the nurses' station. If Meggie had come to hurt me or my baby, would I have time to shout for help? Would they have time to run to my assistance? I clutched Callie closer to me. No one, not Meggie, not Jude, not my father, no one was ever going to hurt my child.

'May I sit down?' Meggie asked.

I nodded warily. Meggie sat in the chair at the side of my bed.

'Can I hold her?' Meggie asked, smiling at my baby.

I eyed her uncertainly. 'Mrs McGregor, I—'

'My name's Meggie. And that's my granddaughter,' Meggie told me. 'I love her already.'

I still wasn't sure, but something about the look in her eyes made me believe her. Slowly I handed over my baby. Meggie's eyes lit up as she settled Callie into her arms. I recognized the expression on her face. It was the same one my mother had worn when she first held her granddaughter. And then I knew that Meggie was telling the truth. She really did love Callie already. Very much.

'Her eyes are blue,' Meggie said surprised.

'All babies' eyes are blue,' I told her.

'But I thought that Cross babies' eyes turned

brown within a few hours or days. You've been in hospital quite a while now,' said Meggie.

I shrugged.

'She's very beautiful,' smiled Meggie, her eyes on her granddaughter.

'I think so,' I said.

Only then did Meggie look at me. 'Thank you for calling her Callie.'

I shrugged, remembering how Callum hadn't wanted me to. Rose had been his idea. Callie had been mine.

'Callie Rose suits her,' Meggie smiled.

We were talking about nothing, both of us too afraid to say what was really on our minds. I took a deep breath, gathered up my courage and went for it.

'Mrs . . . Meggie, do you blame me for Callum's death?' I asked.

Meggie looked at me and shook her head. 'No. I never blamed you for what happened to my son.'

'Why not? Jude does.'

'Jude still hasn't found what he's looking for,' sighed Meggie.

'And what's that?'

'I don't think even Jude knows that. But until he can make sense of his own life, he'll blame you and every other Cross for everything that's wrong in it,' said Meggie.

'And you don't?'

'No.'

How wonderful it would be to believe that— even for a moment. With a sigh, I settled back against my pillows.

'Besides, I think you're probably blaming yourself enough for the both of us,' said Meggie.

'You know me so well.' I smiled without humour.

'I should do, Miss Sephy. I brought you up, didn't I?'

Which was no less than the truth.

'Please don't call me Miss Sephy,' I asked. 'Just Sephy will do.'

Miss Sephy . . . I wondered if she hated calling me that as much as I hated to hear it. It was almost like a member of my own family calling me Miss Sephy. Funny, but when I think of my early childhood, I remember my nanny, Meggie, being there more often than my own mother. Meggie and Callum were my closest friends—until the day Meggie left our house with Callum and hadn't been invited back. After that it was just Callum and me. Meggie and my mother had been so close, but it'd changed in a moment. Funny how life pivoted on single moments, single choices.

'So when d'you think you'll go home?' asked Meggie.

'They've said I can definitely go home tomorrow morning,' I told her.

She looked at me. 'Are you still in your flat?'

'Yes.' I frowned. 'How did you know about that?'

'A friend told me.'

A friend . . . Jude?

106

'No, not Jude,' said Meggie, reading my mind. 'I haven't seen him . . . to speak to since before Callum died.'

Did I believe her? I had no reason not to.

'I've got a suggestion,' said Meggie.

'What's that?'

'You could move in with me.'

'Sorry?' I was sure that I must've misheard her.

'If you don't like the idea of being alone in a flat, I thought perhaps you could move in with me,' said Meggie. 'I could help you and Callie Rose. I wouldn't try and take over. I just want to help.'

'Oh, but Mother's already—'

'It's common knowledge how your mother feels about you and Callie Rose. But that's not how I feel,' Meggie interrupted. 'Just hear me out. I've thought and thought about this and as we're both alone now, I thought it'd be the ideal solution.'

My heart began to pound inside me—long, loud thuds mocking every breath I took.

'But what about your sister? Aren't you living with her now? I'm sure she won't want me and a baby under her feet,' I said.

Tell her. You're going to move back home with Mother. Tell her.

'I live in my own place now,' said Meggie. 'It's not big or fancy but it's home. And you're welcome to share it with me.'

'Why . . . why d'you want to do this?' I asked, bewildered.

'You and Callie are all the family I've got left,' said Meggie.

Just a few words but they echoed with such longing and loneliness that my eyes instantly began to sting. I looked from Callie to Meggie and back again.

'And I'm sure it's what Callum would've wanted,' said Meggie, playing her ace. 'For us to live together as a family.'

My face felt like it was going to crack. But what could I do? I wanted to go home to Mother. I'd set my heart on that.

But Meggie needed us.

So did Mother.

I groaned inwardly. No matter what I decided, I'd end up hurting someone.

All the family I've got left . . .

The simple truth was that Meggie needed Callie and me more than Mother did. And I owed her.

'Please, Sephy?'

'Are you sure you won't mind being kept awake by a crying baby and having a house smelling of dirty nappies?'

'I'd love it,' Meggie grinned.

'Then I guess you've got two lodgers,' I replied. 'But only on one condition.'

'What's that?'

'You let me pay rent and half of all the bills.'

Meggie looked like she was about argue, but she regarded me and changed her mind. 'OK. That's all settled then.' She handed Callie back to me. 'Thank you, Sephy. I'll come and pick you up first thing tomorrow morning.' Meggie beamed at me. 'Having you and my granddaughter in the house will give me a reason for getting up in the mornings again.'

And with that she set off down the ward. I watched Meggie until she disappeared through the double doors at the end and even then, I couldn't tear my gaze away. What on earth had I done?

'I know this is none of my business,' said Roxie from the bed next to mine, 'but I couldn't help overhearing. I thought you were going home with your mother tomorrow?'

'I guess not,' I said, my voice clipped.

'Who was that woman then?' Roxie asked.

'Meggie McGregor. Callie's grandmother.'

'Why did you say you'd go with her?'

'She needs me.'

'What about what you need?' Roxie asked.

I had no answer.

twenty-three. Jude

Cara and I have been going out for a couple of weeks now. I decided to be patient. I'm after more than just a day's takings from the local hairdresser's. I have my eyes on bigger fish now—like the money from the whole Delany hairdressing salon account. There must be hundreds of thousands of pounds in it. I've seen Cara constantly have to turn people away so she has to be raking it in. Getting my hands on all her money shouldn't be too tricky.

For the simple reason that she cares about me. A lot.

I've tested her out. Sometimes, I let two days pass without phoning her. On the third day, like clockwork, she phones me on my mobile and suggests we hook up. And every time I see her, I give her flowers or chocolates or cheap bits of jewellery and she laps it up.

And the questions have started.

'How many brothers and sisters do you have?'

'Steve, what're your mum and dad like?'

'Steve, what exactly d'you do for a living?'

'What did you want to be when you left school?'

'Where d'you see yourself in five years' time?'

All those searching female questions that girls ask when deciding whether or not to get serious about you.

And the funny thing is, I haven't done a single thing to encourage it. Definitely no sex, very few kisses, limited handholding.

But I'll say one thing for Cara—she's intelligent. She knows how to have a proper conversation—unlike Gina. And she has opinions of her own. Gina would always ask me what I thought before venturing an opinion, invariably the same as mine. Cara isn't afraid to disagree with me. It's been a while since I sat down and talked about politics

110

and religion and films and life with someone outside the Liberation Militia. And it's been for ever since I discussed any of those things with a Cross.

'D'you get many noughts in your shop?' I asked over dinner one night.

'Not many—no,' said Cara. 'Not as many as I'd like.'

'I bet some of your Cross patrons don't like you doing nought hair in the same salon,' I said.

'Then they're free to go somewhere else,' said Cara immediately. 'I can't stand that kind of thinking around me. It's such a waste of time.'

'So if I asked you to cornrow my hair, you'd do it?'

'In this restaurant—no!' said Cara dryly. 'But in my salon or at my house? Yes, of course I would. Why wouldn't I?'

'You don't feel we noughts are trying too hard to take over the Cross style?' I said, careful to keep my tone even.

'The Cross style? What's that when it's at home?' Cara asked, leaning in to hear my answer, her expression alert.

'Everything that's you and not us,' I told her.

'For example?'

'Walk into any nought clothes shop and you can buy padded knickers so nought women can have more of a curvaceous bum—like Cross women. Everything about our lives, the style of clothes we wear, even down to the food we eat,

111

it's all dictated by Cross aesthetics, by the way Crosses see the world. Rich nought women aren't dressed without collagen implants to give them fuller top lips and melanin tablets or expensive sun bed treatments to make their skin darker. And what about Hartley Durrant?' I said warming to my theme.

'What about her?'

'She's the only nought woman to make it into this year's list of the one hundred most beautiful women in the world. And d'you know why? Because she looks like a Cross.'

'No, she doesn't,' Cara argued.

'Yes, she does.'

'D'you think she's attractive?' asked Cara.

'Yes, she's gorgeous. But that's not the point,' I replied impatiently.

'Don't you think that beauty is as beauty does?'

'What does that mean?'

'It means too many people, Nought or Cross, are caught up in the things that don't mean a damn—like how people look and how much money they have. Who cares!'

'So what does matter then?' I asked.

'What people are on the inside,' said Cara.

What a load of naïve, happy-ever-after nonsense, I thought sourly. And easy for you to say.

'Yes, I know it's easy for me to say.' Cara smiled, reading my mind. 'I'm on the inside. I'm part of the majority—I know that. Most magazine covers have Cross women and men on them, not Noughts. Most film stars are Crosses, most TV dramas are about Crosses. I know all that. I'm on the inside but that doesn't mean I can't see what's going on outside. And it doesn't mean I approve of the status quo.'

'Why not? Why should you care?' I couldn't help asking.

'Because my mum and dad brought me up to believe that people are different but equal. And that I should treat everyone, no matter who, with the same respect I'd like to be shown,' said Cara.

'So you're with me to show you can put your parents' philosophy into practice?' I could've bitten off my tongue the moment the words left my mouth.

'Is that what you really think, Steve?' Cara asked seriously.

I took a sip of my wine. I'd said far too much already.

'Is it?' Cara persisted.

'I don't know,' I said, looking her straight in the eye.

To my surprise, she smiled and sat back in her chair. 'Thanks for being honest. Now I'll be equally honest. I'm here with you because I like you—very much. And that's the beginning, middle and the end of it.'

But you don't know me, I couldn't help thinking. And the thought didn't bring me the satisfaction it should've done.

Sometimes when we're chatting or laughing

113

together, I actually forget that she's a Cross. But only sometimes. When that happens, I force myself to look at her and concentrate on her skin colour and nothing else. And that usually does the trick. I focus on the things that are totally different about us. What surprises me is that sometimes I actually forget about our differences. Not for long—but it does happen. And it shouldn't. I'm going to have to make my move soon. I'm in danger here. Because I've started to think about the things we have in common rather than the things we don't. It's time to cut and run with whatever I can get from her.

twenty-four. Sephy

Mother didn't understand my decision. How could she, when I barely understood it myself?

'You said you were coming home with me,' Mother reminded me.

'There's been a change of plan. Callum's mum said I could stay with her so I've decided to . . . to live with her instead.'

'Why?' Mother asked quietly. 'To punish me?'

'It wasn't like that,' I insisted.

'Sephy, d'you want to live with Callum's mother?'

'She's got no one else,' I replied.

'That doesn't answer my question,' said

114

Mother.

She'd noticed.

I'd taken the coward's way out and phoned Mother on the morning of my departure from the hospital. And even though I couldn't actually see her, I could still hear the hurt in her voice. And in some ways it was worse because my imagination filled in the blanks. My mind painted a picture of the bewilderment on her face, the disappointment clouding her eyes.

'I'm sorry, Mother,' I tried again.

'I thought you were serious about the two of us putting the past behind us and starting again . . .'

'I was. I am.'

But Mother wasn't listening. And I couldn't really blame her.

'So you'd rather live in some hut with a nought than come home with me?' asked Mother.

'I'd rather go where I won't hear comments like that,' I replied. 'And I thought Meggie was once your friend?'

'I didn't mean it,' Mother said instantly. 'I just don't understand you, Persephone.'

'You never tried to in the past and it's too little too late now,' I lashed out.

Silence.

'I see,' Mother said at last.

'Mother, I don't want to fight with you. I'm too tired. I'll come and see you as soon as I get settled,' I told her.

'Goodbye, Persephone,' said Mother.

'Bye, Mother.'

Mother put the phone down first—but not before I heard her sniff and caught the catch in her throat. She was crying. It made me want to cry too. Mother was crying.

I'd done that.

*   *   *

So Callie, here I am at Meggie's. I've been here for almost a month now. She lives in a two-up, two-down house but it's warm and clean and better than I've been in recently so I can't complain. Meggie sleeps in the smaller bedroom upstairs. I have the bigger one. We argued about that until Meggie put her foot down and said that there were two of us and only one of her so it was only right we had the bigger bedroom. The bathroom is opposite my bedroom which is handy. Downstairs, there's a kitchen and a living room with a burgundy sofa and a light beige armchair which don't match—but who cares? The TV sits self-consciously in one corner. The ancient music centre sits in another. Meggie has a courtyard garden. It's smaller than her living room, but it's enough to dry your clothes when they've just come out of the washing machine. So the house is fine. The area is something else again though.

When I phoned Minerva to ask about her new job at the *Daily Shouter* and to check that

Mother was OK, she was horrified when I told her where I was going to live.

'But it's really rough around there,' she told me.

'No rougher than anywhere else,' I replied.

'Are you kidding?' Minerva scoffed. 'My first assignment was to interview a woman just a couple of streets away from where you are now. On the way back to the office I was ambushed.'

'What d'you mean?' I asked sharply. 'Are you all right? Were you hurt?'

'No. Some nought creep pushed me against the wall and asked me what I had for him,' Minerva said with disgust.

'What happened?'

'He took my purse and my mobile phone, then ran off,' said Minerva. 'Bastard! But it could've been worse.'

'You were unlucky—' I began.

'Sephy, the majority of the rapes and murders in this country are committed by noughts. You remember that,' Minerva told me.

'That's such a simplistic argument—and you know it,' I shot back at her.

'It's the truth.'

'The truth or manipulated statistics? Besides, even if that's true, which I don't believe it is for a second, that doesn't mean that every nought is a criminal.'

'But the ones that are don't walk around with the word stamped on their forehead,' said

117

Minerva.

'So you're saying I shouldn't trust any nought?'

'I'm saying you should be careful,' said Minerva.

'I prefer to trust people no matter who they are until they give me a reason not to—not the other way round,' I told her.

'Which is why you always end up getting hurt,' Minerva told me.

And I couldn't think of a single thing to say to that. I decided to change the subject before we ended up screaming down the phone at each other.

'Congratulations on getting your job,' I said.

'I'm on six months' probation,' Minerva told me. 'I won't get the really big stories for a while yet. Like I said, I'm only a junior reporter at the moment.'

'You'll breeze through it,' I said.

'I hope so. I've reported on two nought assaults and a fire at a warehouse so far—as well as a kitten stuck in a tree and the local sweet shop being flooded out.'

'Two assaults? They're launching you in at the deep end, aren't they?'

'Not really. They were both nought-on-nought crimes and no Crosses were involved, so they were minor league stories,' Minerva dismissed.

'Not to the Noughts involved,' I replied.

Couldn't Minerva hear herself? Could she sound any more like Dad?

Minerva sighed. 'I didn't mean that the way it sounded.'

I let it slide. We chatted for a few more minutes until I learned that Mother was really down but not drinking. I was grateful for that at least.

Meggie and I still haven't quite settled into a routine yet. To be honest I feel like I'm tiptoeing across eggshells around her. And Callie, you cry such a lot. I feed you and change you and try to make sure you're not too hot and not too cold but you still cry. And after hours and hours of crying, I just want to scream at you to please, *please* stop. I don't know what you want. I don't know what I'm doing wrong and I feel like such a failure. I pick you up and hold you to me and that usually—eventually—calms you down. But then as soon as I try to put you back in your cot, you start up again.

'You shouldn't keep picking her up all the time,' Meggie told me. 'That's why she cries whenever she's away from you. If you just left her, after a day or two of crying, she'd soon get used to not being held all the time.'

'I'm not going to leave Callie crying in her cot,' I told Meggie.

'It works,' Meggie insisted. 'Callum was exactly the same when he was a baby and . . .'

Meggie's voice trailed off. What was she going to say? It never did him any harm—in fact it did him good? Made him self-sufficient? Self-reliant?

119

'I'm sorry,' said Meggie unexpectedly. 'I'm doing exactly what I promised you I wouldn't do. You do what you think is best.'

I watched as Meggie left my room, before picking you up, Callie. I walked round and round the room, whispering soothing things into your ear and praying that you'd soon get tired enough to go to sleep. I felt like I was about to drop. It wasn't just the regularly interrupted nights. More wearing than any of that was the gnawing guilt I felt every second of every day. So many things to feel guilty about. And not being able to stop my own baby from crying just added to my sense of worthlessness.

It was like the first time I bathed you, Callie. I was so scared. Meggie asked me if I needed any help but I turned her down. I didn't want her to think I didn't have a clue, when in truth that was exactly how I felt. I ran the water in the bathtub and checked the temperature whilst you lay in your carry-cot on the linoleum bathroom floor. I did all the things I was supposed to do. I checked the temperature with my fingers, the back of my hand and my elbow. Then rechecked the temperature. I undressed you and put you carefully into the water. And then it all went wrong. I tried to hold onto your arm, whilst supporting your head with my forearm, but when you started to mew, I realized I was gripping your arm too tightly. I slackened my grip and turned to grab the soap from the side of the bathtub with my other hand, but then your head flopped off my forearm and your whole body started sliding further into the water. Panicking, I yanked you back up again but I did that too hard and you let me know it. You howled. I took you out of the water, your wet body dripping down my shirt—and burst into tears. I couldn't even give my own daughter a bath. How pathetic was that? Meggie came in and took a nanosecond to realize I was in a right state.

'Let's bathe her together—OK?'

I nodded, gulping down my tears. Meggie kneeled down beside me and supervised whilst I had another go at bathing you, Callie. And this time I did better.

I never realized before just how exhausting looking after a baby would be. I never realized how you never get a break, how you have to be on call twenty-four hours a day, seven days a week. And babies don't understand 'Just give me five minutes' or 'Not now, I'm tired'.

I try to catch up on all my other household stuff when you're asleep, Callie—like the washing and ironing—but I move like a tortoise, I'm that tired. If it wasn't for Meggie helping or insisting that I try to get some sleep when my daughter does, I don't know what I would've done. Thank goodness I didn't have to take you back to my bedsit. I can't imagine how I would've coped if I'd been alone with you.

Then I think of Callum and what we're all missing because we're not together. How much more fulfilling it would've been if Callum was here to share it with me. With us. Then all my problems would've shrunk to the size of full stops. Those are the worst times, when I hold you, Callie, and think of your father. Or when I lie in bed and dream of him.

Why is nothing ever easy, Callie? I so wanted you to have your dad's surname of McGregor. You'd think I'd be able to declare your name was Callie Rose McGregor and put that name on your birth certificate and that'd be the end of it. But no. Apparently, as Callum and I weren't married, I need Callum's permission to use his surname. I explained to the woman at the registry office that Callum wasn't in a position to give his permission but she wasn't having any of it.

'You'll have to consult a solicitor then,' she told me. 'But I warn you now, it's a lengthy and complicated process.'

So I'm waiting to get more settled and then I'll go and see a solicitor about having your surname changed legally. But what a big song and dance about something which should be perfectly straightforward.

I stopped walking and glanced at you. You weren't asleep but at least you were no longer crying. I'd taken just a step towards your carry-cot, when the peal of the doorbell made me jump. And you started crying again. I cursed. Meggie didn't get many visitors. I didn't get any. So why did someone have to come calling at just that moment? I carried on walking

122

around the room.

'Callie, please stop crying,' I pleaded.

As if you heard me, you began to quieten down. For once.

'Sephy, it's for you,' Meggie called upstairs.

Frowning, I carried Callie downstairs. Had Mother finally decided to come and see me in person in an effort to change my mind? But it wasn't Mother at all. It was Jaxon, the boy with the guitar I'd met in the hospital.

'Hello,' I said, eyes wide.

'Bet you weren't expecting to see me,' Jaxon grinned up at me.

'You've come to see me?'

'That's right,' Jaxon nodded.

'Is something wrong with Roxie?' I asked.

Roxie, his sister must've sent him. She was really nice but we hadn't been in touch since we'd both left hospital on the same day.

'No. She's fine. In fact—perfect,' said Jaxon. He looked around. 'Any chance of a sit down?'

'Sorry. Through there.' I indicated the living room on my left.

'Anyone for a cup of tea?' Meggie called out from the kitchen.

'No, thanks,' I replied.

'I'd love one,' Jaxon called out.

Jaxon sat down at one end of the burgundy sofa. I think he expected me to sit down at the other end of it, but I sat in the armchair instead. He regarded me speculatively. I bent my head to kiss Callie on her forehead, mainly so that Jaxon wouldn't see the unease in my

123

eyes. What did he want? I forced myself to look straight at him. He smiled at me. I didn't smile back as I waited for him to speak.

'I'll get right to it then,' said Jaxon.

'I'm listening.'

'You've got a good voice.'

'Pardon?'

'A good singing voice. In fact you have a great singing voice,' Jaxon explained. 'And I've got a band together but we need a female singer. We'd split all the money we make four ways. Equal shares.'

'Wait,' I frowned. 'You want me to join your group?'

'That's right.'

Except he hadn't actually asked me anything yet. I sat back in the armchair, unimpressed.

Jaxon regarded me in silence, then sighed. 'OK. Can I start again?'

'I think you'd better.'

'I play the guitar in a group. My mate Rhino plays the drums and Sonny plays the keyboards and bass guitar.' Jaxon was now talking to me like a human being. I started to listen. 'We've been told we'd get more gigs if we had a female singer. When you sang with me in the hospital, you were good.'

Right up until Jaxon had verbally abused the poor Cross nurse who'd only been doing her job.

'I've discussed it with Rhino and Sonny and we've all agreed that we'd like you to join us,' said Jaxon. 'Like I said, everything we earn would be split four ways.'

'What kind of places d'you play at?'

'Clubs, pubs, weddings, parties—anywhere that pays,' Jaxon told me.

'And what kind of music do you play?'

'Like I said, anything that pays,' Jaxon said.

'Don't you write your own songs then?' I asked, surprised.

'Yeah, but no one wants to hear them,' said Jaxon, a trace of bitterness in his voice.

'Why not? I don't understand.'

'We sing lots of cover versions. Club managers like the old standards,' Jaxon explained. 'We try to slip in a couple of original songs towards the end of our set but we don't always get the chance.'

'So why me?' I asked.

'You can sing . . .'

'So can lots of other girls. Why me?'

'D'you want the truth?'

'Always.'

'We'd get more gigs in Cross clubs if we had you as our lead singer,' said Jaxon.

I'd asked for honesty and I'd certainly got it. The bottom line was that Jaxon wanted to use me. Well, that was OK, because I'd be using him and his band to make some money of my own. It was definitely tempting. I'd be making a living of sorts and it wouldn't be something I'd have to do every day so I wouldn't have to be away from Callie for more than a few hours at a time. If I did this, I could keep my word to Meggie and chip in something towards the cost

125

of the bills.

'D'you have a gig lined up?' I asked.

'Is this Saturday too soon?' Jaxon grinned at me.

'Saturday? You mean the Saturday in four days' time?' I squeaked.

'Yep!'

'But I don't know any of your songs or your arrangements,' I panicked. 'You might all play in a key I can't reach or sound awful in. I might . . .'

Meggie came in with a cup of tea and handed it to Jaxon.

'Thanks,' Jaxon smiled at her.

'Everything OK?' Meggie asked me.

'Jaxon wants me to join his group,' I told her.

'What kind of group?' Meggie asked sharply.

'A musical group,' Jaxon provided.

'Singing?' Meggie visibly relaxed.

'That's right,' I told her.

'Does that mean you'll do it?' Jaxon asked.

I considered. I'd be earning money, which was a plus, but I'd have to sing in front of other people to do it. And I'd have to sing with Jaxon, who had a temper like an active volcano and a chip on his shoulder about Crosses the size of a giant redwood. Was it worth the hassle?

'I don't think so,' I said.

'Why not?'

'This isn't chopped liver in my hands, you know. I've got a baby to look after,' I told him.

'I can look after Callie for you,' Meggie leapt

in.

I frowned at her. 'No. She's not even two months old yet. She needs me.'

'It would only be a rehearsal or two a week after work and then a gig on a Friday or a Saturday night,' Jaxon persisted. 'That's not too much to ask, is it? And we could make some serious money.'

'I've got a baby to look after,' I repeated.

'Sephy, it'll do you good to get out and about,' said Meggie. 'You've barely left this house since you came home from the hospital.'

Was I suddenly talking Martian? I didn't want to leave the house. I didn't want to go anywhere. And I certainly didn't want to stand up and sing in front of a load of strangers. What was this about? Was Meggie fed up with our company already?

'It's not that I'm chasing you out. Far from it. I love having you and Callie living here with me,' Meggie told me. 'But I'm worried about you, Sephy. You don't want to go anywhere or do anything.'

Well, I certainly wasn't going to argue in front of Jaxon.

'Thanks for the offer, Jaxon, but no thanks,' I told him.

Pursing his lips, he stood up. 'Look, if you change your mind, this is my address and phone number.' He handed over a business card, one of those you can get in any newsagent's where you key in your details and get a lot of cards for not much money. I took it without even looking at it. I wasn't going to sing in his band or anywhere else—and we both knew it.

I let Meggie see him to the door whilst I hugged you to me, Callie, nuzzling your forehead.

'What shall I tell you about your daddy today?' I asked you.

You looked up at me like you were ready to drink in every word.

'Callum's favourite food was roast lamb. He thought astrology was a load of bosh! Didn't believe in stars and planets telling his fortune or anyone else's. He once told me that the silliest thing a girl could ask a boy is "What's your star sign?"! I must admit I don't believe in that stuff either, but Callum was really scathing about it. He loved to draw. Animals pouncing mostly. And trees. Always lone trees in bleak landscapes. I didn't like them much . . .'

I trailed off when I realized I had company. Meggie was back in the room and watching me.

'Why were you so curt with that poor man?' asked Meggie.

'I wasn't aware I had been,' I told her. 'But I don't want to sing with him and I don't like being manoeuvred into something I don't want to do.'

'Sephy, you need to get out again. You haven't even taken Callie to see your mother yet. And you need to decide what you're going to do with your life,' Meggie told me. 'What're
128

you going to do for money?'

'Oh, so that's it,' I said. 'Worried I won't pay my way?'

'No, of course not,' Meggie denied. 'But it's like you're closing in on yourself. You're letting your whole world revolve around Callie and that's not healthy.'

'When she's older then I can sort out what I'm going to do,' I told her.

'How much older?' asked Meggie. 'A month? A year? Ten years? Fifty years? When?'

'Meggie, stop pushing me!' I shouted. 'Why can't you just leave me alone?'

I obviously scared you, Callie, because you started crying.

'See what you've done,' I hurled at Meggie.

And before she had a chance to reply, I raced out of the room with you in my arms. Why didn't she understand? If I could've gone to Callum's grave and crawled in beside him with you in my arms, Callie, then I would've.

Why didn't anyone understand that?

twenty-five. Jude

Cara phoned me on my mobile and asked me to meet her outside Chamber Lane station at seven o'clock this evening. I'm not keen on going into town too often. There are CCTV cameras everywhere so you never know who's watching you but Cara cajoled me into doing it. And I couldn't say no.

After all, how could she understand my reluctance? I couldn't exactly tell her that I was still a marked man—one of those wanted for the abduction of Persephone Hadley. So I did as Cara asked. My uniform for the day was an ordinary pair of jeans, an ordinary T-shirt, an ordinary jacket and a cap pulled down low over my forehead. I kept my head down as I came up the escalator from the underground platform. Something in my gut told me that this was madness. If I ever got caught it would be in a place like this, in town with lots of people around where I could be easily surrounded and it would be hard to take cover. So what was I doing here? I still didn't know— apart from the fact that Cara had asked me.

Cara was already waiting for me. I put my ticket through the machine and then stood against the wall out of everyone's way as I watched her scan left and right as she looked for me. She was wearing navy-blue, tight-fitting trousers and a white, sleeveless T-shirt. Her arms were so sleek and well defined, they looked like they'd been expertly carved out of dark wood. For once she wore her braids loose and they hung down past her shoulders, framing her face when it was in profile.

I just stood and watched.

And watched.

But then she spotted me.

'Steve! Hello, Steve.' There it was again. That smile on her face which was brighter and

130

warmer than summer sunshine.

'Hello, Cara.' I moved towards her.

'I'm glad you could make it. I've got a surprise for you,' she told me.

'I don't like surprises.'

'You'll like this one.'

We walked for a couple of minutes before Cara unexpectedly linked her arm with mine. At my nonplussed look, she just smiled and carried on leading me. We finally stopped outside one of the most prestigious, not to mention luxurious cinema complexes in town.

'What're we doing here?' I frowned.

'I got us two tickets to *Strange Days, Strange Ways*,' Cara beamed at me.

'But it only opened a couple of days ago.'

'I know.'

'And you hate science fiction films,' I said with suspicion.

'But you love them,' Cara told me. 'So this is for you.'

My stomach flipped. Then, for just a moment, it flashed through my head that maybe this was a trap. That maybe the police were watching and waiting. But one look at the expression on Cara's face and I knew it wasn't. It couldn't be. Cara's face was like an open picture book. I genuinely didn't know what to say. And the smile of pleasure on Cara's face just seemed to make the hollow feeling inside of me grow rather than diminish.

'Won't you be bored?' I said at last.

'Not with you,' said Cara. 'OK?'

I nodded. My stomach flipped again as we went inside. We were half an hour early so we had to wait in the bar. I bought us a couple of drinks and we sat down.

'After our talk the other day about this film in particular, I was worried you might guess what I had in mind,' Cara admitted after a sip of her mineral water.

I shook my head. 'Didn't have a clue.'

'Good.'

'Cara . . .'

Cara smiled at me expectantly. I looked around but the nearest other people were at the bar several metres away. I wanted to ask her about her day, her parents, her friends, her hobbies, her last holiday, anything and everything except what came out of my mouth.

'Why're you with me?'

Cara looked puzzled. ' 'Cause you wanted to see this film and I thought we could go for a meal or maybe for a walk around the park afterwards.'

That wasn't what I meant. 'Why don't you mind being seen with a nought?'

Cara sat back in her chair and regarded me, a strange look on her face. I'd probably blown my chances by asking that question. I mean, if she could pretend to be colour-blind then why couldn't I?

'Does it bother you that people look at us then?' said Cara at last.

'Sometimes.'

'Steve, when you look at someone, what's the

132

first thing you notice, the first thing you latch on to?'

I shrugged, unsure how to answer.

'I always notice a person's eyes. Not just the colour but the shape and the thoughts and feelings behind them. Does that make sense?'

I nodded.

'And then I focus on that person's mouth— whether or not it smiles a lot,' Cara continued. 'I like mouths that know how to smile. You know how to smile, you just don't do it very often.'

Where was she going with this? More people were beginning to arrive and some sat down close to us. I began to feel uncomfortable, sorry I'd broached the subject in the first place.

'Then I see if they have anything to say for themselves, anything going on upstairs,' Cara continued. 'Anything else is irrelevant.'

'Fair enough,' I said. 'They're taking the tickets now.'

Cara tilted her head to one side. 'Steve, would you rather we left?'

'No. Of course not.'

'I don't want you to do anything you're uncomfortable with,' said Cara seriously.

'I'm not uncomfortable with you,' I told her.

'D'you promise?'

'I promise.'

'And just so you'll know,' Cara began seriously, 'I'm with you because I like being with you.'

'That's because you have excellent taste,' I joked to lighten the mood, not to mention our

133

conversation.

'I'm glad you approve!' Cara smiled, then stood up. 'Ready?'

I finished my lager and joined her. 'Ready.'

We went in to see the film.

twenty-six. Sephy

Callie, isn't it a beautiful day? Those white things up there are clouds. And the blue thing beyond is the sky. And that green stuff around us is grass. And we're sitting on a bench in the park and just enjoying the day. You like it when I tickle your tummy, don't you? You love it! Callie, d'you think I'm a coward? D'you think I should've taken Jaxon up on his offer? I admit, part of me wanted to. But to sing in a group in front of people—I've never done anything like that before. Then there're a lot of things I'm doing now that I've never dreamed of before. I'm still a teenager and I've got a daughter of my own. Sometimes I wake up in the middle of the night for no reason and just for a split second, it's as if the last few years haven't happened. I wake up and Callum's still alive and I'm still at Mother's and my life is very simple again. But just for a split second.

I shouldn't've shouted at Meggie like that. She was only trying to help. And she does care about you, Callie Rose. Very much. We'll go and visit my mother soon. She loves you very much too. You hold onto that, Callie. Love is all that matters. Believe me, I know.

twenty-seven. Jude

I surprised Cara at work one afternoon by turning up unannounced at her salon with a picnic basket. Cara looked beautiful. She had on a dark-blue cropped top which showed off her midriff and a matching blue, flouncy skirt with gold thread running vertically through it. Long, thin gold earrings framed her face and she looked so animated, so *alive*. It made me smile just to look at her.

'Steve, it's a wonderful idea, but I just can't pick up and leave,' Cara protested.

'Why not?' I asked. 'Will this place fall down if you're not here for one afternoon?'

'But I've got Mrs Burgess coming in at three and another client due at quarter to four—'

'Someone else can snip their hair or they can come back some other time,' I said. Come on, Cara. Don't make me beg, I thought with irritation.

Cara looked at me, then broke into a smile. 'I'm out of here, everyone.'

And she linked arms with me. We left without a backwards glance. And in that moment I knew I had her. It was only a matter of hours or at the most days before I got hold of every penny she had.

We went to the park and sat on the picnic benches near the children's playground and talked and ate and talked some more.

'When're you going to tell me some more about you?' asked Cara, before biting into an apple.

'What d'you want to know?'

'What d'you do for a living?'

'I'm between jobs,' I said. 'But up until a few months ago I worked in . . . construction.'

'Building work?'

'That's right.'

'Building or painting and decorating or what?' asked Cara.

'Painting and decorating mostly,' I said. 'But enough about me . . .'

'Funny, but after a couple of questions, you always say that,' said Cara. 'I'll have to call you my mystery man.'

'Nothing mysterious about me,' I told her. 'My life's an open book.'

'An open book but in a language I can't read,' Cara said wryly, making me laugh.

After our picnic, we strolled round the park, then caught a film at the local cinema before heading back to Cara's for dinner. An hour later, we both sat down to a meal of ribbon pasta with chicken and a bottle of reasonable red wine.

'Steve, d'you like me?' Cara asked without warning.

I groaned inwardly. Why did girls always

want to talk about relationships and feelings? Why couldn't we just get on with our evening without all this introspective crap?

'Of course I like you,' I replied.

'Then why've you never tried to do more than kiss me?' Cara asked, unable to look me in the eyes.

Her head was bent and she was obviously embarrassed. I put down my fork, my appetite vanishing. What was I supposed to say to that?

'I've just had a lot on my mind recently,' I sighed. 'You know, I'm still looking for a job and I've got bills to pay and things aren't going too well for me at the moment.'

'Then please let me help,' Cara pleaded.

'No, I told you—'

'It's only money, Steve.' Cara sprang up and headed for the table in the corner of her living room. Taking off the necklace around her neck, she used the small key on it to open one of the desk drawers. The only drawer in the desk that was locked—as I knew from past experience. I watched as she took out her cheque book, then walked back over to me.

'How much d'you need?' She was signing the cheque before even filling in the amount.

'I'm not taking your money,' I told her quietly.

'Please, Steve. I want to do this. I want to help,' said Cara.

But I hardly heard her. I threw down my napkin onto the table and stood up.

'I think I'd better go,' I said.

137

'Steve . . .' Cara placed a warm hand against my face.

She looked up at me like she really did like me or something. Like I was something special in her life, even after the few short weeks we'd been together. Cara stood on tiptoe and kissed me. I closed my eyes—and found myself kissing her just as passionately as she was kissing me. It'd been a long time since anyone had wanted me like that. I wrapped my arms around her, my eyes still closed and kissed her like this moment was the last thing, the only thing I had left.

And then I opened my eyes. Cara was still kissing me, her eyes shut, but at the sight of her, my soul froze. I pulled away, staring at her.

'What's the matter?' asked Cara.

'Nothing,' I mumbled. 'I really have to leave.'

'Steve, you're hurting about something. Won't you tell me what it is?'

'What're you talking about?'

'I think . . .' I think you're afraid to get close to anyone. And sometimes you look at me like . . .'

'Like what?' I prompted when she trailed off.

'Like you see someone else when you look at me. Like you're looking through me.'

The strangest feeling tingled right through me, like my blood was shivering or something. Had I really let my guard down that much?

'You know about my dad dying of a heart attack. Won't you tell me who you've lost? It was someone you cared a lot about, wasn't it?' Cara said.

I opened my mouth to speak but the words wouldn't come.

'My dad and I were very close,' Cara continued. 'It's not something you ever get over quickly.'

'Why're you telling me this?' The words came out in a whisper, low and racked with pain.

'Have you lost someone?'

'My brother. My brother died . . . He was murdered.'

Cara nodded. She was so understanding, and that was the worst of it, because I knew she did understand me—totally. She was like the calm, sane half of me.

'I'm so sorry, Steve.'

I couldn't answer.

'You look so alone sometimes. So hurt,' said Cara softly. 'It reminds me of me.'

And now my blood was howling around my body, racing faster and hotter. I wanted her to stop. Just stop talking. Stop understanding me. My throat was hurting. My eyes were hurting.

Stop talking. Stop . . . STOP . . .

'Steve . . .' Cara said uncertainly.

I stared at her, not daring to even blink. Her fingers crept back to my cheek. Her touch was soft and warm.

'You and I are so alike,' Cara smiled sadly. 'I guess that's what brought us together. Kindred spirits.'

I had to stop her talking. I had to. I kissed

139

her, with what felt like a fist in my chest squeezing relentlessly at my heart. Cara wrapped her arms around me and kissed me with the same kind of lonely desperation. She was right. I was lonely. I'd been lonely all my life—even before my family had shattered into a million pieces. What was it about me that made it so hard for me to get close to anyone? What was it about me that made it impossible for me to make friends and keep them? What was it about me that had me kissing a Cross and no longer wanting to pull away and wipe my mouth? What was it about me that had me falling for someone I should despise?

My hand slipped from her waist to up under her top. Her bare skin was soft as a whisper and as smooth as quality velvet. I'd never felt skin so smooth. The more I touched, the more I wanted to touch. I pulled her close, my hand moving straight to her breast. My blood was roaring, racing, pumping. I was breathless and more turned on than I'd ever been in my entire life. I wanted to do more than have sex. I wanted to make love, to drown in her.

But then I opened my eyes . . . I straightened up and forced myself to concentrate on her skin. Take it in. Sink into it. But I couldn't see her skin any more. Just her eyes, warm and rich brown, smiling at me with understanding. With love.

With love.

She smiled at me. Total trust, love and devotion. It was too much. I was dying in it. I clenched my fists and hit her. Her whole body fell backwards. She looked up at me, too shocked to even cry out. Her eyes, so warm and rich that I just wanted to pour myself into them, were now stunned and hurt. But the love was still there. I knelt down and hit her again.

And then I couldn't stop.

I punched her over and over again before leaping to my feet. And even then I couldn't leave her alone. I kicked out with all the rage erupting inside me. She had no right to make me care about her. I'd show her, I'd show both of us that she meant nothing to me. I kept hitting her over and over, even when she was screaming at me to stop.

Even when she stopped screaming.

I only stopped kicking and punching when I was too physically exhausted to raise my hands or move my feet. Blood covered my knuckles. I wiped the backs of my hands on my trousers. Then I picked up her forgotten blank cheque from the floor. I went to the drawer she usually kept locked and took out all the money and cheque books and pass books and everything else I could find there. Only then did I leave the house, careful not to look at Cara. Not once. Not even a glance. With each step away from her, I grew colder again—which was just the way it should be. I had money and cheques which I'd cash first thing in the morning and then I'd disappear. I was good at that. I'd walked but a few steps when I realized my face was wet. I looked up. When had it started raining? The night glittered with a thousand and more stars, the air warm around my face.

But there wasn't a single cloud in the sky.

twenty-eight. Sephy

Meggie and I hadn't said too much to each other after our bust-up the afternoon before. Now we were both tip-toeing around each other like we were walking on crisp packets. But she had no right to tell me how to live my life.

I lay on my bed with you on my chest, Callie, and I was reading to you. I wanted you to love books as much as Callum and I did.

When the doorbell rang, I decided to let Meggie get it.

'Sephy, it's for you,' Meggie called upstairs.

Two visitors in two days. What on earth was going on? I put the book down and, holding you to me, got to my feet. We went downstairs. It was some man I'd never seen before. A Cross, middle-aged, greying at the temples with a neat, pencil-thin moustache adding a distinguished air to his face. He was good-looking for an older man. The sort of man my mother would admire. He watched me as I walked down the stairs. If he was another journalist, he'd soon be bouncing down the road so fast, he wouldn't stop moving until the day after tomorrow.

'Yes?' I said coldly. 'Can I help you?'

'Persephone Hadley?'

'That's right,' I replied.

'My name is Jack. Jack Labinjah.'

I waited for him to continue. Meggie stood hovering in the background, for which I was grateful. She'd had a bellyful of journalists knocking on her door as well.

'I'm a prison guard,' Jack continued. 'I was with Callum on his last day.'

My blood turned to liquid nitrogen in my veins, freezing every bit of me. I couldn't breathe. A single breath would have had my body crumbling.

'You were with Callum . . .' My voice, when it finally arrived, was barely above a whisper.

Jack nodded. 'I'm sorry to trouble you, but it's taken me this long to find you. In fact I only managed to track you down because of the birth announcement you put in the paper.'

'Why did you want to find me?' I asked.

'Callum wrote you a letter. He made me promise to deliver it,' said Jack slowly. 'He wrote more than one to you actually, but he didn't want you to have the others. He threw them away. This is the one he wanted you to have.'

And in Jack's hand, an envelope with my name on the front—*Sephy*—written in Callum's bold, slanting handwriting. My hand automatically reached out for it. And the moment I touched it, it felt like Callum was there, standing next to me or watching over my shoulder. No, it was more than that. Stronger than that. It was like Callum was moving around me and through me and I could feel him and smell him and hear his voice whispering in my ear. My legs were turning to water. Meggie rushed forward just as Jack stepped forward to tuck a helping hand under my elbow. Meggie took Callie away from my unresisting hands. I sat down on the stairs, staring at Jack.

'You were with my son? On his last day? You were with him?' asked Meggie.

'I was with him every day until his last day. We became good friends,' said Jack.

'What did he say? What did he do? What was he like? Did he talk about me at all?' The questions tumbled out with a hundred more right behind them.

'He didn't talk about anything else but you.' Jack smiled at me, his smile fading as he looked down at the envelope in my hand.

I couldn't speak. I wouldn't've been able to say a word then, if my very life had depended on it. This man had shared Callum's last few days. He had something I could only dream of. I'd tried so hard to see Callum when he was in prison but I had never got further than the prison gate.

'Tell me why I could never get in to see Callum. Please tell me,' I pleaded.

Jack began to shake his head, but I wasn't going to take no for an answer.

'You must know. You were with him. You

worked in that awful place. Why couldn't I see him?' I begged.

'Orders came from high up that you weren't to be allowed to see Callum under any circumstances,' Jack said at last.

'Orders from who? The prison governor?' asked Meggie sharply.

'Higher than that,' said Jack softly, looking straight at me.

'It was my dad, wasn't it?' It might've sounded like a question, but it wasn't. I *knew*.

'Let's all go into the living room,' said Meggie. 'Then we can discuss this properly.'

'I can't.' Jack shook his head. 'If it gets found out that I was here, I could lose my job. Like I said, I wouldn't've come but Callum made me promise. I didn't want to deliver that thing.'

'Why not?' asked Meggie sharply.

Jack didn't reply.

'You've read it, haven't you?' said Meggie.

'Yes,' said Jack unapologetically. 'In my job, I can't be too careful. I needed to see just what I was getting myself into.'

'I see,' Meggie said icily.

'And I'm sorry I ever agreed to get involved. I'd rather cut off my hand than deliver something like that but—'

'But you promised.' Meggie finished the sentence for him. It was a well-worn refrain by now. 'What does that letter say?'

Jack shook his head. Callum's letter lay, if not forgotten, then dormant in my hand. Jack had been with my Callum. At this moment,

145

that was more important.

'Did Callum know that I tried to see him?' I asked.

'Yes. I told him,' said Jack.

'Did he . . . did he know how much . . .' I shook my head. I was going to ask, did Callum know how much I loved him? But how could Jack answer that? Jack didn't know me. I didn't know him.

'All I can tell you,' said Jack, 'is that Callum never stopped talking about you. You were the most important person in his life. You need to remember that.'

'Sephy, I think you'd better give me that letter,' said Meggie.

I pulled my hand away from her, hugging Callum's letter to me.

'NO!' I exclaimed. 'It's mine. It's the last thing I have of Callum's. I'm going to hold onto it and treasure it and no one else is going to get it. It's mine.'

'I have to go.' Jack was already heading for the door. He turned back to me once the front door was open.

'Miss Hadley, I . . . I'm sorry.' And then he was gone.

I wondered why he was apologizing. Didn't he realize he'd given me so much? In my hands I had a gift I'd never dreamed of. A letter from Callum. The last letter he'd ever written—and it was to me.

I was actually trembling as I opened the envelope. It wasn't sealed, the flap was just

146

tucked in. I took it out and started to read, devouring each word, gobbling up every syllable. I read quickly, eagerly at first but I got slower and slower as each word pierced my flesh like a shark's tooth. As I got to the end, the letter fell from my hands. I turned slowly to Meggie, looking at Callie Rose wriggling in her arms.

Our daughter.

My daughter.

I put out my arms to take Callie from Meggie. She handed her over without a word. I sat on the third step and stared down at my daughter. Meggie picked up Callum's letter.

'Don't read it . . .' I whispered.

Without another word to me, Meggie began to read it out loud. I didn't want her to, but my voice had now gone completely. My thoughts had gone. My skin had gone, to be replaced with the one I was wearing now, made from needles and pins and thorns, all pointing inwards.

Sephy,

I'm writing this to you because I want you to know the way things really are. I don't want you to spend the rest of your life believing a lie.

I don't love you. I never did. You were just an assignment to me. A way for all of us in my cell of the Liberation Militia to get money—a lot of money from your dad. And as for the sex—well, you were available and I had nothing better to do.

Meggie's voice began to falter but she carried on reading.

You should've seen yourself, lapping up every word of that nonsense I spouted about loving you and living for only you and being too scared to say it before. I don't know how I stopped myself from laughing out loud as you bought all that rubbish. As if I could love someone like you—a Cross and, worse than that, the daughter of one of our worst enemies. Having sex with you was just my way of getting back at your dad for being a bastard and your mum for looking down her nose at me all those years. And now you're pregnant.

Well, I'm ecstatic. Now the whole world will know you're having my child, the child of a blanker. That if nothing else is worth dying for. Whether you come to my hanging or not, I'm going to announce to the world that you're having my child. MINE. Even if you do get rid of our child, everyone will still know.

But no one will know how much I despise you. I loathe the very thought of you and now when I think about all the things we did when we were alone in the cabin, I feel physically sick. To think I actually kissed you, licked you, touched you, joined my body with yours. I had to think of my other lovers the entire time to stop myself from pulling away from you in disgust. God knows, I'm disgusted with myself but the object of the exercise was your total humiliation—and at least I can console myself with the knowledge that

148

that's what I've achieved. Did you really in your wildest dreams believe that I could love someone like you? You've got more ego than any fifty people I know. And you've got absolutely nothing to be egotistical about.

I've told Jack to deliver this to you only if and when you have our child. I can imagine your face now as you read this and at least that gives me comfort as I wait to die. Once you've had our child and you've read this, no doubt you'll hate me just as much as I hate you. But just remember, I had you first. Go ahead and try to forget about me. And while you're forgetting, you can do something else. Never tell our child about me. I don't want him or her to know who I am or how I died or anything about me. I don't want you to mention my name ever again. That shouldn't be so hard after all the things I've told you in this letter. All the true things. You're probably so conceited that you're telling yourself what I'm saying in this letter isn't true. That I'm only saying this so you'll move on with your life, but I never for a second doubted you'd do that anyway.

I won't tell you to take care of yourself. You're a Cross who was born with a jewel-encrusted, platinum spoon in your mouth and even if you don't take care of yourself, others will do it for you.

Forget about me.

I've already forgotten about you.

Callum

ORANGE

Wounds

Grief

Evening Sunlight

Dying Down

Setting Sun

Pus

Weeping, Wailing, Sobbing

Curses

Aches and Pains

Spinning, Dizziness

Torrents

Burning

Shrill

Acid

Orange just orange just orange just orange
just orange just orange

Assaulted Woman in Critical Condition

Cara Imega, 26, is in a critical condition today after being viciously beaten up and left for dead. She was found by colleagues yesterday after she failed to report for work.

A spokesman from West Garden Hospital stated, 'It's a miracle she's still alive. She'll be in intensive care for quite some time. Whoever did this to her, needs to be found quickly before he strikes again.'

Shocked colleagues from Delany's Salon in Lexmark Street told the *Daily Shouter* that Cara didn't have an enemy in the world. 'She always went out of her way to help others. She did a lot of charity work and was a friend to everyone.'

The police are seeking Steve Winner, a nought man who is thought to be the last person to see Cara on the night she was assaulted. *(see page 7)*

twenty-nine. Sephy

Jaxon's house wasn't hard to find. In fact it was only a twenty-minute walk from Meggie's house. It was a long walk, though, not in terms of distance, but due to the looks I was getting. Some hostile glares, a few welcoming smiles, but mostly curious stares. There weren't very many Cross faces around Meggie's neck of the woods. And I was already missing Rose—really badly. Callum was right about that at least. Rose is a much better name for her.

Callum . . .

Don't think about him, Sephy. Ever again. He's dead and gone.

I had my daughter Rose. I didn't want or need anyone else.

Not Callum.

Especially not Callum.

I'd snatched his letter out of Meggie's hand when she began to tear it up. I didn't want her to dispose of it. I wanted to keep it, to look at it if ever my heart threatened to rule my head again. It would serve to make me realize just what a fool I'd been. I went to Chivers boarding school and Callum went off to God knows where to do God knows what. I was stupid, stupid, stupid to think he'd feel the same way about me after over two and a half years apart. People can change in the space of two and a half minutes. Callum became a terrorist and worse in those years. No wonder he and the rest of his Liberation Militia group had picked me to kidnap and terrorize. They couldn't've have selected a softer target.

And yet . . . if I were truthful, I couldn't deny that part of me still clung to the hope that it was some kind of sick joke or mistake. Did I really believe what he'd said? Oh, Callum had written the letter all right. I knew his writing too well to doubt it. But he'd never write such a letter to me.

Except that he had. And I had it locked up at the back of my journal to prove it.

Did he mean what he said?

Did he hate me?

Did he mean it?

Or did he love me?

Why'd he write it?

Did he mean it?

Did he spend the entire time we'd been together at the cabin laughing at how he was going to use me?

Did he mean it?

And round and round and round. Why couldn't I get past the letter? Like poison it had seeped into every image and every memory I kept of Callum, polluting them until I couldn't tell what was real and what was just wishful thinking any more. Until at last, I was forced to face the inescapable fact that, for whatever reason, Callum *had* written the letter.

That told me something in itself.

155

Because never in a million years would I have been able to write the same letter to him if our roles had been reversed. Each night I told myself to scrunch it up and chuck it in the bin. Or burn it. Or at the very least—don't read it. But every night, Callum's letter seemed to find its way into my hands. And I was a fish being gutted every time I read it.

But it didn't stop me doing it.

So I wasn't going to think about it. Not any more. I had to get on with my life and stop living a stupid lie. Callum didn't love me, didn't want me, didn't need me. He was just using me to get some kind of revenge against my dad in particular. He was even more ruthless than his brother, Jude. I was tired of being used.

And I was tired of being hurt.

No one would ever do that to me again. Ever.

Time to close my mind and throw away the key.

*   *   *

Jaxon's house was all on one level, a small, neat bungalow with flower boxes outside filled with pink geraniums and yellow polyanthus. He didn't have a bell so I knocked on the door and waited. And waited. I knocked again. Moments turned into minutes. I shook my head as I turned away. I'd only taken a few steps when the front door was flung open.

'Hello,' Jaxon said, surprised. 'To be honest, I wasn't expecting you.'

'Well, like you and Meggie said, I have to do something to earn a living.' I shrugged.

'The gig's tomorrow night.' Jaxon frowned. 'You took your time making up your mind.'

I raised my eyebrows. And sod you as well, I thought sourly. No amount of money was worth the aggravation of putting up with this twerp.

'I'm glad you could make it,' he said quickly. 'And I'm sorry if I'm a little tetchy. It's just the way I am when things haven't been going too well. You'll have to get used to it.'

'Tetchy isn't the word I'd use,' I told him.

He laughed. 'Point taken. Come in and meet the others.'

He led me through his house, which smelled deliciously of beans and toast. The walls were painted plaster, cream-coloured and decorated with cracks just below ceiling level throughout most of the hall. The floor was wooden boards and I could smell lavender air spray. It all felt very homely.

'I like your house,' I said.

'Liar,' Jaxon replied.

'Listen, if I didn't like it, I wouldn't've said anything,' I told him, annoyed.

'In that case, thank you,' said Jaxon.

'Do you live here alone then?'

'No, I live with my family.'

I remembered how Roxie had told me she had a big family.

157

'How's Roxie doing? And her son?'

'Oh, they're fine,' said Jaxon. 'They live just round the corner so she pops in a lot.'

Jaxon took me through the kitchen, where the smell of toast and baked beans was strongest, and out into the garden.

'We practise in the work shed at the bottom of the yard,' said Jaxon.

I nodded, looking around. Threadbare patches of parched grass were surrounded by larger patches of dirt and outdoor toys. At one side of the garden was a swing, dangling from the thick, tall branch of an oak tree.

'Are you going to tell me you like our yard too?' asked Jaxon.

'No,' I said dryly.

'Fair enough.'

We made our way across the dirt to the wooden shed at the bottom of the garden. It was huge. My idea of a shed was a reasonable space to keep the lawnmower, a bench and a few gardening tools. This was bigger than my last flat. As Jaxon opened the shed door, I painted a nervous smile on my face. He was only going to introduce me to his friends and maybe we'd do a bit of singing. They weren't going to eat me, so why did I feel like there were dive-bombers in my stomach?

We went into the shed. Noughts were scattered around the room like points on a compass.

A shorter-than-average skinny boy sat behind a full drum kit. He had crew-cut mid-brown hair and warm dark eyes. His face was lean to the point of being thin. I reckoned he was no older than his late teens. He was reading a girlie magazine which he shoved behind his back as soon as he saw me. If this was Rhino, then it'd obviously been someone's idea of irony. He looked like a gusty wind would whisk him up and away.

'This is Rhino,' said Jaxon, confirming the name. 'And that over there is Sonny, master keyboard player. He's not as good as me on the guitar though.'

'Jaxon, is anyone as good as you at anything?' Sonny asked, making me smile.

Sonny was another blond like Jaxon but he was built like a nuclear bunker. This one could definitely take care of himself.

'Hi. I'm Sephy,' I smiled.

Rhino waved a drumstick in my direction. Sonny came over to shake my hand.

'Welcome to our merry band,' said Sonny.

A redheaded girl with impossibly long, blood-red nails sat on an upturned wooden crate, glaring at me.

'And that over there is Amy,' said Jaxon.

I smiled at her but the temperature of the look she sent my way dropped even further. Was she the girlfriend of one of the band? What was her problem?

'We were just rehearsing before you arrived,' Jaxon told me.

'Well, thanks for inviting me along,' I smiled, before turning to the others. 'Jaxon said you're looking for a singer?'

'What?' Amy jumped to her feet.

'Oh-oh!' Sonny said quietly.

I'd've had to be as insensitive as a politician not to pick up on the sudden atmosphere in the shed.

'What d'you mean—singer?' Amy asked. 'That's what I am.'

'Not any more,' said Jaxon. 'Is there any food? I'm starving.'

'Now wait just a minute, Jaxon,' I began. 'You said—'

'What the hell is going on?' Amy started coming towards me.

I held my hand out. 'Whoa!' I said quickly. 'Jaxon told me he had a band who're looking for a new singer. That's all I know.'

'And it was the truth,' Jaxon shrugged. 'Our group needs a lead singer.'

Amy glared at him and scowled at me and my heart plummeted. So much for that then.

'You have one already,' I pointed out. 'And I don't think she's looking for female company on stage.'

I turned away, ready to head for the door. All the way over to Jaxon's place, I wasn't sure if I was doing the right thing but now that the whole idea had petered out, I felt strangely disappointed. Deflated. Coming over here in the first place had been a big decision.

'Now hold on, Sephy,' said Jaxon grabbing my arm and turning me round again. 'The guys and me have already discussed it. We've been talking about finding a new voice for ages. And Amy just isn't up to it.'

'And you pick *now* to tell her?' I asked.

'Since when have I not been up to it?' Amy quoted back at him furiously.

'Oh, Amy, get a grip! You've got no range— anything half an octave above or below middle C and you're lost. You've got no looks, no figure and worst of all you've got no stage presence.'

'What d'you mean, no looks and no figure?' said Amy. 'That's not what you've been telling me every night for the last few months.'

Jaxon shrugged. 'Winter nights are long and cold. But spring is finally here.'

Both Amy and I gasped at that. Why was he behaving like such a jerk? Or was he always like that?

'Jaxon, that's harsh,' said Sonny. 'There's nothing wrong with Amy's figure.'

I noticed he didn't say anything about her singing.

'Look at her,' Jaxon dismissed. 'Her boobs look like two aspirins on an ironing board and she's got no bum. Her legs stop and her back starts and there's nothing in between.'

'Why, you—'

If Sonny hadn't leapt into the fray and held Amy back, Jaxon would've lost an eye for sure.

'If I had any sense I'd let her go,' Sonny said angrily. 'Damn it, Jaxon. You can't treat people like that.'

'Oh Amy, grow up. We had fun but you knew

161

it wasn't going to be for ever,' said Jaxon.

'You are a pig, Jaxon Robbins, and I hope this girl rips your heart out,' Amy spat at him.

She stormed out of the shed and I for one didn't blame her. I scowled at Jaxon, wondering if he realized how lucky he was? He'd got off light. If he'd done that to me, he'd be rolling on the floor clutching his tenders.

'Jaxon, what's wrong with you?' Sonny shook his head. 'Amy's been good to you. She deserved better than that.'

'Oh come on. We all agreed that we couldn't carry on with Amy as our lead singer,' said Jaxon.

'That's not what I'm talking about and you know it,' said Sonny.

He looked at me like somehow what had just happened was partly my fault.

'Jaxon, when you said you wanted me to sing with your group, I thought that was the A to Z of it. I didn't realize you were going to use me to get rid of someone else,' I told him stonily.

'That wasn't meant to happen,' said Jaxon. 'You said you weren't interested. If you'd phoned me first to let me know you'd changed your mind then she would've been long gone before you got here.'

'Your relationship with Amy is your business and I'm not getting involved,' I told him. 'But if I join your group and you ever try to deal me out that way, you'll regret it.'

'Ooh! The mother is a lioness as well, is she?' Jaxon pretended to quake in his walking boots.

I shook my head. What a horse's arse!

Turning to Sonny and Rhino, I said, 'If you two would rather I left so you can get Amy back or bring in someone else, just say so.'

'I'll reserve judgement until after I've heard you sing,' said Sonny. Which was fair enough.

Rhino didn't say anything. I might've been slow on the uptake but I always got there eventually. Rhino wasn't convinced about me, to say the least.

'If you don't think this is a good idea, please say so,' I said to him directly.

'It might work,' said Rhino carefully, leaving a lot unsaid.

'So what do we do now?' I asked Jaxon.

'D'you want to sit down for three hours and talk so we can all get to know each other?' asked Jaxon.

'Hell no!' The words were out before I could stop them.

'Neither do we,' Jaxon laughed. 'So let's get to it. D'you know *Red to Green*?'

'The Gibson Dell song?'

'That's the one,' nodded Jaxon.

'Yeah, I think so,' I replied.

'Let's try that first then. D'you play any instruments?' Jaxon asked.

I shook my head. Three years of saxophone lessons couldn't compare to what professional musicians like this lot could do.

'OK, let's do it!' said Jaxon. 'Sephy, your microphone is in the middle there.'

I walked over to it, my heart pounding. What

163

was I letting myself in for? I sang when the mood took me, like in the bath or the shower or in front of the mirror when I was messing about. What was I doing here? I was about to make a damned fool of myself, that's what I was doing here!

Jaxon counted the others in. I waited for my musical cue, my heart bouncing. I was so wound up, I missed the start of my line completely and tried to cram the first two lines of the song into about two seconds.

'Hold it.' Jaxon put up a hand to stop the others.

'Sorry,' I mumbled.

'Let's try it again,' smiled Jaxon.

I took a couple of deep breaths to steady my nerves and my voice. Then I launched in. I was so determined not to miss my cue this time that I belted out the first line of the song— only the microphone couldn't take it. It squeaked and hissed in protest.

'Sorry,' I muttered.

'Jaxon, this is hopeless,' said Rhino, opening his mouth for the first time. 'She doesn't have a clue.'

'Give her a chance,' said Jaxon. 'Let's take it from the top.'

I glanced around at Rhino and Sonny, who were both looking incredibly unimpressed. I turned back to the mic and closed my eyes. Jaxon came over to me, surprising me with the genuine smile on his face.

'Sephy, forget we're there. Just sing it for

164

yourself. And have fun. OK?'

I nodded. Jaxon went back to his mic and the music started again. My cue came up. I started singing in my normal voice. The mic didn't squeal at me, so I carried on singing, my eyes still closed. *Red to Green* is one of those songs that starts off softly but gets louder and louder, just the way I like it. By the time I hit the second verse, I'd forgotten about everything but my enjoyment of the song. It took a few seconds after the song had finished for me to realize that I wasn't alone. The shed echoed with the dying strains of the guitar which finished the song. I forced myself to turn and look at the others. If they started laughing, I'd walk straight out of there.

But they weren't laughing. They were staring at me.

Silence.

'Was I that bad?' I asked after no one said a word.

'Wow!' Sonny breathed.

'I think we've found our lead singer,' grinned Jaxon.

And without being prompted, Sonny and Rhino started clapping and cheering. OK, so Rhino started hitting his drumsticks together but it meant the same thing.

'Not bad,' said Rhino.

'Thanks!' Coming from him that was high praise indeed. A warm rush of pleasure swept over me, before I felt a warm rush of something else start to leak from my boobs.

'Hell!' I exclaimed.

'What's the matter?' Jaxon asked.

Milk from my boobs was beginning to show on my shirt. I was lactating.

'Have you got any tissues?' I asked.

'Why?' frowned Jaxon.

'Jaxon, mate, when a girl asks for tissues you don't ask why,' said Sonny. 'You just hand them over.'

I couldn't help but smile at the sudden look of panic on Jaxon's face.

'Do you really want me to tell you?' I asked in a sudden fit of mischief.

'On second thoughts—no.'

'Because I really don't mind—' I began. Part of me just longed to pull him down a peg or two. I bet if I told him, he'd be just as grossed out as any other guy—Nought or Cross. Not so different, after all.

'Please don't!' Jaxon put out a hand. 'The tissues are over there.'

He pointed to a work bench at the side of the shed.

'Once you've sorted out . . . whatever it is you have to sort out, we'll do a full rehearsal of all the songs we'll be singing tomorrow,' Jaxon rushed on.

'Not too many all at once,' I told him as I headed for the bench. 'My voice won't take it.'

'Then we'll do a full rehearsal now and you're not to do any talking or singing until our gig tomorrow night,' said Jaxon. 'We're singing at the Dew Drop Inn at eight.'

166

'Fine.' I turned my back on all of them as I folded up the tissues and slipped them into my bra. 'Ready?' I turned round, then burst out laughing as they all made a great show of looking everywhere except at my front. And the sound felt strange and alien to my ears, as if it was coming from someone else and me— the real me—was just standing back and watching. But that was OK. I could do that. I could be two people if I needed to be. The real me deep inside, and the false, fake one that would hide the real me from the world.

'So what's the band called then?' I asked.

'The Cockroaches,' said Sonny.

His straight face told me he was serious.

'That's dire!' I sniffed. 'Who likes cockroaches, for heaven's sake?'

'What would you suggest then?' Sonny asked me.

'How should I know? The Midges,' I replied to be flippant.

To my surprise, Jaxon, Rhino and Sonny actually considered it. Then they looked at each other and nodded.

'The Midges it is then!' said Jaxon. And just like that, it was agreed.

'And by the way, I don't want to use my real name in the band,' I told them.

'What's wrong with your name?' Jaxon said quickly. Too quickly.

'I mean it, Jaxon,' I said with belligerence. 'If you're hoping to make some money off my name, then forget it.'

'So what d'you want to be called?' Sonny asked before Jaxon could argue.

I considered. 'Ridan—if anyone asks. Which they won't.'

'Ridan? What's that supposed to mean?' said Jaxon.

'It means nothing at all,' I told him. 'It's just an end-of- sale name.'

'A what?'

'A rock bottom, all-time low name,' I smiled.

He glowered at me, still disappointed he couldn't announce that he had Kamal Hadley's daughter up on stage with him.

'It's Ridan or I walk,' I told him straight.

'Ridan it is then,' said Sonny quickly.

'It doesn't even mean anything . . .' muttered Jaxon.

I shook my head. 'No, it doesn't. And that's the point.'

thirty. Jude

She's still in hospital. She's still unconscious. Cara Imega. She cared about me. She cared about all the things I said, and all the things I didn't say. She cared about what I showed on the outside and what was hidden on the inside. *If* is such a big word. *If* she was a nought or I was a Cross . . . *If* we lived in a different world . . . *If* I didn't hate Crosses so much . . .

I've kept the picture of her that was in the newspapers the day after she was found. Just a souvenir. It doesn't mean anything. I could throw it away any time if I wanted to. It's just that I'd never seen that photo of her before. She looked like she was almost praying. I wonder what she was thinking when that photo was taken. It was a good photo, a good likeness. She was just like that really.

Calm.

Quiet.

I cashed her cheques in a number of different banks around the city. All on the same day before her bank could put a block on them. Some I made out to cash. Some I had paid into a holding account and as soon as the cheques cleared, I withdrew the money. She was in hospital, not dead, so the banks had no reason not to clear them. And I was careful to backdate them. She'd signed one cheque so it was easy enough to forge her name on the others. And she had quite a bit of cash in that drawer as well. By the end of the week, I was several thousand pounds better off.

I should've been better off all round.

Except that it won't stop raining.

Especially at night when I'm alone again and lonely again and there's not a cloud in the sky.

And deep inside, it feels like I'm never going to see the sun again.

thirty-one. Sephy

'Sephy, when're we going to talk about this?'

'About what?' I asked Meggie.

She frowned at me. 'Sephy, that letter was a lie. Callum loved you. You shouldn't need me to tell you that.'

'So Callum didn't write that letter?'

'It looked like his writing,' Meggie conceded. 'But if he really wrote that then he was forced to write it or there was some other reason we haven't figured out yet.'

I tilted my head as I looked at Meggie. Did she really believe any of the crap she was coming out with? Forced to write it! What next?

'Sephy, Callum loved you. And if you never believe anything else in this life, you should believe that,' Meggie persisted.

But I hardly heard her. Now that she knew there was nothing between Callum and me except lies, maybe she'd changed her mind about us living with her.

'Would you like Rose and me to move out? I could go to Mother's,' I added, so that she needn't worry that I'd end up on the street.

'No, of course not,' said Meggie. 'This is your home for as long as you want.'

I shrugged, telling myself I wasn't bothered one way or the other.

'Sephy, did you love my son?'

'Of course I did. I wouldn't've let him touch me otherwise.' The words came from my heart rather than my head and I cursed silently as soon as I said them. My cheeks were on fire. I looked away from Meggie, unwilling to look at her after revealing something so intimate.

'Then why're you so desperate to believe that he meant what's in that letter?' Meggie asked.

Desperate to believe it? Everything I was and everything I had, clung to the prayer that he hadn't written it, but it did no good.

'Because Callum did write it,' I told her, anguished. Why couldn't she understand that? 'Callum wrote that hateful, hurtful letter—and he did it deliberately. And can you honestly say, hand on heart, that he didn't mean every word?'

Meggie opened her mouth to argue.

'You don't know what he was thinking when he wrote it,' I interrupted. 'He was in prison and about to hang. It's only natural that he would blame me. That he would hate me.'

'Callum wouldn't do that,' said Meggie. 'You've got so used to blaming yourself for what happened to my son that you can't believe everyone else isn't doing the same thing.'

'Sometimes . . . sometimes I think I've got it wrong. That Callum really did . . . love me. And then I read his letter again . . .'

'Then stop reading it and tear the damned thing up,' Meggie insisted. 'Or give it to me

171

and I'll do it.'

This was getting us nowhere.

'It's time for Rose's feed,' I said, standing up.

I really didn't want to listen any more. And I had no intention of arguing with her. Besides, I had to save my voice for my gig later that evening. As I went upstairs, I forced myself to concentrate on the forthcoming gig and nothing else. Which wasn't the best thing for my mood, to be honest. The gig was still a couple of hours away and I was already feeling almost physically sick with nerves. I was actually going to do it. I was going to stand up and sing in front of a club filled with strangers. Mind you, none of them knew me so if I was ruddy awful at least I'd never have to see any of them again. Funny, but if it was a choice between singing in front of hostile strangers or reading Callum's letter again, I knew which one I'd rather do. I'd been in my room less than a minute when Meggie knocked at my door. With a sigh I opened it.

'D'you want me to get you something to eat before you go out?' asked Meggie.

I shook my head. We both knew that wasn't the reason she'd knocked on my door.

'Sephy, will you please give me the letter?' said Meggie. 'The longer you keep it, the more damage it will do. You'll start to believe it . . .'

'Meggie, I already believe it,' I told her silkily. 'I was stupid to believe anything else.'

'Don't you have any faith in my son at all?'

asked Meggie.

I considered. 'I had faith in a lot of things. Faith in my family. Faith that God wouldn't let Callum die. Faith that Callum loved me. Faith in love. Now I know better. Now I know there's no such thing.'

Meggie and I regarded each other. Then Meggie shook her head and walked away.

I shut the door behind her.

thirty-two. Jude

'Fancy some company?'

I looked up from the beer I'd been nursing for at least an hour. A woman with shoulder-length light-brown braided hair and pale blue eyes was smiling at me. She wore a navy-blue T-shirt with white handprints over her boobs and denim jeans. Was she a skank? I couldn't be sure.

'What?'

'Fancy some company?'

The automatic shake of my head turned into a nod.

'You look like you've got the weight of the world on your shoulders,' the woman said as she sat opposite me.

I shrugged, wondering why I'd agreed to company when all I wanted was to be left alone. I took another sip of my beer.

'My name's Eva,' she told me.

'I'm . . . Jude,' I told her.

The pause before saying my name had her smiling dubiously.

'Hello . . . Jude,' she said formally. I knew from her tone that she didn't believe for a moment that Jude was my real name. How ironic! 'So what d'you do . . . Jude?'

She was getting on my nerves already. 'I'm a painter and decorator.'

'Really? D'you work on a building site or for yourself or what?'

'I go where the work takes me.' I shrugged again. 'What d'you do?'

'I'm a nurse,' Eva said.

I looked at her then. Really looked at her. She didn't look like a nurse. She didn't look like anything much.

'Look, d'you want to get out of here?' I asked.

'Pardon?'

'D'you want to leave? Go somewhere else? Do something else?' I asked.

Where'd that come from? This sudden urge to get out of my body, to get out of my head?

Pause. 'OK then,' said Eva after a quick assessment.

I put down my warm beer and stood up. Eva stood up too. I put out my hand. Would she take it? She didn't have to. She looked straight at me as the seconds ticked by. Then she put her hand in mine.

'D'you have somewhere we can go?' I asked.

I knew what I needed and Eva would do as

well as any other woman.

'Whoa there! D'you wanna slow down a bit?' said Eva.

'I want to be with you tonight,' I told her. 'If that's not what you want then say so now.'

'And you can't ask me any better than that?' Eva frowned.

'I don't feel like playing games,' I said.

'But you don't know anything about me,' said Eva in a typical girly fashion.

'But I know I'd like to,' I lied. 'And I need to be with someone tonight.'

'Have you just split up from your girlfriend or something?' asked Eva.

'Or something,' I agreed.

Eva regarded me long and hard. This was where I either got my face slapped or I pulled.

'Can I see your hands?' Eva asked.

Frowning I held them out. She turned them round so that my palms were facing upwards, and studied them intently.

'What're you doing?' I asked.

'Eyes and words can lie but hands never do. I'm into palmistry,' Eva explained.

I almost groaned out loud. Horoscopes and palmistry and runes and all that other bollocks left me cold. Usually when a girl started spouting on with that nonsense, I ran in the opposite direction. One of the few things Callum and I had in common. What a turn-off! But I looked at Eva and decided that beggars couldn't be choosers.

'You have a very prominent love line. You

feel things very deeply. You love for ever and hate for ever. You have good hands. Strong hands,' Eva told me.

The image of Cara cowering before my hands flashed unbidden and unwelcome in my mind.

'D'you have somewhere we can go?' Only intense restraint kept the impatience out of my voice. What a ridiculous conversation. At least Cara and I had had real discussions—not like this nonsense.

'We can go back to my place,' Eva whispered.

No slapped face. I'd pulled.

We walked back to her place arm in arm.

'It's a shame you don't have a car,' she told me. 'These shoes are killing my feet.'

'Why wear them then?' I asked.

'They look good,' Eva told me.

I mean, how stupid can you get? Cara wouldn't wear shoes just because they looked good, but then Cara had more sense. Cara . . . The direction in which my thoughts were taking me made me start.

'What is it?' Eva asked.

'Nothing,' I dismissed. 'Someone just walked over my grave, that's all.'

Eva laughed. I didn't.

'So d'you have any brothers or sisters?' asked Eva.

'No, I'm an only child.'

'Do you live around here?'

'About an hour away.' I sighed inwardly. What made her think that by asking me a few

176

questions, she'd get to know me better? A few questions and she could tell herself we had some kind of relationship before we crawled into bed together. How pathetic was that? Throughout our walk, she asked me questions and I batted back so-called answers. I smiled into her eyes and laughed at her jokes as she held onto my arm and I held onto hers. When she finally drifted into silence, I knew we were close to her flat and she was beginning to rethink the wisdom of what she was doing. I could feel she was close to bottling out. Time to pour out the charm.

'You're very beautiful,' I whispered to her. 'I thought that the first time I saw you.'

And I bent my head and kissed her. Slowly her arms snaked around my neck. I wrapped my arms around her body. Not too tight, but not too loose either. I made it seem like I didn't want to crush her but I was loath to let her go. The girls like that one and it works every time. Jude's law number twelve: *The key to a girl's heart is through her vanity.*

Except with Cara.

When we both finally came up for air, Eva beamed at me, reassured.

'Here we are,' she said, almost immediately.

We stood before a seedy, rundown block of flats. A couple of old jalopies sat in designated parking bays around us. The majority of windows facing us were lit. I knew they'd be lit whether or not the flats were occupied. Unlit flats were an invitation to burglars as they signalled that the owner might be out.

'This is me,' said Eva. 'I'm up on the third floor.'

And she led the way. I watched her, wondering what the hell I was doing? Now it was my turn to have doubts. But it was simple. I needed some company. I followed her into the block. We turned the corner and headed up some stairs. The walls were covered in graffiti and the whole place stank of pee. But it was nothing I wasn't used to.

'No point in trying the lift,' Eva shrugged. 'It never works. And when it does, it's always covered in puke and worse.'

'The stairs are fine,' I told her.

On the third floor we went along a walkway with a waist-high wall on one side and a number of evenly spaced doors on the other. We stopped outside a dark-green door lit by a single bulb above it on the walkway.

'Well, this is me,' Eva said again as she fiddled with her key in the door.

Not much I could say to that so I didn't bother trying. She unlocked the door and we went inside. The door opened into a small hallway, with doors off the right side of it only. Eva led the way into the first room on the right, the living room. The walls were painted cream with a couple of cheap posters put up to try and cover the cracks and damp patches on the walls. A grey and red, ill-fitting, threadbare carpet covered most of the floor.

'Would you like something to drink?' Eva

asked, unable to hide the nervousness in her voice.

'No,' I said. I walked over to her and kissed her again. Part of me wanted to have sex with her but part of me was sorry I'd come to her flat. I just wanted to get this over and done with. So I kissed her like a drowning man who'd just been thrown a life ring.

The strange thing was, that's exactly how she kissed me as well. With the same kind of panicked desperation. I started to pull her T-shirt over her head.

'Let's go to the bedroom,' Eva broke away to whisper.

'What's wrong with right here?' I asked, looking pointedly at the sofa.

'The bedroom,' Eva insisted.

I let her take my hand and lead me out of the room and further down the hallway. We passed two closed doors and an open door leading to a small bathroom, to reach the last door down the hall. Eva went in first but waited until I was inside before shutting the door behind me. This room was smaller than the living room. A double bed filled three-quarters of the space. The walls were light blue, but not light enough. The wooden floor was painted matt white. The whole room felt enclosed and cold. A railing with clothes on it was pushed against the far wall. Eva went over to the dark-blue curtains and closed them. She came back to me with a smile and we started kissing again.

Less than five minutes later we were both

lying on the bed, naked. I closed my eyes. I couldn't stop kissing her and touching her and stroking her. I was burning up for her. I kissed her shoulders and her neck and her ears, whispering the meaningless words that girls like to hear. Until she suddenly froze beside me.

'What's the matter?' I opened my eyes to ask.

'What did you just say?' She frowned at me.

How on earth should I know? Nothing of consequence. Just pre-sex talk, that's all. What was the big deal?

'What's wrong?' I frowned.

'You called me Cara,' Eva told me.

I've never been turned off so fast in my life. I moved away from her. 'I never called you that.'

'Yes, you did,' Eva argued. 'You called me Cara.'

'You're mistaken.'

Eva didn't argue, but her expression said it all.

'I'd better go,' I said, pulling on my boxer shorts. I couldn't've had sex then if my life had depended on it.

'You don't have to go,' said Eva.

'I think I'd better,' I said, pulling on my trousers.

'Was Cara your ex?'

'I never called you Cara,' I turned my head to tell her insistently. 'I don't know any Cara.'

'If you say so.'

'I do.'

180

I pulled on my shirt and headed out the door.

'You don't have to go,' Eva called after me. 'I don't want you to leave.'

I walked out. Then I ran.

thirty-three. Sephy

Well, here I was outside the Dew Drop Inn and I was so nervous I felt like I was about to pass out. I mean, it was only a club for heaven's sake. It wasn't exactly the Royal Capital Hall so why was I getting so worked up? The fact that it'd taken me over an hour to get ready earlier didn't help to steady my nerves. I'd tried on my favourite cream-coloured dress, followed by beige jeans and a black shirt but neither outfit did the trick. I finally settled for my black jeans and a loose-fitting sparkly silver top. I didn't want anything hugging my boobs too tightly.

I took a step back to get a better view of the Dew Drop Inn. At least, that's the reason I told myself. It took all my willpower to stop myself from walking backwards until I could turn and run. It really wasn't a bad setting though—a club opposite the common with now closed and boarded-up shops on either side. Not too many residents to complain about the noise then.

Jaxon and the others were trying to find

somewhere safe to park the van as it had all the equipment in it. Sonny brought his own portable keyboard and Jaxon brought his guitar. Even though the club already had a drum kit, Rhino insisted on bringing his own drumsticks. When I asked him why, he told me very condescendingly, 'I'm a professional. My sticks are an extension of my hands. So where I go, they go.'

That's me told! I thought as he walked off. Rhino definitely didn't like me. But I wasn't about to burst out crying over it.

I'd insisted on getting out to get some air and stretch my legs. Really I just needed to get away from the lads and their talk of gigs past, present and future. They didn't seem to realize that each word was just making me more and more panicky.

The queue was beginning to build up so I thought I'd better join it and keep a place for the others. Five minutes later I was still waiting for the guys to turn up and I was almost at the front of the queue. Two lean, mean Cross bouncers, dressed in black suits and wearing discreet headsets, stood at the door, selecting who could go in and who couldn't. One of the bouncers had on a purple shirt; the other one's shirt was dark blue but they both looked remarkably similar. Was it some kind of bouncer uniform then? Looking around, I couldn't help noticing though that the queue consisted solely of Crosses, except for the occasional Nought girl.

'All alone, love? In you go.' Purple Bouncer smiled and waved me inside.

I looked around desperately. I couldn't go in without Jaxon and the others. I didn't have a clue where I was meant to go once I was inside or what I was meant to do.

'Are you going in or not?' said Blue Bouncer impatiently. 'You're holding up the queue.'

And then I saw the guys running towards me.

'Where did you park?' I asked. 'The other end of the country?'

'It's no joke trying to park around here,' Jaxon told me.

We all started to go in together. The bouncers leapt in front of us.

'It's OK,' I told them. 'We're all together.'

'They're not coming in here,' Purple Bouncer told me.

'Excuse me?'

Purple Bouncer looked at me with undisguised disdain. 'They can't come in here. You can. They can't.'

'Why not?'

'Those are the rules,' said Blue Bouncer, adding for my benefit, 'Maybe you should select your . . . friends with more care.'

'Listen, you tosser, we're booked to play here tonight,' said Jaxon. 'We're the entertainment.'

The bouncers exchanged a look. 'You'll have to go in round the back.'

'So we can sing here, but we can't dance or drink here? We can't even enter through the front door. Is that it?' Jaxon asked furiously.

183

'Those are the rules,' Blue Bouncer repeated.

I was about to tell him exactly what he could do with his rules when he added, 'Are you part of this band then?'

'Yes, I am,' I said through gritted teeth.

'Well, you can come in this way. But you others will have to go round the back,' said Blue Bouncer.

I stared up at him, speechless.

'Come on, Jaxon,' said Rhino, cold, hard resignation in his voice. 'We need this gig—remember?'

Sonny, Rhino and Jaxon headed off without even waiting for me. They'd just taken it for granted that I'd go through the front entrance and leave them to find the back door. So I went through the front entrance. But I wasn't going to leave it there. No way was this the end of it.

'Are any other bands due to sing tonight?' I asked the bouncers from over the club threshold.

'Yeah, one other. But they've already arrived,' said Purple Bouncer. 'They're in the changing room behind the stage.'

'Where can I find the owner of the club?' I asked with a smile.

Blue Bouncer looked me up and down then obviously decided I was too weedy to pose any real threat. 'Mr Kosslick is in his office—the room above the bar. But he doesn't like to see anyone without an appointment.'

184

'Oh, don't worry. I'll certainly make it worth his while,' I said silkily.

I walked into the club. There were toilets to one side of the corridor and a cloakroom on the other, with Nought staff to take the coats. The double doors straight ahead revealed an open space beyond with a dance floor. On the other side of the dance floor was a raised stage with tables and chairs all around the edges of the room. Spotlights lit up the stage and the dance floor. Against the far left wall was a long bar which was already doing a roaring trade, if the number of people standing over there waiting to be served was any indication. Most of the bar staff were Noughts, as were most of the waiters and waitresses as far as I could see. I looked above the bar. Two large lit windows looked out over the people below, like the eyes of some predatory animal. But from where I was standing, it was hard to see past the windows as the blinds in the office were semi-closed.

I made my way to the bar, working out en route that the stairs were to the left of and slightly behind the bar. I waited until the bartenders were busy then ran up the uncarpeted stairs. I knocked on the door and waited. A few seconds later, the door opened.

'Mr Kosslick?'

'Yes?' A Cross man in a quiet but very expensive suit opened the door.

'I'm Ridan.' I put out my hand.

He shook it even though he obviously didn't

185

have a clue who I was.

'What a lovely office,' I said, brushing past him before he could protest.

'Can I help you?' he asked, shutting the door behind him.

My heart was pounding by now but I was going to go through with this. Nothing could make me back out now.

'Well, I was hoping we'd be able to help each other.' I turned to him with a smile.

'Oh yes?'

I'd definitely aroused his curiosity now. He looked me up and down. And I let him do it. I knew I looked good. My figure was right back to what it'd been before I'd got pregnant, except for my breasts. They were still two sizes bigger than normal but this git wasn't about to complain. I was wearing black jeans and a silver-coloured top and my make-up had been carefully applied to instil confidence if nothing else.

'I'm with the Midges,' I explained. At his blank look, I continued, 'One of the groups you hired to sing for you this evening?'

'Oh yes,' said Mr Kosslick. 'You've got three blankers backing you up as I understand it.'

Careful to keep the smile on my face, I replied, 'Yes, that's right. That's why I'm here actually.'

'I'm listening.'

'Well, Mr Kosslick . . .' I sat on the edge of his vast table and crossed my legs. I stuck out my chest and hoped fervently that the breast

186

pads wouldn't slip out of my bra before I'd finished. 'I was wondering if I could pick up our fee for the night now?'

'Why?' Mr Kosslick's smile vanished.

'If I tell you, d'you promise you won't think badly of me,' I asked coyly.

'I doubt if I could do that,' said Mr Kosslick, but he still looked suspicious.

'It's just that, well, I want to be a solo singer. But a girl has to start somewhere,' I began. 'So I was thinking that once you've heard me sing, if you like what you hear—and see—then maybe you could sign me up to sing regularly in your club. Without the others—if you follow my drift.'

'Oh, I'm way ahead of you,' smiled Mr Kosslick.

I doubt that, I thought sourly. But I kept on smiling.

'But that still doesn't explain why you need your fee up front,' he continued. 'That's not how I do business.'

'Oh and I can understand why if you're dealing with . . . blankers. But I'm a Cross, Mr Kosslick, so I'm not about to run out on you,' I said. 'I know you'll want me once you've seen me sing, so I want to tell the guys that I'm gone once we've finished our set. I thought if I could pay them off immediately then they won't come up here and cause any trouble.'

When Mr Kosslick opened his mouth to argue, I rushed on. 'I'm sure you can take care of yourself and you've got those lovely, muscled bouncers on the door but I don't want to cause you any more trouble than necessary. Otherwise you might change your mind about hiring me.'

'I see.'

'Please, Mr Kosslick. You won't regret it, I promise,' I said, trying to make my expression as vacuous as possible. 'I'll make sure the guys get paid off and they head out the back door like meek little lambs. Deal?'

'I don't know . . .'

'I really can sing,' I carried on. 'D'you want me to prove it for you here and now? 'Cause I will.'

'Go on then.' Mr Kosslick sat back in his chair.

My heart sank. I was afraid he'd say that.

'Anything in particular you want me to sing for you?' I asked, trying to muster my courage, which seemed to be oozing out of every pore in my body.

Mr Kosslick considered. 'Sing *Fantasy*.'

This wasn't what I'd been planning at all, but I could hardly back out now. Ignoring the elephants stampeding through my stomach, I took a deep breath and started. I'd got the first verse and chorus out of the way before I realized that Mr Kosslick's frown was deepening. I trailed off, my heart thumping.

'What's the matter?' I asked.

'This is a nightclub, not a CD-player,' he told me.

'I'm not with you.'

'You've got a voice, but what about the rest? You've got to move, dance, do something to show a little stage presence,' Mr Kosslick told me. 'Otherwise you might as well be a song on the radio.'

'I see,' I said. And I did see. 'Can I start again?'

'Go on then.' Mr Kosslick now looked distinctly unimpressed.

I took another deep breath, smiled at him and started singing. But this time I moved with it. I swayed and danced along to my own singing, pretending I was a real pop star in front of a crowd of adoring fans. And I got into it surprisingly quickly. But then I'm good at pretending. Always have been. This time, I finished the song. And by the time I got to the end, Mr Kosslick was grinning at me.

'That's more like it,' said Mr Kosslick. 'Come and see me after your set and we'll sort out your contract.'

'So I can sing at your club on a regular basis?' My surprise wasn't feigned.

'Of course. You have a great voice,' he told me. 'You still need a lot of work with your delivery but I can help with that. Once you've signed up with me, we can get down to some serious work. You've definitely got something . . . I'll send you for singing and dancing lessons and teach you everything you need to know. You won't learn a damned thing hanging around with blankers.'

'Thanks, Mr Kosslick,' I smiled. 'I won't let

you down.'

He opened a drawer and threw a plain brown envelope at me with *The Midges* written on it in spidery writing.

'Thanks ever so much,' I grinned.

'Here's a little extra something just for you,' said Mr Kosslick, digging into his pocket and pulling out a couple of extra notes. 'And once you've signed on with me, there'll be plenty more where that came from.'

'You won't be disappointed, Mr Kosslick,' I said, fluttering my eyelashes.

Clutching the envelope in one hand and my bonus in the other, I made my way out of the office and down the stairs, knowing full well he was watching me every step of the way. As I made my way backstage, I checked the envelope to make sure it had every penny of the money we were owed in it. It did. I made my way to the one changing room that everyone had to use. It was large, with mirrors lining three of the four walls. A fold-up screen hid one corner of the room. I figured it was so that if men and women were sharing the changing rooms at the same time, then it'd provide some privacy if you needed to change your clothes. The room was basic but comfortable.

The other band was already there—five Nought men in matching, dark-blue leather outfits. Jaxon said we should dress smart but not dress up, otherwise it would look like we were trying too hard. This lot obviously didn't think the same.

'Hi, I'm Ridan. My band were going to play here tonight as well, but we've decided to abandon ship.'

'Why?' the tallest Nought asked me sharply.

'Don't you know?' I said, astounded. 'Mr Kosslick has been warned that the Liberation Militia are going to make an appearance here tonight. That's why they've got all that heavy security on the door. But the L.M. are determined to cause trouble—and I'm not going to be anywhere near this place when the bullets start flying. Good luck.'

'Are you serious?' one of the other Noughts asked.

'Is this something I'd joke about?' I said. 'See you.'

And I headed towards the back door.

'Marty, I'm not playing in some place where the L.M. are going to come calling. I've got a wife and kid, mate,' said one of the Noughts.

Less than a minute later they'd stuffed their ordinary clothes back into their bags, had their instruments under their arms and were out the back door. I watched them leave just as Jaxon, Rhino and Sonny came in.

'Where're they going?' Jaxon frowned.

'They got a better offer,' I told him.

I took out my handbag, ready to apply my make-up. And I pretended I couldn't see or feel the others watching me with varying degrees of contempt.

191

thirty-four. Jude

I raced along the walkway and half-jumped, half-fell down the stairs, taking them three and four at a time. I ran. Away from Eva and her pale-blue eyes. I ran till I doubled over with the stitch from hell stabbing its way out of my side. Dragging the cool night air into my lungs, I fought to get my heartbeat back under control.

What was the matter with me? Going with Eva had been a big mistake. What was supposed to be half an hour's oblivion had turned into anything but. It was as if I hadn't even allowed myself to inhale until I'd left her and her seedy flat. That's how bad it was. I didn't want to even share the same air as her. I started walking in no particular direction, feeling like nothing on this earth. I took out my mobile and phoned directory enquiries to get a phone number. After I'd got the number, the operator asked if I wanted to be connected to it. I almost said yes. Which just goes to show how switched off I was feeling. I declined the offer and wrote the number on the back of my hand. It took me ten minutes to find a working phone box.

I phoned the hospital.

'Could you put me through to your intensive care unit please?' I asked.

'Just a moment,' the receptionist said, her tone bored.

Moments later I was talking to someone else.

'Intensive care. Can I help you?'

'How is Cara Imega?' I asked.

'Are you a member of the immediate family?' the male voice asked.

'Yes, I'm Joshua Imega, her uncle. I only just heard what happened,' I said without even blushing. 'I'm on my way down to see her now but I wanted to know how she was doing.'

Silence.

'Hello?'

'She's not doing very well,' the male voice said with apologetic sympathy. 'We can't really give out much information over the phone, but if I were you, I'd get here as soon as possible.'

'I see,' I said.

And I put down the phone.

thirty-five. Sephy

'Can we sing *Bad Attitude* first?' I asked Jaxon.

'That's the highlight of our set,' Sonny pointed out, looking at me like I was some kind of maggot who'd just crawled across his top lip.

'I know. But I do have a good reason for asking.'

'I don't know about that—' Jaxon began.

'Give the Cross lady what she wants,' Sonny interrupted.

So this was the way it was going to be. In the

changing rooms, I'd re-applied my lipstick whilst the guys changed their shirts in an all-enveloping, chilly fog of silence. The others had made a particular point of ignoring me completely. And I didn't expect it to, but it hurt. I looked across at Rhino on the drums. He wouldn't even look at me.

'Rhino, can you start us off? I really want to get the crowd going,' I said to him.

He looked at me with such malevolence, I actually shivered. Then he started drumming. Slow and steady. I turned and walked back to my mic. Jaxon stood on one side of me, holding his guitar. Sonny stood on the other side of me behind his keyboard. I was getting third-degree burns from the loathing radiating off all of them.

'How're you all feeling?' I called out.

The crowd packed around the stage cheered.

'I said—HOW'RE YOU ALL FEELING?'

The cheer this time was even louder.

And Rhino's drumbeat was getting faster and faster. I nodded at Jaxon who let rip with his guitar. Sonny came in a bar later. *Bad Attitude* was pop candyfloss but it was popular pop candyfloss. I watched the crowd, who were already getting revved up as the music took them higher and higher. And as I watched, the silent rage inside me took root and spread throughout my entire body. I despised everyone in the room at that moment— Noughts and Crosses alike. I loathed all the pettiness and narrow minds and narrow visions. Why was hatred so easy?

You can't come here.

You can't play there.

No mixing.

No matching.

Stay on your own side.

Stay in your own country.

Stay off my planet.

And I wasn't any better.

And I wasn't any different.

Of everyone in the place, I loathed myself most of all.

I took a deep breath. I had to make this good. Better than rehearsal. Better than I'd ever sung it before. Better than anything anyone in this club had heard in a long time. So I started to sing. And anger gave me a voice. And rage took away my fear. And fury took away my doubts. I wasn't Sephy any more. I was Ridan, a girl with no hesitations and no apprehensions. A girl with nothing to gain and nothing to lose. I really let rip. By the time the song had finished, the crowd were cheering so loudly my ears were ringing. They loved us. *Bad Attitude* had been just the right song to sing. It was a popular, fast, up-tempo dance track that always got people on their feet. We had the crowd right where we wanted them.

'D'you want some more?' I shouted.

'Yes!' they screamed back.

'I said—D'YOU WANT SOME MORE?'

'YES!'

For the first time that evening, the smile fell

off my face.

'Well, it's not going to happen,' I said.

The cheers fell away into confused whispers. The crowd weren't the only ones who were puzzled. I had the full attention of Jaxon, Rhino and Sonny as well.

'When we came here tonight, we were going to sing a whole load of songs, each of them bigger and better than the one we just did,' I said into the mic. 'But we weren't allowed to come in through the front door. We were told to go around the back. Well, if we're not good enough to come through the same door as you lot, we sure as hell aren't good enough to sing to you. So peace out and goodbye.'

And I headed off stage. But then I remembered something and went back to the stage.

'And it looks like you'll be without any live music this evening because the other band were so disgusted by the way we've been treated that they've already left the building.'

And this time I did make it off the stage. Jaxon and the others had no choice but to follow me. The stunned silence was beginning to be punctuated with a few boos. But even if only one person in the audience understood what I was saying, it would've been worth it.

'What the bloody hell d'you think you're doing?' asked Jaxon. 'We haven't been paid yet.'

'Oh yes we have,' I said waving all the money that slick git Kosslick had given me. I dug into

196

my pocket and took out the extra money I'd been given as well. 'You'd better hold onto that, Sonny. I don't think anyone will be getting anything off you that you don't want to give them.'

And I handed it over. He immediately stuffed it into his trouser pocket.

'Shall we go?' I smiled.

Rhino, Jaxon and Sonny all stood there staring at me. But every trace of their earlier contempt had gone. This was much better!

'I know you guys don't know me from a crisp packet but we all go through the same door, or we don't go in at all. OK?'

'OK!' agreed Sonny with a smile.

Outside the booing and cat-calls were almost as loud as the previous cheers and whistles.

'We'd better get out of here before—' But I didn't get any further.

'What the hell d'you think you're playing at?' Mr Kosslick had arrived with a couple of heavy-duty minders.

The guys moved to stand in front of me, but I pushed my way through to stand with them.

'We're not playing,' I told him.

'You bitch! You were paid to play for me tonight,' said Mr Kosslick, glaring at me.

'And we did. We played one track so we've fulfilled our part of the deal,' I told him.

'I want my money back,' said Mr Kosslick, waving one of his muscle-heads forward.

'I wouldn't do that if I were you,' I warned him as Sonny tried to push me back out of harm's way.

'But you're not me—blanker-lover,' Kosslick hissed at me. 'I'm going to take pleasure in dealing with you personally—'

'Try it,' I challenged. 'My real name is Persephone Hadley and my dad's Kamal Hadley, the Deputy Prime Minister. And I promise you, if any of us gets so much as a chipped fingernail, you'll all be swinging from a rope before the week's out. So just try it.'

The muscle-head looked back at Mr Kosslick for guidance. Mr Kosslick didn't take his eyes off me. I looked straight back at him. He decided I wasn't bluffing.

'Let them go,' he told his minions. Then he turned to me. 'But don't you ever set foot in my club again.'

'Don't worry,' I said. 'We Midges are too good for this dump anyway.'

'You haven't heard the last of this,' Mr Kosslick called after us. 'Especially you, Miss Hadley.'

'I'm shaking,' I called back with contempt before we all entered the changing room.

But here's the funny thing—I *was* shaking inside.

We gathered up our stuff and left, across the stage and through the front door. And although we got a few boos and hand gestures, no one made a move to stop us. I have to say we got one or two genuine hand claps as well. One or two.

No one spoke. It was as if each of us was

holding our breath until we got out of the club. And only when we were outside on the street and walking back to the van at the back of the club did we all fall about with spontaneous laughter—brought on by relief more than anything else.

'Oh my God! I thought we were dead!' I admitted.

'"My father's the Deputy Prime Minister!"' mimicked Sonny. 'I thought you didn't want anyone to know who you really were?'

'I don't. I didn't,' I shrugged. 'But I didn't fancy getting my head ripped off either, thank you very much. Sonny, don't forget that a quarter of that money in your pocket is mine.'

'I won't forget,' Sonny said wryly.

'Would your dad really have ridden to the rescue?' Jaxon asked.

'Are you kidding?' I told him, my smile disappearing. 'He'd probably have held their coats for them.'

I turned to Rhino, who hadn't said very much at all. My smile went unanswered, but I didn't mind. Rhino still didn't know what to make of me, but I wasn't public enemy number one any more. Maybe public enemy number two or three.

'Sephy, I think I underestimated you,' said Sonny.

And coming from him I knew it was a compliment. I didn't reply. I didn't need to.

Like I said, no one would ever play me for a fool again.

thirty-six. Jude

I've done absolutely nothing this weekend. Just sat around the flat, watching telly and eating and scheming. Andrew Dorn, the traitor in the L.M. is back at the top of my priority list now. I have money. Now I just need to figure out how to get to him. I still have friends in a few L.M. cells. Friends who would go out on a limb for me. And others who might, if the price is right. I want to get as close as I can to Andrew Dorn. I want to be the one to make him pay.

And I will.

The news is coming on now. I can't believe it's so late. But I don't want to see the news again. It'll be the same old, same old. Except for one of the later items first announced this evening. News about the hunt for Cara Imega's murderer.

Cara died this morning in hospital.

thirty-seven. Sephy

What a weekend! Yesterday's gig was a non-starter, but Jaxon phoned me earlier today to tell me another club, Russell's, has us booked for a fortnight on Saturday.

'But Russell's is a Nought club, isn't it?' I asked.

'Their money's just as good,' Jaxon told me icily.

'That's not what I meant and you know it,' I said with patience. 'They're not going to want me in a Nought club.'

'Once you start singing, they won't care,' said Jaxon.

'Oh great! And that's meant to be reassuring, is it?'

'You're worrying about nothing,' Jaxon dismissed.

And after that, I knew it was pointless arguing with him. Russell's was a very popular club, frequented by Noughts. And it was one of the few clubs in town actually run by a Nought but that's all I knew about it.

'Look, this gig was booked almost a month ago,' Jaxon said. 'Mind you, what happened at the Dew Drop Inn didn't hurt us.'

'They know about that?' I asked, aghast.

'Are you kidding?' Jaxon laughed. 'The word has already spread.'

'Do they know who I really am?' I panicked.

' 'Course not. You're Ridan, our lead vocalist, as far as anyone knows. But Russell's is the main rival around here to the Dew Drop Inn and Alice loves to get one up on them.'

'Who's Alice?'

'She owns Russell's,' Jaxon informed me.

All kinds of bells were pealing in my head.

'Besides you can't drop out now. We need the money,' said Jaxon.

And he had a point. The money from the

201

Dew Drop Inn wouldn't last very long at all. But I couldn't stop those warning bells jangling. Jaxon and I discussed our rehearsal dates and that was the next gig sorted out. Now I just needed to sort out the rest of my life.

I've decided to stop breast-feeding Rose. I've been feeding her myself for a few weeks now. I think that's long enough.

'I thought you were going to feed Callie yourself for a year, not a couple of weeks,' Meggie argued when I told her.

'The sooner she starts feeding from a bottle the better,' I replied. 'Then you can feed her and look after her whilst I'm out working.'

'I'm not her mother, Sephy,' said Meggie.

'Meaning?'

'Meaning feeding her and looking after her is your job,' said Meggie. 'I offered to help, not to take over.'

'Rose is your granddaughter,' I pointed out icily. 'Callum's precious child. But if you don't want to look after her, just say so.'

'I never said that. And isn't she your precious child too?' Meggie asked with sarcasm.

'What's that supposed to mean?' I frowned.

'It means Callie's a baby and she needs her mother.'

'I'm here, aren't I?' I shouted at her. 'And apart from a couple of rehearsals and my gig on Saturday, have I been anywhere without her?'

Meggie regarded me. 'You're determined to

pick a fight with someone, Sephy, but it's not going to be me.'

'I wouldn't start an argument with you, Meggie. After all, it might give you an excuse to turn on me the way Callum did.'

Meggie handed Rose back to me, saying frostily, 'I have to go shopping.'

Our first major disagreement.

Meggie went out for hours, packed away the shopping when she finally came back home and went out again. I was stuck with Rose all day. So I put her in the scrubbed- up second-hand buggy I'd bought and went for a walk. I actually took the time to notice the world around me. I'd visited Callum in Meadowview plenty of times as a child, but then the world was a beautiful place, as was everything and everyone in it. Then I saw only the poster-paint blue of the sky and the sun-kissed green of the leaves on the trees and a smile on every face.

But now I was older.

And Meadowview was no longer beautiful. The paving stones were uneven and cracked and broken. Wheeling Rose in her buggy was like manoeuvring over an obstacle course. I'd come out in four-centimetre-high shoes. All the Noughts around wore trainers. Now I could see why. The pavement was speckled with dried chewing gum, most of it so old as to be on a level with the surface of the paving stones beneath. Five minutes didn't pass before another police car or ambulance whizzed past me. Trees were few and far between, their roots surrounded not by soil or grass but by tarmac or steel grilles. Everyone looked so tired.

And no one smiled.

As I pushed Rose in her buggy, I couldn't help but be aware of the looks we were getting. A lot of the Noughts we passed did a double-take when they noticed us. One tall Nought woman, in her mid-thirties, I'd guess, with black hair and dark eyes even turned round and started to follow me. I instinctively knew she was behind me. Some sixth sense like an inner radar jangled my nerves. A stillness settled over me as I turned my focus outward instead of inwards. It was like the world slowed down so I could notice everything in it. A horn beeped two or three cars behind me. A man ran across the road, dodging in front of one car, waiting for another to pass before he chanced trying to reach the opposite pavement. A pneumatic drill sounded relentlessly in the background.

And the woman was still behind me, following. And getting closer. I took a deep breath and turned to face her, standing between her and my baby with one hand clutching at the buggy's handle.

'Can I help you?' I said with belligerence.

'I'm sorry but are you . . . Persephone Handley?'

It's Hadley, I thought sourly. But I had more sense than to answer.

'You are, aren't you?' she said, scrutinizing me. She took a step closer. I took a step back.

Here we go, I thought, my heart sinking.

What was it that made people think that just because I'd been in the paper, they were entitled to stop me in the street and verbally abuse me? When I'd been pregnant, one woman had even slapped my face, calling me a traitor and telling me I was 'no better than I should be'—whatever that means. The woman's face broke into a broad smile, taking my silence for assent.

'Can I say something?'

'If you must,' I mumbled, bracing myself.

'I just wanted to say—good for you!'

'Excuse me?'

'Good for you,' she repeated.

And with that her face whooshed red. She turned and almost stumbled in her embarrassed haste to get away from me. Astonished, I watched her walk quickly away. It took a few seconds before her words sank in. I wanted to call after her, but she was out of earshot. I smiled and said softly, 'Thank you.' Then I turned round and carried on with my walk—still puzzled, not just by what she'd said but also by my automatic assumption that she'd been winding up to say something nasty to me. When did I get so distrustful? I smiled at the next Nought I walked past. She looked from Rose to me and gave me the filthiest look I'd had in, oh, at least a day. I sighed inwardly. No more smiling. No more catching anyone's eye. The thing to do was keep myself to myself. Growing up was just a euphemistic way to describe growing more cynical and inhibited.

After about forty minutes, we went back home. And Rose chose the moment I put the key in the door to bawl her head off. I fed her and changed her and put her down but she wouldn't stop crying. Meggie said I should leave her to cry in her cot, but after half an hour of listening to her scream, I couldn't handle it any more. So I picked her up and rubbed her back.

And when that didn't work, I whispered in her ear.

And then I looked at her. Looked at her properly for probably the first time since I'd read her dad's letter. And only when I looked into her eyes so that she could look straight back into mine did she stop crying. Only then.

I sat down and held her in my arms, long after she'd fallen asleep. Her eyes were still a deep, dark blue. I hadn't realized. Her hair was already longer than when she was first born, and she felt chunky and solid—just as she should. She'd put on so much weight, it was almost as if she was growing before my eyes.

Who could I tell about it?

I felt so alone. It was loneliness, not blood that coursed through my veins. I finally put her back in her cot. It was easy to forget everything else when she looked at me and I looked at her. But it was all too easy to remember when we were apart. I needed to think, away from Rose, away from any distractions. I decided to have a bath, to calm down and consider. I had a lot of thinking to do. Meggie arrived home and went straight to her room so I was left alone.

I lay in the deep, warm, lavender-scented bath water knowing I wouldn't be disturbed. Meggie was obviously still mad at me. Well, that was her business. I had to think about what I was going to do next. But I felt so relaxed for the first time in a long time that it was hard to think at all. I gently undulated my thighs so that the water would wash over my stomach and breasts. And it was so soothing. I closed my eyes and tilted back my head. And still my thighs moved in and out gently, slowly, to keep the water lapping over my body. I drifted away to golden beaches strewn with smooth pieces of driftwood, spring in Celebration Park when the air smelled of fresh wet earth and abundant wild flowers, blissfully ignorant childhood Sunday mornings under the duvet curled up with a good book. I gathered up all the good memories I could as I moved further down into the bath water. I drifted away to a cold cabin in the middle of some dark, nameless forest.

With Callum.

Kissing me.

Touching me.

On me.

In me.

*'I love you, Sephy . . .' he whispers against my
mouth.*

*I'm too breathless, too overwrought to say
anything in reply. I cling onto him, my arms
around him, loving him so much I think I'll die
of it. Can he hear my scattered thoughts? Or just
read what I'm feeling in my eyes? Just one look
to drink me in. Just a touch to eat me up. Carry
me away. Your hands are so hot against my skin,
burning me wherever you touch. But don't stop
touching me. Never stop loving me.*

*Oh Callum, I love you so much. And what
you're doing to me . . . My blood is on fire. Each
kiss, each caress robs me of another piece of my
heart, another part of my soul. There's no you
and me any more. There's just us—as one. I
return your kiss, our lips pressing together harder
and harder until we can't breathe, until I can't
tell where I stop and you start. Lost in a dream
and carried onwards and upwards, until we're
both so high we're touching heaven. Knocking on
heaven's door.*

Callum, I love you . . .

Callum, I love . . .

Callum, my love.

I opened my eyes to find myself half in the
present, half in the past. My hands moved out
of the cooling bath water to grip the sides of
the bath.

Oh Callum, my love . . .

My body trembled with pleasure as every cell
of my body remembered him, all of him. And
with each quiver of my body, the past faded

and the present reclaimed me. When the quivering stopped and the shivering started, I sat up and buried my face in my hands, unable to stop the tears running down my face. The real world buried me and once again I remembered how desperately alone I was. This loneliness would drive me insane, if it didn't kill me first.

I climbed out of the cool bath water, putting on my dressing gown. I sat at the edge of the tub for I don't know how long, staring down at the lino. I only got up when I began to get pins and needles in my feet. After pulling the plug and cleaning the bath tub, I headed back to my room. It was lit by a single lamp on the table by my bed. I peeped into Rose's cot and watched her sleep, trying to resist the temptation to pick her up or stroke her cheek. After drying my skin, I put on my cotton pyjamas and slipped into bed.

Tired as I was, I knew I wouldn't be able to sleep. My mind was racing. I found myself wishing there was some pill or potion I could take which would make me forget about Rose's dad for long enough to get some rest. Giving up, I sat up in bed wondering what to do next. I thought about reading but I wasn't in the mood. I didn't know what to do with myself. My mind was wading through treacle. I wanted to talk to someone but there was no one. Meggie was in her room, probably asleep. And I couldn't phone Minerva or Mother at this time of night. However, I needed to talk to someone. Anyone. In desperation, I picked up my notebook from off the floor and hunted around for something to write with. Retrieving a pen from the pocket of my jacket hanging on the wardrobe, I got back into bed. Now what? I wanted to write something but I had no idea what. Something that was pure fantasy. Something that would take me away from the words in Callum's letter. Something that would stop me wishing there were no words left in the world.

Don't think about it, I told myself. Just write.

So I did. I wrote down *'No Words'* and underlined it twice. And then I wrote with my heart before my head could censor me. I just let the words pour out. Pure fantasy.

No Words
We had something special.
I still can't believe it's gone.
For once I left your loving arms
Everything went wrong.
We danced upon a rainbow
And chased the clouds away.
But now that you're not with me,
There's no more left to say.

For love's first kiss
No words.
Just one night of bliss
No words.
What we had is gone
No words.

It's time to move on
No words.

No one promised us for ever
But we thought it'd never fade.
Now all I do is close my eyes,
To feel the love we made.
You were and are and will be
My one and only lover
You held me in your palm, my dear,
So how can there be another?

For the long, cold night
No words.
When wrong was right
No words.
I live in the past
No words.
Long may it last
No words.

And can you feel my heart beat?
And can you feel it soar?
One kiss, one night was not enough,
You've got me wanting more
You've got me needing more
You've got me craving more.

So here I am without you
Was this really meant to be?
Let's pretend we're still together
In love, eternally.
But here I am without you

And it doesn't matter why,
There are no words that can explain
And memories make me cry.

I can't move on
No words.
I'm not that strong
No words.
I need you so
No words.
Why did you go?
No words.

No words that can be whispered,
They fade upon a sigh,
There are no words to sing or say
Except my love,
Goodbye.

I put down the notepad and switched off my light. I stared into the inky darkness of my room.

'Can you see me, Callum?' I whispered. 'Can you see how you've ruined my life? I wonder, does it make you laugh or does it make you cry?'

YELLOW

Blinding

Closed off

Burning

Cowardice

Lightning

Lasers

Screams

High Frequency

No Hope for Peace

Scorching, Scolding

Fire

Sulphur

Stench

Too Light, Too Bright

Noughts in Stop and Search Protest

The controversial Stop and Search bill made it through Parliament last night with a comfortable majority of twenty-two. This new bill now gives the police the right to stop and search any nought who is genuinely believed to be carrying drugs, excess alcohol or components which could be used in the manufacture of explosives.

Alex Luther, leader of the non-violent Lutherian Coalition, stated last night, 'This is a grave day for all of us—Noughts and Crosses. This immoral, unjust law is a charter for the police to treat every nought as a criminal, based on nothing but their own suspicions and prejudices. Justice in this country has been set back one hundred and fifty years.'

Yesterday, nought protest groups were out in force up and down the country, reacting angrily to the proposed legislation. Inevitably, some noughts used this as an opportunity to run riot, causing criminal damage and looting in most major cities up and down the country. The police were out in force and several arrests were made. *(The Editor says—page 4)*

thirty-eight. Meggie

Our days filled with platitudes. We both talk, but neither of us says much. The evenings are mostly filled with silence. Like last night. There we were again, sitting down, watching the telly. Sephy was sitting in the armchair she's made her own. I sat on the sofa. Callie was asleep in her cot in Sephy's bedroom— bless her. And thus our evening in began. After an hour, Sephy hadn't said much. In fact she hadn't said anything at all. When she first moved in, we'd talk. We'd discuss telly programmes, the things we'd heard, the things we'd seen, items in the news. Now there was only silence. Finally I couldn't stand it any longer.

'Sephy, you mustn't believe what was in that letter—'

'I've already told you,' Sephy interrupted without looking at me. 'I don't want to talk about it.'

'I just want to—'

Sephy stood up and headed for the door.

'OK. Have it your way. I won't say another word.'

Sephy looked at me, trying to gauge whether or not I meant it. She finally decided I did because she sat down again. And there we sat, in silence. And I didn't dare say another word. Because I was afraid Sephy wouldn't just walk out of the room, but would walk out of my house taking my granddaughter with her. I try my best not to criticize, not to interfere—but it's hard. I don't want to drive Sephy out by nagging her too much, but sometimes I look at her and I could swear that we're both feeling the same, both going through the same, but neither of us has the courage to just come right out and say so. Sometimes, I see Sephy's eyes cloud over. It might be for a minute or a moment, but it's enough. I know she's trying to match the memory of Callum against the words in his letter.

That bloody letter.

I don't believe for one second that Callum wrote those hateful, hurtful things—not for a second. Callum loved Sephy. I don't know much in this world but I do know that. He loved Sephy the way my husband Ryan loved me. The way Lynette loved Jed. The way Jude could love too, if he'd just let go of all the hate inside him first. It must be a McGregor thing—love all the way, hate all the way. Nothing in between.

No matter what anyone else says—like my sister, Charlotte—my family were lucky in one way at least. We loved each other very much and no one can ever take that away from me. My husband Ryan would've done anything for me and our kids. Anything. When I think of my family, it makes me realize that there's not much in this life that remains constant. The only thing that never changed in our lives was our love for each other. When the memories come and threaten to wash me away, I hold onto that one thought for my life and my sanity.

Sometimes I catch Sephy watching me, a puzzled look on her face. She looks away when she realizes I've caught her but that expression on her face has been there more times than I can count. I think she swings between not quite believing that I don't hate her and wondering why, if I don't, then why I don't? I hope she didn't agree to stay with me out of some need to do penance or as her stint in purgatory for some imagined sin. Sephy never did understand just how much she means to me. She is almost as dear to me as my own daughter, Lynette. I can't tell her that though. She'd never believe me. I look at her sometimes, when she's eating or reading or when she's nodded off on the sofa and I go through in my head all the things I'd like to tell her.

Like how much I love and admire her for what she did on the day they hanged my son. Like how much I love and cherish her for having my grandchild, Callie Rose. I know she could've had an abortion. I'll bet that's exactly what her bastard father wanted. Or she could've put her child up for adoption. But she didn't. Does she have any idea how strong she is? I hope so, I really do.

And as for Callie Rose, well, every time I look at her I can see Callum. The same eyes, the same expressions, the same tilt of the head when puzzling out something. I look at Callie and I want to just gobble her up or hug her tight and never let her go or wrap her up and put her in my heart and never let her out. I'm so desperate to keep her safe and wrapped in love. Because I know she's not going to have it easy. She's neither nought nor Cross. And in a world desperate to pigeon-hole and categorize and stereotype, she may feel forced to come down on one side or the other.

And the truth is, she's both.

And the truth is, she's neither.

She's new and special and different and individual and herself. Maybe that's what we all need—to be mixed and shaken and stirred as vigorously as possible until 'nought' and 'Cross' as labels become meaningless. But what I wish for, and what is, are worlds apart.

Sephy has me worried. She's changed. And Callum's letter is the thing which changed her. It's difficult to put into words, but it's as if something has gone out in her. She was ready to take my head off before when I suggested that it wouldn't hurt Callie to be occasionally left in her cot when she cries. But that was before Callum's letter. Now she follows my advice a little too often. Sometimes I sit in the living room with Sephy, whilst Callie cries in her cot in Sephy's bedroom, and I have to bite my lip not to say anything. I want to scream at Sephy to get up and take care of her child. There've been plenty of times when I've been close to doing just that. Then with a sigh, Sephy manages to drag her backside out of the armchair and she heads towards the bedroom. Before Callum's letter, Callie couldn't cry for longer than five seconds before Sephy was at her side.

But that was before Callum's letter.

And this is most definitely after.

Take what happened yesterday afternoon. Sephy was in the kitchen, making herself a sandwich, and I was in the living room watching a chat show when Callie Rose began to grizzle. I glanced down at my watch. It was about time for her next feed. Less than a minute later, the grizzling turned into a full-blown, full-throated bellow. Callie wasn't happy at being ignored—and I couldn't blame her. I stood up, wondering if and when Sephy was going to sort out her daughter. Callie's cries continued. I sat back down. For heaven's sake, if I could hear Callie then so could Sephy. But Callie carried on crying. And on. And on. I couldn't stand it any more. I stood up and went upstairs to comfort her. Sephy had obviously decided that her sandwich was more important than her daughter.

But I was wrong.

Sephy was in her bedroom with Callie. But she stood at the foot of the cot, staring down at her. I watched Sephy, wondering when she was going to do something about Callie's cries. She continued staring down at her—and my blood ran cold at the expression on her face. Because there was no expression on her face. Not love. Not tenderness. Not hate. Just a blank.

'Is everything all right, Sephy?' I asked.

She turned to me and it was like shutters coming down. She smiled with her mouth, not her eyes, and nodded.

'Yes, Meggie. Everything's fine,' she told me.

And only then did she pick up Callie Rose. I backed away, feeling a chill that had nothing to do with the temperature around me. I'm losing Sephy, losing her to that letter. But worse than that, Callie is losing her too.

And I can't for the life of me figure out what to do about it.

thirty-nine. Sephy

Russell's was the first Nought club I'd ever been to. We entered the place—through the front door—to be greeted by one of the broadest, strongest women I'd ever seen. She wasn't fat as such, more built like a armoured truck. She had dyed red hair and must've put on her make-up with a trowel 'cause it was that thick.

'How d'you do?' I said, offering her my hand.

'My! Aren't you polite?!' the woman laughed. 'How do you do yourself! I'm Alice.'

And she gave me a bear hug that crushed my ribs and left me in quite a lot of pain. I tried for a smile, afraid to open my mouth again for fear I might give her something else to laugh at.

'Let me warn all of you, the crowd tonight is a little rowdy,' said Alice, turning to the others. 'We've got a couple of birthday parties in, plus a hen night.'

'A hen night. Oh no!' groaned Jaxon.

At my look of confusion, Alice told me, 'Hen nights are the worst. I can deal with men who get out of line but even I can't cope with the women. I have to call in my bouncers.' She turned to Jaxon and the others. 'You're all in for quite a time.'

For one brief second I thought, I *hoped* she was joking. The look on the guys' faces said otherwise.

'Great,' Sonny growled. 'Just great.'

'Hey!' said Alice. 'That's why you earn the big dosh!'

Sonny just snorted at that.

We were escorted through the club and to the changing room. The place had a different odour to the Dew Drop Inn. Russell's reeked with the sweetish smell of beer and the sharp catch of cigarette smoke and other less legal aromas. I looked around the club, which was already three quarters full even though it'd only been open for about half an hour, and my heart sank. I was the only Cross in the place and I stuck out like a throbbing thumb. At least there had been Nought staff in the Dew Drop Inn, so that Jaxon, Rhino and Sonny wouldn't feel totally isolated. OK, so the

Noughts were waiters and serving behind the bar but at least they had been present. In this place, it felt like all eyes were upon me and I could feel myself getting hotter and more uncomfortable.

'What's she doing in here?'

'Who's the dagger?'

A number of the comments being made about me reached my ears. Goodness only knew what was being said that I couldn't hear.

'Are you the dance act then?' called out one woman as we walked past.

'Don't you wish!' Jaxon shot back.

'You look like you're hiding something.' A nought man looked me up and down as I walked past him. 'How about if I stop and search you?'

A few catcalls and whistles began to follow us across the floor. I was already nostalgic for Meggie's armchair in front of the TV. We entered a small room with PRIVATE on the door. It was in between the men's and women's toilets, which were already smelling pretty ripe. Alice led the way into the private room first and we all trooped after her. I looked for somewhere at least screened off where I could change. There was nothing. Six chairs, a wall mirror, a lino-covered floor, a dangling light bulb and a box of tissues on the shelf-like table beneath the mirror—that was it. Not even a fan heater to take the chill off the place or a lampshade over the bulb. That would teach me. I should've worn the outfit I wanted to perform in to the club, but I had thought, facilities-wise, this one would be on a par with the Dew Drop Inn. It wasn't even close.

'You're the warm-up act for tonight so you're on in five minutes—and you'd better be good.' The last was said directly to me.

And if I was nervous before, it was nothing compared to just how sick I now felt. Every nerve clanged and jangled like a bad orchestra warming up. I'd been anxious in the Dew Drop Inn but when they wouldn't let us in the front door, my anger had taken over and got me through my one song. But that wasn't the case now. As I watched Alice leave, I half wanted her to turn round and say something to piss me off. At least then, I'd have something more than this feeling of panic to concentrate on. But she just headed straight out of the door without so much as a backwards glance. The moment Alice left the room I turned to Jaxon, Sonny and Rhino.

'Where am I supposed to change?'

'At home?' Sonny ventured.

I glared at him. 'I'll remember that for the next gig, but in the meantime?'

'In here, with us then,' Jaxon said impatiently.

'I'm not showing you three what I haven't got,' I protested.

'Then what would you suggest?' asked Sonny.

I was about to propose that they turn their

224

backs or maybe leave the room, but I could imagine how that one would go down.

'I'll go and change in the toilets,' I said with a sigh.

Gathering up my small holdall, I headed out of the room. I felt like saying that Sonny, Rhino and Jaxon should've been the ones to leave the room, not me. But there was more chance of blue snow falling in summer than that happening. I walked into the women's toilets deep in my own thoughts. So I didn't realize I had company until a bony finger prodded my shoulder blade. I spun round.

It was Amy, the singer with the band before I arrived. She'd followed me in. And from the look on her face she was after blood. My blood.

'You think you're real slick, don't you?' Amy told me.

I didn't answer. Instinct told me to keep my mouth shut.

'You think Jaxon cares about you? He's only using you so that the band can play in Cross clubs. You're just his meal ticket.'

Well, I already knew that. If Amy thought I was going to get all worked up over that fact then she was about to be very disappointed.

'And he reckons you'll be easy to get into bed,' Amy continued, when I still didn't speak. 'You've been to bed with one nought so what difference would another one make? You obviously like your meat rare—that's what he said.'

225

Which was so ludicrous I almost laughed out loud. I didn't much care if Jaxon said it or if Amy was making it all up but I didn't like the look on Amy's face when she saw she wasn't getting to me. I took a quick look around. Amy and I were alone, worst luck. Mind you, in this place I couldn't guarantee that I'd have too many allies. I was sure Amy wasn't the only Nought in the place ready to kick my butt.

'You lot make me sick.' Amy came closer so that she sprayed my face with saliva when she spoke. 'Our club, our music and you're still in here trying to take it over. I should be with the band, not you.'

I wanted to tell her to take it up with Jaxon. I wanted to tell her to back off and leave me alone. But I said nothing, sensing that she had a lot to get off her chest. Why had she picked me instead of Jaxon to have a go at though? Maybe because I was the softer target. Maybe she thought I'd care more or that she'd be able to get through to me.

Or just get to me.

'You make me more than sick,' she repeated.

'Look, Jaxon asked *me* to sing with the band, not the other way round.'

'You could've said no. You should've,' Amy shot back. 'You don't belong here. And you certainly don't belong with the band. I don't know what Jaxon sees in you.'

I frowned, not happy with the way she was making it seem like there was something more between Jaxon and me than a business

226

relationship.

'Jaxon likes the way I sing. That's it. End of story. Bye bye. See you later,' I told her.

'Yeah, right,' Amy scoffed. 'We both know it's just a matter of time before you end up in his bed. From what I've heard you don't mind a bit of slumming. You were with that terrorist Callum McGregor, weren't you? Even I wouldn't crawl into bed with someone from the Liberation Militia.'

Enough was enough.

'If you've finished, I need to get changed,' I told her.

She glared at me, hatred personified, and I knew the split second before she did it what she was about to do. She pounced. There's no other way to describe it. She jumped at me, ready to scratch my eyes clean out of their sockets.

But that wasn't going to happen.

I raised my right arm to block her hands and shoved her to one side. A few years earlier, I'd been jumped in the girls' toilets at my school and had the crap beaten out of me. After that I swore no one would ever do that to me again. Ever. And I meant it. Amy fell against the wall, then turned and was stupid enough to come at me again. I twisted my body round so that I was sideways on to her and she'd have less of a target before directing my fist down and out. I connected with her stomach and sent her crashing backwards. She lay sprawled on the ground, dazed.

'I'd quit whilst you're behind if I were you,' I told her quietly. 'Because I'm not going to let you lay one finger on me. That's not going to happen.'

'You'll be . . . sorry,' Amy coughed. 'If it's the last thing I do I'll make sure you're sorry.'

I sighed inwardly. Was I ever going to get through one of these gigs without someone threatening me? It certainly hadn't happened so far. Amy got to her feet and stumbled out of the room, just as two other Nought women walked in. They looked me up and down before heading into the two toilet cubicles.

I pulled off my T-shirt, unzipped my holdall and pulled on my shirt in double-quick time before anyone else could interrupt me. I was just buttoning it up when one of the Nought women emerged from the cubicle. But instead of washing her hands, she leaned against one of the two sinks watching me.

I carried on buttoning up my blouse. The other Nought flushed the loo and came out of her cubicle. She washed her hands, shaking her head at her friend. I picked up my holdall and headed out of the door, making sure that I didn't hurry or look in any way flustered—even though my stomach was turning over inside me. I had my hand on the door marked PRIVATE when the others trooped out.

'Let's do this,' said Jaxon.

'Is five minutes up already?' I groaned. Just a minute's peace to collect my thoughts would've been welcome.

228

'Are you OK?' Sonny asked.

'Why?'

'You look a little . . . flustered,' said Sonny.

At that, Jaxon peered at me anxiously.

'I'm fine,' I told him.

' 'Course you are. It's show time,' Jaxon told me with an inane, show-business grin on his face.

I glanced up at Sonny. A slight frown turned down his lips as he regarded me. I turned up my lips to resemble some kind of smile. He didn't say anything but I could sense he wasn't convinced. I threw my holdall across the room and headed out after them. The guys looked relatively relaxed. But then they would. They weren't the ones being glared at and assaulted in the toilets before even one note was played. I was about to be greeted by an audience full of malice. Something told me this wasn't going to be the best night of my life.

forty. Meggie

Sephy's out tonight at her gig at Russell's and to be honest, I was glad. During the last two weeks, things had gone from bad to worse. Sephy changes Callie's nappy, she feeds her, she bathes her but she won't hold her. Hugs and cuddles are a thing of the past. And Callie cries a lot more often now. It's a vicious circle. Sephy doesn't want to hold Callie, so Callie cries harder and longer and more often to be held. I've picked up Callie more in the last two weeks than Sephy has. Sephy's been at rehearsals with that Jaxon Robbins—who I wouldn't trust with one of my used tissues—or else she makes excuses to leave the house. She tells me she needs to go for a walk or she's going shopping or she's visiting friends, but what it boils down to is Sephy isn't here. And her daughter is. So I've made a decision. I had no choice but I knew Sephy wouldn't see it that way.

I pressed the digits on my phone and placed the receiver to my ear. My heart had leapt up to my throat so I wasn't sure if I was going to be able to squeeze a word out anyway. The phone rang twice only.

'Good evening. The Hadley residence.'

My heart plummeted to my heels, then bounced like a super ball inside me at the sound of Sarah Pike's voice. So she still worked for Jasmine, did she? I guess she was just niftier than I was at keeping her head down and keeping on Jasmine's good side. I'd made the mistake of thinking Jasmine and I were good friends. But one error, one slip-up—and I'd been out on my ear.

'Hello?' Sarah prompted.

I swallowed hard and forced myself to speak.

'Can I speak to Mrs Hadley please?'

'Can I say who's calling?' asked Sarah politely.

She obviously hadn't recognized my voice,

but then why should she?

'Er . . . it's . . . Meggie. Meggie McGregor,' I said softly.

I caught Sarah's gasp, even though she tried to disguise it immediately afterwards by launching straight into a monologue.

'Oh, Meggie. I . . . Hello . . . I'll just go and see if Mrs Hadley is available.' And she put the phone down with a clunk that made my ears ring.

Hello to you too, I thought sourly. No 'how are you?' for old times' sake. Sarah was obviously the same scared little mouse she'd always been. I could just imagine the conversation happening now between her and Jasmine. What was I thinking? This had been a bad idea. But at least I'd tried. Maybe I should just put down the phone now, rather than wait for Sarah to give me some feeble excuse and bounce me off.

'Hello, Meggie.' Jasmine's voice shocked me into silence. 'Meggie, are you there?'

'Hello, Mrs Hadley.'

'Please call me Jasmine. Is my daughter all right? Has something happened?'

'No, she's fine. It's nothing like that. Sephy and Callie are both fine. Everyone's fine,' I blathered.

'I don't understand then,' said Mrs Hadley. I couldn't think of her as anyone but Mrs Hadley.

'I'm worried about Sephy but it's not really something I can discuss over the phone.

231

Perhaps we can meet up?' I suggested.

'Is Persephone ill? What aren't you telling me?' Mrs Hadley said at once.

'I promise you Sephy isn't ill or anything like that.' I took a breath to steady myself before continuing. 'I'm . . . concerned about her behaviour and I'd like to discuss it with you face to face.'

'Shall I come to your home tomorrow?'

Surprise at her suggestion almost made me say yes on the spot. The Jasmine Hadley I knew wouldn't dream of setting foot in any area where the majority of the residents were noughts.

'Er . . . no. Maybe we could meet at a coffee shop?'

Pause. 'Would you like to come to my home? We could have coffee here. You'd be more than welcome.'

'No. I don't think so,' I shot back.

Too much time had passed and the water under the bridge was too deep to go back to her house. That place would stir up too many bad memories.

'Java Express then. The coffee shop on the high street, next to Markman's bookshop,' Mrs Hadley suggested.

'Ten o'clock?'

'Ten will be fine. I'll see you then. And Meggie?'

'Yes?'

'Thank you for phoning.'

Even as I put down the phone, I wondered

about the wisdom of what I was doing. Sephy was going to hate me for it.

But what else could I do?

I had to think of Callie Rose. Callie came first. No ifs, ands or buts. And she always would.

forty-one. Sephy

I walked up onto the stage to the sound of stony silence. Every eye was upon me. I walked over to the microphone with a sudden banging headache which I knew was purely down to nerves. An audience of Nought men and women stood before the stage and they gave out nothing. No expectation, no welcome, no anticipation—nothing. Jaxon walked over to me.

'We can do this,' he whispered into my ear away from the mic. 'Blow them away like you did in the Dew Drop Inn. We'll start with a ballad, *Spontaneous.*'

Jaxon walked back to his own mic. And it was just me and the crowd. No one standing in front of me, or around me to hide me. Jaxon was a metre to my left and Sonny was a metre to my right and Rhino was a metre behind us all. They might as well have been kilometres away. Looking out over the audience, I felt like a hunk of bloody meat in a den full of hungry lions, each waiting for the other to pounce first before they joined in.

Jaxon, Rhino and Sonny started playing *Spontaneous*. The tone from Sonny's keyboard was rich and mellow. Rhino's drumsticks whispered across the drum skin. Jaxon's chords on the guitar could break your heart. But my mind went blank. The music was approaching my cue and I couldn't remember a word of the song. Sweating like a saucepan lid, I opened my mouth hoping the words would fall out at the right moment—and nothing.

'Boo-ooo!'

The catcalls came immediately, led by Amy, who stood before the stage with a malicious smile all over her catlike face. The music trailed away. I stared out into the crowd, who were either whispering together or looking at me with derision.

And I was a girl again at the funeral of Callum's sister, Lynette, being told to leave.

I was a girl again in the school food hall being dragged away for sitting at Callum's table.

I was a girl again, being beaten up in the school toilets for not hiding the fact that Callum was my friend.

And the scary thing was, I hadn't changed. Inside, I was still that same bewildered little girl.

'What the hell are you doing?' Jaxon hissed at me. 'For God's sake sing, or we won't get out of here in one piece.'

After nodding at the others, the guys started

playing the introduction again. But I could hardly hear them as the boos got louder and the whistles got shriller and the jeers got sharper.

'Go back to where you came from . . .'

'Get out of here . . .'

'We don't want any daggers in here . . .'

'Dagger bitch. Get off the stage . . .'

And once again I missed my cue. Someone threw something small and hard which hit me on my forehead. A coin. I staggered backwards, my hand flying to my temple. It was bleeding. In the audience, some people started to laugh. I looked down at the blood on my fingers, red and vivid. The music trailed off again. Jaxon came over to me, pulling me back away from the mic.

'We'd better go,' he said, already taking off his guitar.

I didn't look at him. From the other side of the club, I could see Alice coming towards us, but even she was having trouble moving through the crowd.

'You see,' Amy shouted at me. 'You're not wanted. Go home, dagger bitch.'

Blood trickled down my cheek. I wiped it with my fingers then, after a moment's thought, slowly smeared it across my cheeks. And I had no idea why. But it seemed like the thing to do. I raised my hand to show the mob the blood on my fingers. The crowd were baying for my blood so I'd give it to them. The noise from the crowd before me died away to nothing as I watched them, catching and holding the eye of as many of them in turn as I could. I stepped up to the mic.

'OK, you win. I'll get off the stage,' I announced. 'But after this.' I turned to Jaxon and said, 'I want to do *Bad Attitude*!'

Jaxon came over to me, keeping a wary eye on our so-called audience.

'Are you mad? You can't sing that. This lot will think you're singing about them,' Jaxon whispered for my ears only.

'It got them going in the Dew Drop Inn, didn't it? And what's good enough for that place is good enough for this.'

'It doesn't work that way,' Jaxon protested.

'*Bad Attitude* or I walk,' I told him.

Jaxon gave me a long, hard look. 'I hope you know what you're doing.' He shook his head before going over to Rhino and Sonny to tell them what our first number was going to be.

Moments later, they started playing. I placed myself squarely in front of the mic and waited for my cue. I wasn't going to miss it again.

You've got logs on each shoulder,
And hatred up your sleeve.
They say you think you're owed it all
And that I can believe,
With your bad attitude.
You've got 'why me?' on your left hand
'Why not me?' on your right.
Why bother talking to me,
When you can stand and fight?

236

With your bad attitude.

You've got a back-stabbing
Money grabbing
Fast living
Never giving
Smooth talking
Night stalking
Bad attitude.

You tell me I'm not living,
That what you've got is life
And I'd be so much better off
If I took your advice,
And had a bad attitude.

But your heart is closed not open
And your soul is made of stone,
You'll always be a winner
But you'll always be alone
With your bad attitude.

You've got a back-stabbing
Money grabbing
Fast living
Never giving
Smooth talking
Night stalking
No sharing
Past caring
Never crying
Start dying
Bad attitude.

237

There's nowhere you can run to,
No direction you can turn.
There's nothing that can reach you,
I guess you'll never learn
With your bad attitude.

You've got a bad attitude
A sad attitude, you've got a bad attitude.

The boos started somewhere around the second verse so that by the time the song was finished, I could hardly hear the music above the whistles and catcalls. Well, I didn't write the ruddy song! I smiled inwardly but it was without real humour. I'd deliberately tried to provoke a reaction—and now I had exactly what I'd wanted. A room filled with hatred, sweeping up to me and over me. I glared out, returning it tenfold.

But then I thought of Rose. Her sleeping, smiling image came unbidden and unwelcome into my head. And everything else I was feeling began to recede. Something hard hit me on my shoulder. More missiles were being thrown. I was still standing—just. And the boos were getting louder. Amy was right. I wasn't wanted. But then, I never had been. Except by Rose. Only Rose. I wasn't fool enough to believe Meggie wanted me with her. Her only interest was her granddaughter. My daughter, Rose. That was the one thing, the only thing in the world at that precise moment that made any sense. The only thing that mattered. And in that second, I would've sold my soul to be back at Meggie's and in my bedroom, holding Rose tight to me. Rose was the present and the future. Her father was the past. Could I hold onto that? Or would Callum always come between me and my daughter. I had a choice. Bury myself in the past—with him. Or hold onto Rose and let go of everything else. But it was so hard. And I didn't know what to do. I was so confused and oh so tired.

'I've got one more song for you,' I said into the mic, but I doubt if anyone even heard me. 'This song is *Rainbow Child* for my daughter, Rose.'

And I didn't even wait for the others to start playing behind me. I just closed my eyes and started to sing. Somewhere in the middle of the song, Jaxon and the others started playing their instruments but I hardly heard them. I wasn't in Russell's any more. I was with my baby, holding on tight, spinning round and round. Or were we the ones standing still whilst the rest of the world whirled around us?

The song finished and I was still with her, holding her so tight that she could hardly breathe. Holding on so tight because I was terrified of what I'd be without her. I had no life without her. And all around me it was strangely quiet. Eerily so. But my heartbeat was steady and my headache had gone. Far away from me, someone booed. Maybe Amy.

Maybe not. It didn't last long. And then came the sound of clapping—again muffled and far away from me. Alice stood on stage clapping. Jaxon came over to me and was patting me on the back. He was talking to me but I couldn't hear what he was saying. His mouth was opening and closing, his lips were moving, but no sound was coming out. At least he looked happy.

And then I stopped trying to make out what he was trying to say.

Take a step back, Sephy.

I was outside and beyond myself and watching it all from a distance. As if it had nothing to do with me. All I wanted to do was go home. I so desperately needed to see and hold and smell and touch and kiss my daughter. I so desperately needed to lock her up in my arms and never let her go. I looked down at Amy, who was scowling at me. Most of the others in the crowd were clapping. Why were they still clapping? I turned to Jaxon— and my legs crumpled under me as all the lights went out.

forty-two. Meggie

The doorbell rang. I knew who it'd be but that didn't stop what felt like an eagle tearing at my insides. Holding a sleeping Callie in my arms, I went to open the front door.

'Hello, Mrs Hadley.'

'Hello, Meggie. Hello, Callie darling.' Mrs Hadley stroked Callie's cheek before kissing it.

And all the while, I never took my eyes off her. It'd been a long, long time. A voice on the phone couldn't compare to seeing Sephy's mum in the flesh. Mrs Hadley was immaculately dressed as always, but even her skilful make-up couldn't hide the fact that here was an unhappy woman. And a woman who'd been unhappy for quite some time. The lines around her eyes were longer. The grooves at the side of her mouth were deeper. Her hair was flawlessly braided as always but the silver streaks were only too prominent. She wore a burgundy-coloured trouser suit with matching court shoes and a gold scarf tied around her neck.

'May I come in?'

'Of course.' I stepped to one side so she could move past me. Mrs Hadley hesitated in the hall as I closed the door. The moment I turned round, there she was looking at me.

'It's really good to see you, Meggie. You have no idea how many times over the last few years I've wanted to come and see you.'

I wasn't sure what to say to that. Then, quite unexpectedly, Mrs Hadley hugged me. Stunned, both my arms stayed around Callie and Mrs Hadley soon let me go. Where had that come from? I looked away, embarrassed, waiting for my red cheeks to cool down.

'How's my daughter?' Mrs Hadley asked.

'She's fine. Sephy and I both think she fainted rather than having been knocked out or anything like that,' I said. 'Jaxon brought her straight home and she's been in bed ever since. That's why I phoned you to ask if we could meet here rather than at the coffee shop. I didn't like to leave her.'

'She's been doing too much,' Mrs Hadley sighed. 'She's only just had a baby, for goodness' sake.'

'I've tried telling her that but she won't listen,' I said. 'Sephy's not listening to much of anything at the moment.'

'Can I see her?'

'She's asleep upstairs. I thought maybe we could talk first,' I told her.

She nodded. 'So what's going on?'

'You'd better come through.' I ushered her into the living room, then followed her in. As she looked around, I lifted my chin and looked straight at her. The brown carpet was an obvious remnant and most of the furniture was second- or third-hand. But it was my home. Let her dare say anything about it. She sat down on the sofa and looked around again.

'This is a lovely room,' she smiled. 'Very cosy and inviting.'

I nodded, unsure of what to say. I decided to continue the pleasantries. 'Would you like a cup of tea or coffee, Mrs Hadley?'

'Won't you call me Jasmine?'

'It wouldn't be . . . appropriate,' I replied.

'Very well, Mrs McGregor. No first names

for either of us,' said Mrs Hadley.

I didn't like her calling me Mrs McGregor. No one called me that. Not even Renee in the post office and I only just knew her.

I smiled. 'Would you like a cup of tea or coffee, Jasmine?'

She smiled back. 'No thank you, Meggie, but I'd love to hold my granddaughter.'

I handed Callie over and watched as Mrs Hadley fussed over her. In my head she'd always be Mrs Hadley. She looked at me suddenly as if she knew I was thinking about her.

'Tell me what's been happening with Sephy,' she said.

So I told her. Everything. Including what it said in the letter Callum was supposed to have written. She didn't interrupt once.

'I see,' she said at last. I watched as she looked down at Callie, no trace of a smile anywhere on her face. 'Sephy feels things deeply. Too deeply sometimes, in spite of what she might say.'

I sensed more was coming so I didn't speak. After a long pause, Mrs Hadley looked directly at me. 'Persephone was pretty much left to bring herself up. That was my fault. I wrapped my life around my husband and then around a wine bottle. By the time I was ready to stand on my own two feet, I didn't know my children any more—especially Sephy. And she's more like me than she cares to think. She wrapped her whole life around Callum. He was the

243

reason for almost everything she did, so his letter . . .' Mrs Hadley shook her head. 'She probably doesn't know which way is up at the moment.'

'Callum didn't write that letter,' I interrupted.

'Are you sure about that?'

'It looked like his writing, but Callum wouldn't write that,' I argued. 'He cared too much about Sephy.'

'But whether he wrote it or not is hardly the point,' said Mrs Hadley. 'What matters is that Sephy thinks he did.'

'So what should we do?' I asked.

'The worst thing we could do is badger her,' said Mrs Hadley. 'Take it from me, it doesn't work. Sephy will dig her heels in and always do the exact opposite of what you tell her.'

'We have to do something. Callie deserves the best we can all give her—and that includes from Sephy,' I said.

'But you don't believe that's what she's getting?'

'Not at the moment, no,' I admitted.

Mrs Hadley shook her head. 'Sephy's just a child herself. And she's been through so much already. There's no way she can cope with raising a baby on her own.'

'I agree. And I'm worried about the way she's treating Callie,' I confessed.

'Why?' Mrs Hadley asked sharply. 'What's she doing?'

'Yes, what am I doing, Meggie?' Sephy's cold

voice rang out behind me.

Dismayed, I spun round in my chair. The look Sephy was giving both of us could've withered concrete.

'Sephy, I didn't mean—'

'How dare you both sit there and criticize and condemn me?' Sephy said with quiet fury. 'Neither of you has any idea what I've been through over this last year. Meggie, you keep going on and on about how that letter wasn't written by Callum. Well, I've got news for you. It *was*. I know his writing better than I know my own. And what's more, deep down I think you *know* he wrote it. You want to make me out to be a liar or deluded because I've accepted that the letter came from him, but you're the deluded one. And Mother, you're sitting there holding Rose and telling anyone who'll listen that you'll do anything and everything for her. Well, you blew it with me and Minerva, Mother. And Rose isn't your second chance.'

'Sephy, we weren't—'

'Sephy, you're not being fair—' Both Mrs Hadley and I tried to protest but Sephy wasn't having it. She was in full flood now.

'I wish you'd all just back off and leave me alone.' Sephy's voice was getting higher and louder. 'It's like no matter which way I turn I can't please anyone. So that's it. From now on, sod you all. I'm going to please myself. And both of you can go to hell!'

Sephy stormed out of the room, slamming

the door behind her with such force that it ricocheted against the frame and bounced open again. I turned to Mrs Hadley and we looked at one another, each, I suspect, mirroring the other's expression. Moments later the front door was opened, then slammed shut with enough force to make the glass in it rattle. And we were left with an atmosphere in the room like nothing I'd ever felt before. Cold, sad and threatening.

Like something around us had changed for the worse, and with a sense of foreboding I wondered if anything could change it back.

forty-three. Sephy

I've been singing with the Midges for over a month now. So far we've played exactly four gigs, which apparently is really good going. We've played two Cross clubs, one Nought club and a birthday party. And when we play at any club we never use the front entrance— Russell's was the exception not the rule in that at least. The clubs insist that all 'artistes' must use the back entrance—with no exceptions. I don't really care. I rehearse, do the gig, then wait for the next one. None of us talk about what happened at Russell's, which is fine with me. I'm trying my best to put that place out of my head—for ever. But I'm not very good at forgetting or letting things go. I wish I was. We played a Cross birthday party last week. A children's birthday party. What a nightmare!

I came so close to throttling some of the little brats, but I had to bite my tongue and smile when all I wanted to do was give some of the kids what Meggie used to call 'an attitude adjustment clap'! The birthday party was definitely the worst. It was a ten-year-old girl's party. I think her name was Romaine. But she was so vile I've tried to blot her from my memory. As it was a beautifully sunny day, Romaine's parents asked if we'd mind singing outside in their back garden. Well, their back garden was the size of a football pitch so there was no problem there. We had to be close to the house so we could plug in our equipment but it'd all been very efficiently set up beforehand. We even had a raised platform to stand and sing on. Everything would've been fine—if it hadn't been for Romaine herself. She stood in front of me the entire time I was singing, screaming her head off.

'I wanted Scarletter to sing at my party,' she shrieked, 'not them. No one's ever heard of the Midges. I wanted Scarletter. I WANTED SCARLETTER.'

Yeah, right! Like a chart-topping group like Scarletter would be caught dead at a kid's birthday party.

'Now, darling, Mummy and Daddy have explained that Scarletter weren't available,' her mum tried to explain. 'But the Midges are very good.'

'No, they're not. They *puke*!' Romaine insisted, scowling at me in particular. 'I wanted a boy band not a girl singer. She pukes.'

Just at that moment, I wished I did have a queasy stomach. And that Romaine was standing in just the right position before me. Then I'd show her the true meaning of the word 'puke'. Romaine's mother smiled apologetically but by then I was in no mood to smile back. So I kept singing and the guys kept playing even though none of the kids were taking any notice of us. They were running up and down the immaculately laid out lawn, into their own games and totally not into us. In between numbers I went over to Jaxon, annoyed.

'Was this your bright idea?' I asked. 'The kids are bored stupid with our music and I can't say I blame them.'

'I didn't choose the music, Romaine's mum did,' Jaxon replied.

'But the stuff we're singing is the kind of stuff my mum would like,' I pointed out.

'Take it up with Mrs Debela, not me,' said Jaxon. 'On second thoughts, don't. I'm trying to impress her husband.'

'Why?'

'He's a big-shot music producer,' Sonny informed me. 'Why d'you think Jaxon took this job? Normally he wouldn't be seen dead singing at something like this. It's beneath his dignity.'

After a swift look around, Jaxon's fingers

told Sonny where to go.

'If you're trying to impress someone, let's try one of Scarletter's songs. How about *Dear Diary*, the one that's in the charts now,' I suggested.

'That's not on Mrs Debela's list.'

'Stuff her ruddy list. I'm putting myself to sleep so God knows what I'm doing to the kids.'

'She's not going to like it,' Jaxon sighed.

But he knew me well enough to realize that not much shifted me once I'd made up my mind about something. The band started up and I went over to the mic. A decent song at last! I came in on my cue and Jaxon came over so that we could share the mic as the song was a two-hander. By the time we got to the chorus we actually had all the ankle-biters gathered around us and dancing. By the time we'd finished the song, Mrs Debela was up on stage with us, asking us very politely but firmly not to sing any more 'inappropriate' songs.

'How is it inappropriate, Mrs Debela?' I asked.

She came over to me and lowered her voice. 'I don't want my Romaine exposed to nought songs with slack lyrics.'

'Pardon?' I stared.

'All noughts ever seem to sing about is s-e-x, if you know what I mean,' she said for my ears only.

I didn't have a clue what she was talking about. *Dear Diary*, the Scarletter song, was
249

about love—not sex. And even if it was about sex, what was wrong with that?

'Romaine is far too young to be exposed to songs with those kinds of sentiments,' sniffed Mrs Debela. 'So if you could just stick to the playlist I gave you.'

Jaxon and I exchanged a look but we had no choice but to do as we were told—we wanted to get paid. Less than four bars into the next song, the kids had gone. By the time Jaxon announced that we'd be taking a short break but we would be back, no one was around to clap or cheer or boo or jeer. I went into the house to find a toilet. One of the kids was being sick in the downstairs cloakroom so I headed upstairs. The house had at least three or four bathrooms so I wasn't worried. In fact, the first door I opened on the landing just to the right of the stairs was a bathroom. It had black marble-effect tiles from floor to about waist height, finished off with gold, scrollwork edging and golden-yellow coloured walls above. There was a white Jacuzzi bath and a separate walk-in shower cubicle which was big enough for about four or five people to share. The bathroom suite was white with gold-coloured taps and the floor was black and gold. It was a bit too ostentatious for my taste but the Debelas were obviously rolling in money. To be honest, I'd never heard of Mr Debela, but then I was new to this business. I locked the door behind me and leaned against it. Peace at last. For two chocolate biscuits and a ginger beer I would've stayed in there for the rest of the day. But that wasn't going to happen. No need to hurry though.

Ten minutes later as I washed my hands, I wondered for the umpteenth time what I was doing. There had to be easier ways to make money. I left the bathroom only to bump into Mr Debela. Literally.

'Oh, I'm sorry,' I mumbled. 'I didn't realize there was a queue.'

'That's OK,' Mr Debela smiled.

I went to move past him but he side-stepped in front of me. 'There's no need to rush off,' he told me silkily.

Uh-oh . . . Warning bells began to ring-a-ding in my head.

'You've got a great voice. I've been watching you all afternoon,' he said, running his sweaty hand up my arm.

'Excuse me?' I shrugged away from him with a frown.

'I'm a producer at a recording company and I think we could work well together. I could do a lot for you, you know.'

'Thank you,' I said coldly. 'But you'll need to speak to Jaxon. He handles all of our business affairs.'

'The offer wasn't for the whole band. Musicians are ten a penny. But a singing voice like yours is a real find,' said Mr Debela.

When I didn't reply, Mr Debela said softly, 'I could make you a star.'

Yeah, but he'd obviously want to make

something else first.

'No, thank you,' I said, trying to move past him again.

'Don't dismiss my offer just yet. Take my card,' said Mr Debela, pushing his business card down into my trouser pocket—and taking his time whilst he did it. 'Think about it. Ask around. I'm well known in the industry.'

'For what?' I asked, but my sarcasm went totally over his head.

'I'm one of the best producers in the business. And a chance like this comes once in a lifetime, Persephone.'

'Who's Persephone? My name is Ridan,' I told him.

He laughed softly. 'Ridan! Was that your idea? Have the nought nit-wits in your band worked out that it's nadir backwards. Is that really how you think of yourself, Persephone? D'you feel you couldn't get any lower, singing with noughts? Because I can soon sort that out.'

'Ridan is just my name. It doesn't mean anything,' I tried to deny.

'Nadir isn't how I think of you,' Mr Debela said softly. 'You're very beautiful.'

And he bent his head to kiss me. I stepped back and slapped his face about a nanosecond afterwards. His whole demeanour changed.

'What's the matter? D'you only give it up for blankers then?' he asked coldly.

'You touch me again and you'll be singing soprano on one of your own CDs,' I fumed.

252

'Now move out of my way.'

He regarded me and I looked straight back to let him know I meant it.

'I guess you really are a blanker-lover then,' he shrugged. 'Everyone knows you're sleeping with your guitarist. I guess you're not too fussy. But I meant it about working with you. I really can make you a star, Persephone.'

'Excuse me please,' I ordered.

He stepped to one side. Seething, I was about a third of the way down before I realized Sonny was at the bottom of the stairs, in the hall. He'd obviously heard every word. I turned to look at Mr Debela, who was looking at Sonny as if he was daring him to say anything. When I reached him, Sonny turned without a word and escorted me back out into the garden.

'Did you come inside to find me then?' I asked.

'No, I went for a loo break, the same as you. I just happened to hear Mr Debela trying it on.'

'Ruddy creep!' I hissed.

'But he wasn't flannelling you,' said Sonny with a stillness I'd come to associate with him. 'He's very well known in the music industry and if he says he can make you a star then he probably can. He's in a position to make it all happen for you.'

'Not interested,' I dismissed. 'And even if I was, I wouldn't be too attracted to the idea of getting there on my back—which is the only

253

position that toad was interested in seeing me in.'

'Some people would say it was worth it. Whatever it takes and all that,' said Sonny.

'Yes, but I'm not some people.'

'So you don't hanker to be rich and famous?'

'My mother was one and my dad was the other,' I said. 'It didn't make either of them terribly happy.'

'So what d'you want, Sephy?' asked Sonny. 'We've been singing together for a while now and I still haven't figured that out.'

'That's a shame.' I smiled without humour. 'I was hoping you'd be able to tell me.'

'I'm serious,' said Sonny.

He didn't realize that so was I.

'What do I want?' I mused. I had to think about it. Hard. 'I think what I'd like more than anything else is peace of mind. Nothing more, nothing less.'

'And what're you going to do to get it?'

'When I've worked that out,' I replied, 'I'll let you know.'

As we walked back to the others, Sonny asked unexpectedly, 'How's your daughter? Rose, isn't it?'

My face began to get hot.

'She's fine.'

'You don't talk about her very much,' said Sonny.

I regarded him. 'Would you like me to inform you every time I change her nappy?'

'No, thank you,' Sonny replied instantly. 'But

you're not exactly one of those dull, doting parents who breaks out the photo album as soon as their child's name is mentioned, are you?'

'I can bring in some photos if you're feeling deprived.' I brushed off his comment.

'Don't put yourself out,' said Sonny.

'All right then, I won't,' I told him.

'Everything all right at home?'

'Why d'you ask?'

'You don't talk about it much.'

'I don't want to bore you,' I said. 'What's all this about? Why the sudden interest in my family life?'

'Just being nosy,' said Sonny. 'Have you got a boyfriend yet?'

'Are you kidding?' I scoffed. 'I've only just had a baby, for heaven's sake.'

'Well, someone always tries to chat you up every time we do a gig,' said Sonny.

'I'm not the slightest bit interested in dating.'

'Life goes on, Sephy,' said Sonny. 'If you let it. You have to let go of the past and move on.'

'You think I don't?'

'I think you won't.'

'What does that mean?' I frowned.

'It means—' Sonny's mouth snapped shut. 'It means it's time to mind my own business.'

'Sonny, I am trying to get on with my life, I promise. But it's far too early for me to even think about getting involved with anyone. And besides, I'm a package deal—remember? Not too many men are interested in that.'

'I know someone who'd be interested,' said Sonny.

'Oh yeah?' I scoffed. 'Who?'

Sonny looked at me pointedly, smiling at my stunned expression as I finally caught on to what he was trying to say.

'Are you serious?' I still couldn't believe it.

Sonny looked straight at me, his expression now earnestly serious but his eyes full of something I hadn't seen in a long time. He said softly, 'You could do worse.'

'And you could do better,' I told him straight out. 'Sonny, I—'

'It's OK. You don't need to say it. If you're not interested . . .'

'It's not that,' I said unhappily. 'It's just that I'm not ready for any kind of relationship at the moment.'

'Why not?'

How should I answer that? Because I can't trust my own judgement. Because the whole thing brings too much pain. Because I've just had the child of someone who hated me. Because something in me has switched off and I can't find a way to switch it back on. Because what I feel inside is so deeply buried that it can't break out of me. Because I haven't cried since Callum's letter. Because nothing reaches me any more—not even my own daughter. Which answer would he like?

'Because I'm just not ready,' I repeated, eventually.

'Well, just remember, I'll be here when you

are,' Sonny told me.

We regarded each other for a few silent moments.

'Come on, you two,' Jaxon called out.

'So how's your songwriting coming on?' asked Sonny as we carried on walking up to the others.

Puzzled, I looked at him. The abrupt change of subject had thrown me, but I realized that Sonny wanted to keep what we'd just said private. Just something for the two of us. As we joined the others, my teeth worried at my bottom lip. I liked Sonny, but I certainly didn't want to go out with him. And if what I'd read in his eyes was correct, he cared about me a great deal. Love rearing its ugly head again. All I could do was hope that if I didn't encourage Sonny then he'd lose interest and look elsewhere. A relationship with anyone— Nought or Cross—wasn't a road I was in a hurry to travel along again.

forty-four. Meggie

'OK, Meggie. What d'you think of this?' Sephy asked.

I suppressed a smile as she cleared her throat. A fragile peace had broken out between us at last and I didn't want to do anything to jeopardize that. Sephy was talking to me again. We were talking to each other. It wasn't much, but we had to start somewhere.

She began to read:

'Above the wide blue nowhere
I dance upon clouds of dreams
And when the music fades away
My world is only beams
Of light.
The endless night
Stretches on
Lost in a heart
Of words . . .'

'Er . . . what does it mean?' I interrupted, unable to take any more drivel in my ear holes.

Sephy was obviously startled by my question. I saw her frown down at the piece of paper in her hand. Silence. This time I had to bite my lip to stop myself from laughing out loud. How should I say it? What was the kindest way to put it? Sephy's first attempt at songwriting needed a lot of work.

'It's about . . . it's about dreams.'

'Is it?' I asked. 'I'm afraid I wouldn't've guessed that if you hadn't told me.'

'Well, what did you think it was about then?' Sephy asked.

'I wasn't sure. But surely the point of a piece of music or a song is to communicate a thought or a feeling or an emotion to the person listening?'

'Yeah? So?'

'What d'you think your poem, song, whatever

258

is saying to me?' I asked.

Sephy looked down at it again. 'It's saying I'm a pretentious twat,' she sighed before scrunching it up in her hands.

'It's not that bad, Sephy,' I tried.

'Yes, it is. In fact it's worse. I'll try again.'

Sephy picked up her pen from the floor and her notepad from her lap and started writing. I watched her with a smile. There it was again. That will not to give up. My smile faded. Sephy hadn't given up on anything in her life—except my son, Callum. Not a day passed when I didn't think about that hateful letter he was supposed to have written. But I would go to my grave, knowing without a shadow of a doubt that Callum loved Sephy more than logic, reason or life itself. If only I could convince her of that.

She looked up and caught me smiling at her. She tentatively smiled back, looking suddenly shy.

'What's the matter?'

'I . . . I have written some other poems,' Sephy began, almost reluctantly. 'Private poems. About me and . . . Callum.'

I felt like someone trying to feed a timid bird or a doe. One wrong word on my part and she'd skitter away and close up like a telescopic umbrella. I kept my mouth shut.

'I haven't shown them to anyone. Not even Jaxon,' said Sephy.

'D'you want to show them?'

'Yes and no. I want to but I'm a bit . . .

anxious about doing it.'

'Well, Sephy, you have to make a decision. Show them and the rest of the world be damned. Or keep them to yourself but then never get any feedback and never share them.'

'It's not that simple,' Sephy sighed.

'Yes it is. It's entirely that simple. Sephy, you have to make up your mind which one you want to do—and then do it. Either poo or get off the pot!'

Sephy started laughing. After a moment, I joined her.

'The things you come out with, Meggie,' said Sephy. 'You always could make me laugh.'

'How d'you confuse a nought? Lean three shovels against the wall and tell him to take his pick.'

The studio audience cracked up at that one. I turned to look at the TV. So did Sephy. The so-called comedian Willy Wonty (what a ridiculous name! Whose idea was that?) stood like a damn fool basking in the audience's laughter. The nought arse was too stupid to realize that the studio audience were laughing *at* him, not *with* him. I shook my head as he grinned into the camera like a complete imbecile.

'D'you know, a good friend of mine came up to me yesterday, really sad and down in the dumps. "What's wrong with you?" I asked. "My family is a mess," he told me. "My wife has left me for another woman, my dad has gone senile, my youngest son is in prison, my daughter has just

260

had a mixed-race child and my eldest son has just become a Member of Parliament. How will I live with the shame?" So I told him, "Tell everyone your eldest son is a bank robber instead."'

'Why are you watching this crap?' Sephy said, glaring at me, then at the TV. 'And I don't appreciate having my daughter equated to being in prison or someone going senile. And I certainly don't appreciate having her likened to being an MP. Was that joke meant to be funny then?'

'I didn't write the joke, Sephy,' I told her. 'I think the man is just as big an arse as you do.'

'I doubt it,' Sephy sniffed.

'I can guarantee it,' I told her firmly. 'Hearing jokes like that from a Cross is one thing. Having a nought tell jokes like that is something else again. He makes it seem like it's OK to poke fun at us and it's not.'

'Can we turn it over then?' Sephy asked. 'That moron is turning my stomach.'

I pressed the button on the remote to change the channel. The news was on. And then I got the shock of my life.

'Earlier today, the police announced a significant breakthrough in their hunt for the murderer of hairdressing salon owner, Cara Imega. They are now looking for this man, Jude McGregor, to help with their inquiries. The public are asked to keep their eyes open for this man. If he is seen, please contact the police immediately. The police warn that he should not

be approached under any circumstances as he is known to be dangerous and possibly armed.'

The photo of Jude when he was eighteen seemed to burn its way through the TV screen and head straight for me.

'Oh my God . . .' Sephy breathed.

I couldn't say a word. Jude. My son. Wanted for murder. It couldn't be true. Jude was a freedom fighter, not a stone-cold killer. He wouldn't do something like that. Beat a poor girl to death. No one in their right mind would do a thing like that. Jude didn't do it. Did he . . . *Did he?*

Sephy's looking at me. Well, let her look. My boy may have done lots of things I'm not proud of. I know he's not a saint. He's in the Liberation Militia and calls himself a freedom fighter. Freedom first—that's their motto. And as a member of the L.M. he must've done some things, terrible things. But that was and is for a cause. And I know that doesn't excuse it and I know that doesn't make it right, but he is fighting for something he believes in. To kill that girl, though, in cold blood . . . A hairdresser, for heaven's sake. And someone who employed noughts and Crosses on an equal basis. He wouldn't do that. But they think he did. And now they won't stop until they catch him and have him and, oh God, hang him.

I can't lose my last child.

Please don't let me lose my last child.

OH GOD, PLEASE, PLEASE, DON'T LET

ME LOSE MY LAST CHILD.

'Please, God. Please don't let me lose my last child . . .'

'Please God, please . . .'

GREEN

New for Old

Old for New

Changing, Rearranging

Absence of Passion

Human Nature

Mother Nature

Sticks and Branches

Sharp

New Shoots

Creativity

Revelations

The Beginning of the End

The End of the Beginning

Flexing

Olive Khaki Lime Sage Leaf Grass

Noughts to join *Pottersville*

Pottersville, the nation's favourite soap, is to get its first nought family. Catherine Burdon, the show's executive producer, told the *Daily Shouter*, 'We're really excited about the prospect of a nought family joining our cast of regulars. Having a nought family in residence will bring a whole new dynamic to our show. *Pottersville* is number one and our new family will bring us an even wider audience.'

Details of the new family are still being kept under wraps but we can reveal that the family wil be called the Slotters and will consist of a grandparent, father and mother and four children.

forty-five. Jude

The night air had a surprising bite to it. So much for summer. It seemed to be passing me by. I zipped up my jacket and thrust my free hand further into my pocket.

'Hang on a minute, Morgan,' I said into my mobile phone.

I looked around, nervous as a rabbit in a fox's den, but I was in no danger here. The city centre was practically deserted and the few people who were milling around didn't want to linger too long because of the chill in the air.

'So did you do it?' Morgan asked again. 'Did you kill that girl like they're saying on the news?'

'How many times do I have to say no before you believe me?' I snapped.

'I wouldn't put it past you, Jude,' said Morgan.

'Thanks.'

'I mean it. You scare me sometimes and I know you. It wouldn't surprise me if the woman looked at you sideways twice and that's why you did her.'

I stopped walking and took the phone away from my ear at that. At that moment, if Morgan had been standing in front of me, I'd've decked him.

'It's nice to know who my friends are,' I told him pointedly. I still hadn't forgotten how

Morgan had shacked up with my girlfriend, Gina. I didn't care about her so much, but I did care that he'd done that to me. Friends don't do that to other friends. Which just went to prove Jude's law number eight: *There are no such things as friends. Just acquaintances who haven't let you down yet.* With maybe a little of rule number three chucked in for good measure—*Watch your back.*

'I am your friend, Jude. You might not believe that, but it's true.'

'Is that right? So how's Gina?'

Morgan sighed. 'If it really bothers you that I'm with her, then I'll move on. Just say the word.'

He sounded like he meant it.

'You have to make up your own mind about what you want to do,' I told him. I certainly wasn't going to salve his guilty conscience for him. I didn't have enough salve to go around.

'I'll do that,' said Morgan. 'Look, did you know Cara Imega?'

'I might've done,' I replied.

'D'you know who killed her?'

I didn't answer.

'Well, whether or not you did it, you'd better keep your head lower than your heels for the next few months,' said Morgan.

'Now tell me something I don't know,' I said, irritated. 'And Morgan, just for the record—I didn't do it.'

And with that I ended the call. I kept telling myself that I'd done nothing wrong. I'm a

269

freedom fighter. Sometimes we have to do whatever is required by any means necessary. But each time I tried to convince myself of that, the words rang out loud and hollow, clanging like a relentless bell. I looked around again. Ever since the police had issued a Photofit of me and announced my real name to the world, I'd been like a cat dancing on hot coals. I knew it was only a matter of time before they matched up the fingerprints found in Cara's house to the fingerprints they had of me on file. But the delay in announcing my involvement with Cara had foolishly raised my hopes. I'd begun to think that I might just get away with it. I should've known better. So now I'm having to keep my head not just down but out. Out of the spotlight. Out of everyone's gaze. I was holed up in a cheap hotel and I lived like some kind of bat, only coming out at night to lurk in doorways and shadows where my face couldn't be seen.

Which suited me just fine.

Cara was yesterday. I still had today and tomorrow to sort out. For all my plotting and planning and scheming, I was still no closer to exposing Andrew Dorn for the blanker traitor he was. I hadn't even worked out how to do it. I couldn't let them catch me now. I still had so much to do. After pushing my mobile phone deep into my jacket pocket, I rubbed my hands together. Strange, but no matter what I did these days, I was always chilly. Even though it was late summer and supposed to be quite warm, my hands and feet were frequently unpleasantly cold.

'Hello, Jude . . .'

At the sound of my name, I swung round, groaning inwardly a split second later when I realized I'd fallen for the oldest trick in the book. My hand flew towards my jacket pocket—but I was too late. At least eight armed dagger cops sprang out of the doorways and from behind cars and I was surrounded.

'HANDS IN THE AIR. DO IT!'

I stood still, wondering how many of them I could take out before they blew my head off. There was a gun in my jacket pocket; it was on the inside and my hands were on the outside. Could I do it? Should I go for it?

'LIE DOWN ON THE GROUND. NOW!'

Maybe I could get the three directly in front of me, and with luck the one to my left. With an inner sigh, I decided that it was unlikely I'd even get my gun out. I reluctantly knelt down on the ground.

'HANDS IN THE AIR. LIE DOWN. WE WON'T TELL YOU AGAIN.'

Slowly, I raised my arms to about shoulder height. I lay down by falling forward, but making sure my hands hit the ground first. Immediately about four of the daggers jumped on me, wrenching my arms behind my back and handcuffing me. Someone kicked me in the side for good measure. Hands were all over me, searching my pockets, moving up and down my legs and taking both the gun and the knife I kept in its sheath in my left sock. The handcuffs were tight. My arms were being pulled back so hard I thought both my shoulders were going to dislocate. I was yanked to my feet and bundled into the back of a police car with a dagger cop on either side of me.

'You're going to swing for this, McGregor,' said the cop to my left. 'Just like your raping, murdering brother. Must be something bad in your blood.'

'Sod you,' I hissed at him.

He punched me in the mouth, wincing almost as much as I did. I could taste blood in my mouth where he'd split my lip. I watched with appreciation as he had to rub his hand afterwards. The pain in my lip was almost worth it.

'This one will definitely hurt you more than it hurts me,' he said. And he pushed my head forward before punching me in my side—the same side that one of them had kicked just moments earlier. I groaned, much to his satisfaction.

'That's enough, Powell,' said the dagger on the other side of me.

'He deserves it.'

'That's for a court to decide, not you,' the other dagger said.

'You're such a bleeding heart,' Powell said with disgust.

The other dagger turned to look out of the window. I leaned back, knowing that this was it. They'd caught me—and I was as good as dead already.

forty-six. Sephy

Rose was asleep in her carry-cot at my feet whilst I sat in the armchair I'd come to regard as my own, sewing a button back on my favourite shirt. Meggie was in the hall, having got up to answer the phone less than five minutes earlier. She came back into the room and sat on the sofa. Picking up the remote she pressed a button and the TV screen flickered and crackled briefly before showing some programme about the life cycle of a fruit bat. I carried on with my bad sewing, waiting for Meggie to turn it over, but it didn't happen. I glanced at her. She wasn't even watching it; she was staring off into the middle distance somewhere. I frowned at the screen. There had to be something better on, but it wasn't my telly. Once I was out from under and had paid off all my bills and debts, the first thing I was going to treat myself to was a portable TV. Then I could stay in my room and watch what I liked. But one thing was for sure. Fruit bats wouldn't get a look in. Even the programme commentator sounded bored. His voice was a soporific monotone. Finally I could stand it no longer.

'Meggie . . .'

'Sephy, will you come with me to see Jude?'

'Ow!' I popped my finger in my mouth where I'd just stuck it with the needle. I frowned at Meggie, sure my ears needed syringing. 'Pardon?'

'Jude just phoned from Baylinn Police Station. He's been arrested for the murder of that girl, Cara Imega. They're moving him to Bellview Prison the day after tomorrow. Will you come and see him with me?'

I folded up my shirt carefully as I tried to marshal my thoughts.

'I'm sure I'm the very last person Jude wants to see,' I told Meggie.

'You don't have to talk to him. You can wait for me outside or something. But I don't want to go into a police station alone.'

'Your sister—'

'Wants nothing to do with this,' Meggie told me harshly. 'Look, forget it. I shouldn't've asked you . . .'

'Of course I'll come with you.' I tried to smile but my lips felt like they were being pulled down by the weight of my heart sinking. I didn't want to go. I didn't want to be anywhere near Jude. Suppose he'd done it? Suppose he hadn't? This whole situation was something to run away from, not towards. I couldn't blame Meggie's sister. I didn't want anything to do with Jude either.

But Meggie needed me.

'Sephy, I wouldn't ask but—' She didn't finish the sentence; she didn't need to.

'Of course I'll come with you,' I said. 'But what about Rose? I don't want to take her all the way to Baylinn.'

'I'm sure Mrs Straczynski next door won't mind looking after Rose for an hour or two,' said Meggie.

The thought of leaving Rose with someone she didn't know very well didn't appeal—even if Mrs Straczynski was one of the few around here who smiled at me and said hello whenever she saw us.

'Well, if you go and ask her, I'll get Rose's things together,' I sighed.

'Oh thank you, Sephy.' Meggie smiled gratefully. 'I really appreciate it.'

She was already heading out the door to go and talk to our neighbour, so she didn't see that I couldn't smile back.

forty-seven. Jude

'Do you understand your rights as they have been explained to you?' asked Detective Georgiou.

Three. Four. One.

'Yes,' I replied.

I was in a police interview room, with two dagger detectives sitting across the table from me. Detective Georgiou, the woman, was doing all of the talking. The other cop, Detective Zork, hadn't said a word so far. The interview room was bigger than my cell, but not by much. There was a rectangular table with two chairs on either side of it. One of the shorter sides of the table was fixed to the wall—impossible to overturn, I guess. Set into the wall were a series of buttons for recording interviews. And there was a CCTV camera self-consciously adorning one corner of the room just above the door. The walls were painted an over-cooked porridge colour. There were no posters, no pictures, no photos, no prints. Nothing to divert the attention. The floor was lined with a thin, ultra-hardwearing carpet which would probably last longer than the building. I looked straight up at the CCTV camera, which was trained on my position. Did that mean I was safe from having a confession beaten out of me? Somehow, I doubted it. Where there's a will, there's a way. I dragged my right foot slowly back and forth across the carpet beneath the table. Forward for four counts, back for four counts. It was something we'd been taught in the Liberation Militia. A way of focusing the mind and concentrating on answering only the questions you wanted to answer.

Forward for four counts.

Back for four counts.

Nice and simple. Focus on counting. Answer each question on the one count only to give yourself a chance to think. Keep it simple. Short and sweet answers. I can't say the training was all coming back to me, because it'd never left.

Forward for four counts.

Back for four counts.

'Is your name Jude Alexander McGregor?'

Two. Three. Four. One.

'Yes.'

'Do you wish to have a solicitor present?'

One.

'No.'

'The suspect was offered a solicitor and declined,' Detective Georgiou said into the interview microphone.

The interview was being separately videotaped *and* recorded. That must've been quite a new thing. But I guess too many convictions had been overturned recently due to proven false confessions and substantiated evidence of police brutality.

'When did you first meet Cara Imega?' asked Detective Georgiou.

I didn't answer.

'How long have you known her?' The detective rephrased the question like I didn't understand her the first time.

I didn't answer.

The questions came flying at me, faster and faster.

'We found your fingerprints in Cara Imega's house. Why don't you do yourself a favour and confess?'

Likely!

'Where did you meet her?'

'We know you killed her. Just tell us why.'

'Were you burgling her house and she disturbed you? Is that what happened?'

We were at it for over an hour—and after confirming my name and turning down the offer of a solicitor, I hadn't said a word.

Something else my L.M. training had taught me.

'We know it was you,' Detective Zork piped up at last. 'And your impersonation of a clam isn't going to stop us from getting you convicted of Cara Imega's murder and hanged.'

I sat back in my chair. It was entertaining watching the two dagger officers get more and more exasperated. Not very professional of them, but amusing nonetheless. Whilst they asked me more questions, I thought of my mum. I'd reluctantly phoned her but now I was beginning to wish that I hadn't. It wasn't fair to her or to me to expect her to drag herself all the way over here.

'Interview terminated at—' Detective Georgiou glanced down at her watch and gave the time.

Detective Zork pressed a series of buttons. The tiny red LED at the top of the CCTV went off. A faint click came from the wall and the tape was no longer recording. The detectives stood up. So did I.

'Back to your cell, McGregor,' said Detective Zork.

I smiled triumphantly at him. 'Is your name really Zork? That's rather unfortunate, isn't it?'

I got a punch in my stomach which had me doubled over and coughing.

'Still think my name is funny?' asked the dagger, his fists still clenched.

I straightened up slowly.

One. Two. Three. Four. Served me right for saying more than I should've. But I'd got smug at their obvious frustration. It wouldn't happen again.

'Are you going to stand there and let him beat me up?' I asked Georgiou.

'I don't know what you're talking about,' she replied coldly. 'You tripped over and landed on the back of chair.'

'And if he chucked me out of window?' I asked with sarcasm.

'You tripped or tried to get away in a suicide attempt,' Detective Georgiou told me. 'Who knows what goes on in the mind of an ice-cold murderer?'

'I'd love you to make a break for it right now,' said Zork. 'Go on. Make my day.'

We all stood in silence, the two of them daring me to so much as twitch. But Mrs McGregor didn't raise any stupid children.

'Back to your cell, McGregor,' Zork said at last.

And I replied, 'Yes, sir.'

forty-eight. Sephy

'Can I help you?' The police officer behind the desk gave me a friendly smile.

'Yes, er, we're here to see Jude McGregor. Please.'

His smile fizzled out like a candle doused in water. 'And you are?'

I didn't want to give my name. What the hell was I doing here anyway? 'I'm Sephy. And this is Jude's mother, Meggie McGregor.'

'I see. Sephy who?' The officer was trying to pin me to the far wall with the expression on his face. 'I need your full name for our visitors record.'

'Persephone Mira Hadley,' I replied, raising my chin.

Meggie moved to stand before me. 'Can we see my son, please?'

'Take a seat and I'll see what I can do,' said the officer.

The officer made a great show of writing our names down as we sat down on one of the two hard benches in the reception area and waited. After writing, the police officer behind the reception desk didn't move for a good thirty minutes. Then he disappeared for less than two minutes before coming back to the desk. Meggie and I watched as he dealt with other people's problems and complaints and queries. And we waited. And we waited. After two hours of waiting, I was ready to tear someone's head off. I'd had to go through the same crap when Callum was in prison. They'd tell me to cool my heels for hours at a time on the off-chance that I might get to see him, before sending me home after a fruitless day's waiting at the gate. I marched up to the reception desk.

'Are you going to let us see Jude McGregor or not?' I asked.

'We have procedures to follow,' the officer told me.

Meggie came up behind me and put a warning hand on my arm.

'It's OK, Meggie. You have a sit down. I just want to ask a couple of questions.' I smiled at Meggie.

She went to sit back down on the hard-as-nails bench.

'We'd like to see Jude McGregor and we'd like to see him now. I think you've kept us waiting long enough,' I said quietly.

'Jude McGregor is pond slime,' the officer told me, adding *sotto voce*, 'but any Cross paying him a social visit is worse.'

'Now you listen here, Sergeant . . .' I scrutinized the numbers on his shoulder epaulettes and made sure he knew I was doing so. 'Sergeant 2985 . . .'

'Sergeant Duvon, ma'am. D-U-V-O-N,' he supplied.

'If you don't let us see Jude McGregor right now, I promise I'll have your job—and I've got the family connections to do it. So stop pissing us about and let us in.'

Sergeant Duvon drew himself up, straightening his shoulders and lifting his chin as he studied me. But I didn't flinch. If he thought I was bluffing he was in for a shock.

'Follow me, please,' he said, his voice hard and cracked like falling icicles.

'Meggie, we can see Jude now.' I forced a smile onto my face before turning round to her.

Meggie came over to me and briefly placed a hand on my shoulder. Sergeant Duvon opened the security door to let us in before leading us down the corridor.

'Wait in there, please,' he told us, indicating an interview room.

My eyes narrowed.

'Jude McGregor is in a cell,' said Duvon. 'He'll have to be escorted up here and an officer will have to stay in this room at all times.'

'That's fine,' Meggie said sombrely before I could argue.

When Sergeant Duvon left, I said, 'Meggie, I'll wait for you out in the reception area— OK?'

Meggie nodded. I walked out of the room and headed back the way we'd come. Outside I was walking. Inside I was running. My hands were actually shaking. It surprised me how afraid I was of seeing Jude again.

Surprised and, worse still, frightened.

forty-nine. Jude

'Hello, Jude.'

When they told me I had a visitor, I half hoped it'd be Mum. But whilst part of me was glad to see her, another stronger part of me really wished she hadn't come. By visiting me, her card would be marked. From now on, if anything happened within a two-hundred-kilometre-odd radius which had even the slightest sniff of the L.M., the cops would go knocking on Mum's door. I'd warned her of that when I phoned her but she said it didn't matter.

Maybe she didn't understand? Or maybe she just didn't care? I looked around the interview room, more to delay the moment of looking directly at my mum than for any other reason. This was my second interview room today. I studied all four corners of the room until there was nothing left to study. Until I had no choice but to turn and face my mum. I could handle most things, but not the pain in Mum's eyes as she looked at me. Pain and that look of *déjà vu*. How many times had she been in this position before?

'How are you? They treating you OK?'

'Fine, Mum. I'm fine.'

I glanced round. Detective Zork stood by the door, ear-wigging every word. Nosy git!

'Can I bring you anything?'

'No, Mum.'

'Can I do anything for you?'

'No, Mum.'

'What about a lawyer? Have you got one yet?'

'I'm going to get one,' I told her with a forced smile.

Mum glanced down at the table between us. When she looked up again, there was a sheen to her eyes. I looked away from her tears. They couldn't save me now.

'That girl . . . Cara Imega . . . did you know her?'

I shrugged before lowering my voice. 'Yes, Mum. I knew her.'

'Did you do the things they're saying you did?'

How to answer that?

What things are they saying I did?

Why 'things'—plural?

What are they saying?

Who are 'they'?

'Mum, I didn't kill anyone.' I looked Mum straight in the eyes as I said that. Here was the one and only person in the world who kept a corner of her mind open to the fact that I might actually be innocent. At least she'd asked me. No one else had done that. So how could I snuff out the last bit of hope she had? 'I didn't do it, Mum.'

I turned to look at the copper by the door. He regarded me with a mocking half-smile.

284

The look on his face said he'd heard it all before. If there'd been just the two of us in the room, I wouldn't've looked away first. But I had more important things on my mind. Mum sighed wearily as I turned back to her. She tried to smile at me but all it did was twist her mouth as she tried not to cry.

'It's OK, Mum.'

'I don't know what to do.' Mum's voice wavered as she spoke. 'I have to get you out of here.'

'Mum, you don't have to worry. I've got it covered,' I lied. 'A friend of mine is going to get me a lawyer. They'll never be able to convict me 'cause I didn't do it.'

'Well, why do they think you did?'

'I don't know.' I shook my head. 'They won't tell me anything, Mum. They keep saying they've got a mountain of evidence against me but they won't say what it is.'

Mum leaned forward to take both of my hands in hers. Her palms were cool and dry and rough all at the same time. I closed my hands around hers.

'No touching,' said Zork immediately. He moved forward to examine both of our hands, to make sure Mum hadn't slipped something to me or vice versa. I glared at him as he backed off to lean against the wall by the door.

'I'll find out exactly what they think they have against you,' said Mum.

'How?'

'Never you mind. I'll do it though. D'you

trust me?'

'Yes, I do.' I smiled.

'Time's up,' Zork piped up. 'Back to your cell now, McGregor.'

Wasn't he fed up with saying that?

I stood up. 'Don't worry, Mum. I won't go down for this. I didn't do it.'

Mum burst into tears. She quickly wiped her eyes and tried to stop herself from sobbing but it did no good. I tried to get back to her, to comfort her in some way but Zork took my arm and dragged at me, trying to dislocate my shoulder by the feel of it. I tried for one last smile at Mum before I turned and allowed myself to be pulled out of the room. Only then did my smile disappear as if it'd never been.

Sorry, Mum.

But what else could I say? What else could I do? I need you and your belief in the good in me. Sometimes, I dream of that night and it's almost like I'm watching another person in that room with Cara. Like I'm standing back, frozen silent, frozen still, and all I can do is stare. At first I watch Cara, cowering. Afraid. And I tell myself not to look at her. It takes every gram of strength I have to look away. But my gaze always moves to the person hitting her. That person is always me. And then it's like I'm not watching any more, but I've snapped back into my own body. And I'm no longer an observer, I'm the perpetrator. Try as I might, I can't stop hitting out. Lashing out. Smashing out. But the person I'm hammering is no longer Cara. It's me.

Mum, it's funny, but I can't stop thinking of one of the stories you told me and Lynette and Callum many lifetimes ago. A story about a man who goes to hell and who's told by the Devil that there's only one way out. One chance. Just one. Well, Mum, you're my one and only chance. You see, I'll never get out of hell if there's not even you left to pray for me.

fifty. Sephy

I sat down on the hard bench in the reception area of the police station, ignoring the contemptuous looks being thrown in my direction by the desk sergeant. Asking to see Jude was enough to condemn me in his eyes. Guilt by association. I looked down at the carpet, I studied the posters on the wall, I watched a spider scurry across the ceiling until it reached its web in one corner of the room. My gaze went everywhere—except towards the desk sergeant. I watched the people coming in and out of the station. A woman came in crying, holding her young son's hand as she wiped the tears away before approaching the sergeant. A man came in holding a bloody hankie to a gash on his forehead. An elderly Nought woman strode in and went straight up to the sergeant, banging her hand down before she'd even said a word to make sure she had the sergeant's full attention. And all the time I sat and watched but my thoughts were elsewhere. What was Jude saying to Meggie in there? Was he confessing all? Chance would be a fine thing. I had no doubt that Jude would say anything, do anything, be anything in his efforts to satisfy his insatiable hunger for revenge against all Crosses. Could he have killed Cara Imega? I didn't doubt that he was capable of it for a second. He'd shot my sister and he was more than happy to try and kill me.

And maybe if I'd let Minerva tell the police who'd really shot her, Cara Imega would be alive today. Maybe. I didn't like the direction my thoughts were taking me, so I forced myself to let them go and think of something else. I so wanted to get home and hold my daughter.

At last Meggie came out. I stood up with a smile, which faded at the expression on Meggie's face.

'Sephy, I need your help,' she began with obvious trepidation.

'Why? What's the matter?'

'I need to find out what evidence they think they have against Jude.'

I began to shake my head. 'The police are hardly likely to tell me . . .'

'But you know people. Couldn't you find out? I'm sorry to do this but I don't know who else to ask,' said Meggie.

'But why? Does Jude reckon he's being framed?'

Meggie shook her head. 'It's not so much

that. Jude says he didn't do it.'

'And you believe him?' I asked.

'I believe in him,' said Meggie.

Which didn't answer my question. We left the police station and headed along the road to the bus stop in silence. Jude was vicious and vindictive, but Meggie couldn't or wouldn't see that.

'D'you think Jude killed Cara Imega?' I tried again.

'He swears he didn't do it . . .'

'And you believe him?' I couldn't help asking.

Meggie shook her head, looking me straight in the eye. 'He wouldn't lie to me.'

I said nothing.

'Will you help me? Please,' Meggie asked.

I sighed. 'I'll see what I can do, but I can't promise anything.'

'You'll find out the truth,' Meggie said, every word dripping with hope. 'I know you will.'

As I looked at her I couldn't help wondering whose truth she was after. Jude's, mine or her own?

fifty-one. Jude

'Is your name Jude Alexander McGregor?'

'Yes.'

'What is your address?'

'I don't have a fixed address at the moment.'

289

'Where do you currently reside?'

'Room fourteen, Cartman Hotel in Bridgeport.'

'It is charged that on the night of the seventeenth of July you did intentionally and ultimately cause the death of Cara Imega. You are therefore charged with the murder of Cara Imega. Do you understand these charges as they have been read out to you?'

I nodded.

'Could you speak up for the court audio tape please?' ordered the magistrate.

Suppressing the powerful urge to tell him just where he could stick the court audio tape, I said, 'Yes, I understand the charges.'

'Your Honour, at this time my client would like to request bail,' my sad-excuse-for-a-lawyer piped up.

'Request for bail denied,' the magistrate declared immediately. 'Jude McGregor, you are remanded in custody until the date of your court case. Next!'

fifty-two. Sephy

I sat in Anada's, the famous seafood restaurant, waiting. I'd never been in this one before. It wasn't exactly the sort of place I could afford. The walls were an in-your-face sunshine yellow and the carpet on the floor was a deep sea-blue. It was the sort of restaurant where they had tablecloths on the tables and shining silver cutlery. And draped across the ceiling were fishing nets full of shells and starfish and seaweed and other stuff from the sea. The strange thing was, it actually worked. It stopped the place from being entirely too pretentious. I studied the menu as I waited for my sister Minerva to arrive. I'd called her to ask for a meeting and to my surprise she'd jumped at the chance, suggesting this restaurant as a meeting place.

I needed her help. And I wasn't sure if she'd be prepared to give it, so I was going to have to resort to a bit of subterfuge. But the thought of deceiving my sister didn't sit easily with my conscience. So I forced myself to focus on the menu and not on our forthcoming meeting. Desserts were always my favourite part of any menu so I looked at them first. With a start, I noticed they had something called Blanker's Delight. *A light-as-air white chocolate mousse flavoured with brandy and served with cream or crème fraîche.* Charming! I looked around the restaurant. No Noughts eating and only one serving. I wondered how he felt when someone ordered a Blanker's Delight?

Disenchanted, my gaze slid back to the main courses. Big mistake. The whole menu was beautifully presented and had some delicious-sounding dishes on it. But not a single one had the price next to it. After a quick glance around, I picked up my bag and surreptitiously opened my purse. I wondered what my meagre funds would buy me in this place. Maybe half an after-dinner mint—if I was lucky. I could try putting it on plastic but I wasn't sure if the credit card companies would authorize yet more spending on my part. I decided to plead a full stomach and just stick to a glass of sparkling mineral water. Perhaps if I told them to hold the ice and not bother with a slice of lemon or lime then I might just be able to pay for it. This restaurant had been my sister's idea. I might've guessed she'd pick a place where you needed a mortgage to pay for the meal.

'Hello, Sephy. How're you?'

I glanced up, then sprang to my feet. 'Hello, Minerva. Thanks for agreeing to meet me.'

Minerva shrugged. 'Of course I'd meet you. What else did you think I'd do?' No hug. No kiss. We both sat down. 'So how've you been? And how's Callie Rose?'

'Rose is doing fine,' I replied. 'She's with Meggie at the moment.'

'Would Meggie mind if I came round to see Callie Rose some time?'

'Of course she wouldn't.' What a strange question.

'Would you mind?' Minerva asked me.

'No. Why would I?'

Minerva shrugged again, her expression noncommittal. She had some bizarre notions and no mistake. What did she think I'd do? Take one look at her and kick her down the street? Mind you, Rose and I had been living with Meggie for a while now. Strange that Minerva wanted to start visiting us. She studied me critically, her lips slightly pursed.

'Have you lost weight, Sephy?'

'Some.'

Minerva regarded me for a few moments more, then waved at a waiter, who was across the restaurant one second and beside our table the next. He must've hitched a ride on a bolt of lightning to get to us so quickly. It wasn't the Nought waiter; he'd disappeared into the kitchen.

'D'you mind if I order for you?' Minerva asked.

'Well, actually, I was only going to have a mineral water,' I began.

'Nonsense.' Minerva turned to the waiter. 'Can we have the smoked haddock and monkfish chowder to start please. No saffron in mine. And we'll both have the swordfish steaks.'

'Of course. And if I may say so, an excellent choice,' smarmed the waiter.

I mean, could he be any more obsequious? I'd never seen such oily toadying. Just as he was about to slime off, I asked him, 'Don't you think it's rather insulting to have something called Blanker's Delight on the menu?'

The waiter frowned. 'The chef sets the menu.'

'That doesn't make it right,' I replied.

'Blanker's Delight is a dessert that's been served for centuries.'

293

'Then it's about time its name was changed, don't you think?' I said evenly.

'Er . . . I'll see to your order,' said the waiter, keen to avoid any kind of confrontation at all costs.

'Was that necessary?' Minerva said. 'My newspaper brings lots of clients to this restaurant. My editor won't thank me if we upset them.'

'How can a junior reporter afford this place?' I frowned.

'I work for the *Daily Shouter*—remember?' Minerva smiled, a trace of pride in her voice. 'And I may be only a junior reporter but I'm working my way up.'

'So the job is working out then?'

'So far.' Minerva looked me straight in the eye. 'Sephy, I'm ambitious. Very ambitious.'

'Fair enough.' I smiled at her. Her gaze fell away from mine. 'So have I made trouble for you then by complaining about the name of the pudding?'

'I doubt it. And even if you have—I'm a survivor,' said my sister.

'Don't you think this place should drag itself into the twenty-first century like the rest of us? Why don't you write about that?'

'My editor wouldn't publish it,' said Minerva calmly. 'It's not news.'

Which I could've guessed. The status quo is never news, only challenges to it.

'Besides, you have to be patient, Sephy. No one can change things overnight—not even
294

you.'

'But it's not overnight, is it?' I argued. 'We've had decades, *centuries*, to change people's attitudes but things are getting worse, not better. D'you know I went shopping in town with Rose two days ago and three different people asked me whose child she was? And when I said mine, one man actually had the cheek to tell me it would've been better if I'd put Rose up for adoption with a blanker family—his words, not mine.'

'So what did you say to him?' Minerva asked.

'If I repeat it, they'll chuck us out of this restaurant,' I said.

Minerva laughed. 'Good for you. Stand your ground. But the ones who speak the loudest don't necessarily speak for the majority.'

'No? Most people would rather cross the street than get involved. This man stood in my way, shouting verbal abuse at me and not one person helped out. They all walked around us whilst that bastard stood there telling me I should've had an abortion or never gone with a Nought in the first place. He actually told me Rose would be better off dead.'

'But you told him where to go, didn't you?'

I sighed, trying to calm down. ' 'Course I did. And he's not even the one who really upset me. It was all the ones who walked past, or crossed the street and let it happen. They're the ones I'm angry with.'

'Don't give them another thought,' said Minerva. 'They're not worth losing sleep over.'

'Easy for you to say.' I was going to argue further but sighed and let it go. I didn't want to ruin Minerva's lunch with my woes.

Minerva said, 'I hope you don't mind me ordering for you. All the food is good here but I can recommend the soup and swordfish I ordered.'

'It sounds fine,' I said, 'but I really was just going to have some water.'

'The bill gets put on my company's credit card so we can both enjoy ourselves,' said Minerva. 'And if the paper cuts up rough, I'll pay for it out of my own pocket.'

'The *Daily Shouter* pays you well then?' I asked, surprised.

'Are you kidding? Hungry junior reporters are ten a penny,' Minerva frowned. 'If I didn't get my allowance from Dad each month, I don't know how I'd manage.'

A sudden flare of pain shot through me. It wasn't so much the money, although that would've been wonderful, but the fact that Dad could so easily forget he had two daughters, not one. In spite of everything that'd happened, all the things that we'd both said and done, a part of me still missed my dad. I'd be lying if I said otherwise.

'So Dad's still looking after you, is he?'

Minerva's eyes widened. 'Oh Sephy, I'm sorry. I didn't think.'

I shrugged. 'Don't worry about it. If lunch is on you, then I'll enjoy myself.'

I sat back in the chair, trying to relax.

'So have you heard about Jude McGregor being arrested?' asked Minerva, smoothing her napkin down on her lap.

'Of course. I haven't just arrived from the South Pole, you know.' Funny, but Jude was just who I wanted to talk about as well. Quite a coincidence.

'So how d'you feel about that?' Minerva asked.

'About Jude?'

'Yeah.'

'Are you interviewing me, Minerva?'

Minerva suddenly found the tablecloth fascinating. She couldn't tear her eyes away from it.

'You are, aren't you?' I persisted. 'Is that why you agreed to meet me for lunch?'

'It wasn't the only reason,' she told me.

'But it was high up on the list, wasn't it?'

'It's my job, Sephy.'

'To use your own sister to get a story?'

'It's not like that,' Minerva protested.

'Then what is it like?'

'I need your help, Sephy.'

I sat back, waiting for Minerva to grow enough of a backbone to get to the point.

'I've got something to ask you and I just want you to hear me out—OK?' said Minerva.

I didn't reply. The flutterings in my stomach were beginning to make me feel nauseous. That in itself was enough to warn me that Minerva was about to hit me with something that I wasn't going to like. But before she could continue, a man wearing an apron and a spotless white T-shirt was fast approaching our table—and he had a face like thunder.

'You are the woman who complained about my menu?' he asked me directly.

'Mr Sewell, my sister didn't complain about your menu as such.' Minerva tried to soothe his ruffled feathers. 'She agrees with me that your cooking is second to none.'

I stared at Idris Sewell. I had no idea he was the head chef of this place. He was a famous chef who was on the TV regularly. He was a lot taller in real life than he appeared on the box. And at this moment, a lot more menacing.

'You criticized my menu,' he challenged me, ignoring my sister completely.

I took a deep breath. 'I just think it's a shame you have something called Blanker's Delight on the menu.'

'The recipe for Blanker's Delight was handed to me by my grandmother, who got it from her mother before her,' Idris informed me. 'So what is wrong with it?'

'I'm sure it tastes wonderful,' Minerva interjected.

'Yes, but its name is insulting,' I said, warming to my theme.

'Sephy!' Minerva pleaded.

I shrugged. 'He asked for my opinion so that's what he's getting.'

And I must admit that part of me was enjoying the confrontation with the chef. I wanted to shout at him and everyone else in the restaurant. I wanted to shout at the whole world for the casual way they condemned me and dismissed my daughter.

'It's just a name,' Idris Sewell told me with belligerence. 'There are nursery rhymes and songs and ads on the telly that all feature blankers. What's wrong with that?'

'They may feature "blankers" but they don't use that word,' I replied coldly. 'They're Noughts, not blankers.'

'If you have a dessert named after you, you ought to be glad. We've had milk-white noughts in here who didn't complain,' said Idris stonily. 'And if they didn't complain, then why should you?'

'Because I can't speak for anyone but myself and I find it offensive.'

'Perhaps you'd like to dine elsewhere if my menu offends you,' Idris suggested.

I looked around. Most people were listening if not watching. 'You don't get rid of me that easily,' I told him. 'I'm here to eat, if you don't mind serving someone whose daughter is half-Nought, half-Cross.'

'I don't care if your daughter is a duck, as long as you pay the bill at the end of the meal,' said Idris. 'But I don't appreciate having my food disrespected.'

'I'm not disrespecting your food, just your menu.'

But the chef was already stomping back to the kitchen.

'Oh dear,' sighed Minerva. 'He'll probably

curdle his béarnaise sauce or something now and it'll be all your fault.' But the last was said with an amused smile.

'Are you sorry you invited me here?' I asked.

'No. This has been the most entertaining lunch I've had in a long while.'

'It may be just entertainment to you, Minerva, but it's my life. I can't walk away from it—and neither can my daughter.'

'Of course.' Minerva's smile faded. 'I didn't mean to be insensitive.'

Let it slide . . . I shrugged to imply that it was OK.

'D'you think the chef is going to spit in our soup?' I teased to ease the mood.

Minerva laughed. 'No way. It'd be beneath his dignity. Besides,' she leaned in closer, 'I'll make sure it's known that I work for the *Daily Shouter*. He won't risk a bad write-up.'

The power of the press.

'Is working for the *Daily Shouter* all you thought it would be?'

'It's better. I've still got a couple of months left of my six months' probation. But at least they're giving me a chance,' Minerva replied carefully.

'But how did you get the job in the first place?' The *Daily Shouter* was the most popular tabloid in the country. They could pick and choose who they wanted working for them.

'Sephy, use your brain. Dad is the Deputy Prime Minister. Mother is Jasmine Adeyebe-

Hadley. I have connections,' said Minerva. 'Less than I implied at the job interview, to be honest, but still more than most junior reporters.'

'I see,' I said. And I did see.

'Like I said,' Minerva looked at me with defiance, 'I'm ambitious.'

I shrugged. Who was I to argue with her about what she wanted to do with her life? At least she had a purpose, a goal that wasn't wrapped around someone else. 'So what were you going to ask me?'

'You first,' said Minerva after a brief but distinct pause. She smiled. 'Why did you want us to meet up—apart from my scintillating company?'

'I wanted to talk to you about Jude as well,' I admitted.

'Oh! Well, that makes things easier,' said Minerva.

'Did he do it?' I came straight to the point.

'The evidence seems to indicate he did.'

'What evidence would that be exactly?'

Minerva studied me, trying to decide whether or not to part with the information.

'I don't intend to broadcast what you tell me,' I tried to reassure her. 'But I have a good reason for asking.'

'Look, this is all confidential,' Minerva said earnestly. 'I'm not supposed to tell anyone, so you're not to pass this on. Not even to Meggie, OK?'

I nodded.

'The *Shouter* will bounce me straight out of there if they think I'm passing on information I pick up at the paper.'

'Minerva, I get it,' I said patiently.

'Well, all I know is Jude McGregor's fingerprints were found all over Cara Imega's house. He gave Cara a false name but the police know it was him. He called himself Steve Winner when he was going out with her—'

What on earth was she talking about? 'Jude was dating Cara?'

'That's right. They were an item apparently.'

'No way. Jude would never date a Cross. Never in a million years.' I wanted to put her straight on that one.

'Well, I must admit, I thought the same when I heard. But the senior editor got this straight from a friend of his who's a police officer working on the case. Apparently several witnesses at Delany's hair salon where Cara worked have identified Jude as Cara's boyfriend. They've signed sworn witness statements to that fact. And after Cara's death, a number of her cheques were cashed at banks throughout the city.'

'And that was Jude?'

Minerva shrugged. 'It's inconclusive but the police intend to make the case that it was. The CCTV footage from the banks shows a nought man cashing the cheques but he invariably wore a cap and sunglasses and kept his head down. The general height and weight match though.'

'But none of the tapes really show his face full on?'

'I don't think so but I'm not sure,' said Minerva after a noticeable pause.

'Did they find any bloody clothing? Any DNA evidence?'

'They didn't find any clothing but he had plenty of time to get rid of what he was wearing. He's not stupid. Evil—yes; stupid—no,' said Minerva. 'And he didn't leave much by way of DNA evidence but the forensic scientists are still working on it.'

I sat back in my chair.

'Why all the questions?' Minerva asked.

Our soup arrived in teacup-sized bowls. It looked and smelled absolutely delicious but I didn't have much of an appetite.

'In your opinion, is the evidence enough to convict him?' I asked.

'From what I've seen so far—yes,' said Minerva. 'And good riddance.'

'Isn't it all a bit circumstantial—apart from the fingerprints?' I asked. 'And they only prove that he was in Cara's house at some point. They don't prove he killed her.'

'True. But all the other evidence, including the eye-witness statements, seems to indicate that he did. And the police are confident that forensics will turn up more evidence against him eventually.'

'And what does Jude say?' I asked.

'How would I know?' said Minerva. 'I'm not

his lawyer.'

'I know.' I couldn't keep the trace of impatience out of my voice. 'But you must have heard on the journalists' grapevine what's going on.'

'Last I heard, Jude's not saying a word. He admits that he knew Cara but that's it. Unless his lawyer surprises everyone by coming up with an alibi or something, I reckon Jude's got no defence.'

'If he's found guilty, will he hang?'

Pause. 'Almost certainly.'

'I see.' I sipped at my soup, which might as well have been wallpaper flavour.

'Why're you so concerned about Jude?' asked Minerva. 'The bastard shot me and threatened you and your baby—remember? And he meant every word. He's dangerous.'

'I know that.'

Minerva scrutinized me. 'Are you going to answer my question now?'

At my feigned puzzlement, Minerva smiled. 'Nice try, Sephy. But I'll ask you once again, why all the questions?'

Prevarication or the truth. I decided I was too tired to beat around the bush.

'I just wanted to know for Meggie's sake. No one will really tell her what's going on so I said I'd try and help.'

'Don't get involved, Sephy,' Minerva warned. 'It has nothing to do with you and if you stick your nose in, Jude will grab it and drag you down with him. And for God's sake, please don't pass on what I've just told you. And it's not as if any of it would make Meggie feel better even if she did know.'

'I just want to help her. She's lost so much already. And ever since Jude was arrested, she hardly goes out of the house and she's barely said a word to anyone—except Rose, her granddaughter. I'm worried about her.'

'Jude's actions are his responsibility, not hers.'

'Meggie lost her daughter Lynette in a road accident. Her husband Ryan was electrocuted trying to escape from prison and . . . and her youngest son was hanged. If Jude were to die, I think it'd just about finish her off. You weren't there when it came on the news that the police wanted Jude in connection with Cara Imega's death. She broke down completely.'

'I'm sorry, but if Jude's guilty—'

I interrupted harshly. 'Her other son was innocent and that didn't get him anywhere, did it?'

Minerva let her spoon clatter back down into her now empty soup bowl. She regarded me speculatively. I didn't flinch from her gaze.

'Sephy, don't make the mistake of confusing one brother for the other.'

'What?'

'Jude isn't Callum. Don't start looking for the good in him 'cause you'll go blind trying to find it. He tried to kill us—remember?'

'I'm not likely to forget.'

'I hope not—for your sake. Callum had his

305

faults but—'

'I'm not here to talk about . . . him,' I dismissed.

Minerva studied me. 'Why are you finding it so hard to even say Callum's name?'

'I'm not finding it hard at all,' I denied.

'Say it now then.'

'Why? What's the point? Because you tell me to?'

'No, but because if you can open up and tell someone how you feel about Callum and how you feel about . . . his death, then maybe you'll be able to move on with your life—and Meggie'll be able to do the same. That way you might both stand a chance.'

'Neither of us wants to live in the past,' I said. 'Meggie reckons we should both move on.'

'Unless you can both fully discuss what happened to Ryan and Callum and then let it go, wherever you move on to, you'll just drag the past behind you. And it'll get heavier and heavier,' Minerva said seriously.

'Studying psychology on the side, are you?' I challenged.

'No. But it's obvious. No one's asking you to forget the past. I'm saying both you and Meggie need to let it go.'

How do I do that? I wondered. 'Out of sight is out of mind' sure wasn't working. Not when every time I looked at my own daughter, all I could see was Callum. At times I almost wondered if Callum's soul had been born into

306

Rose's body. Then I'd tell myself I was being fanciful. But then I'd ask myself—why not? Callum's soul might've entered Rose's body. It was possible. After all, Rose laughed the same way as Callum, she looked more and more like him with each passing day, and her eyes . . . It was so much like looking into Callum's eyes that it scared me. Rose's eyes were a different colour but that was irrelevant. Everything else about them was the same—the shape, the lashes, the way they looked at me with that contemplative stare.

'Are you close to Meggie?' Minerva asked.

I shrugged. 'I guess.'

'Then I'm glad you're going to be there for her,' Minerva said sombrely. 'Because, make no mistake about it, Jude is going to hang.'

The main course arrived. We both picked at our fish in silence. All I could think was that if I didn't try to do something, Meggie was about to lose the only child she had left.

'Your turn now. You still haven't told me why you wanted to see me,' I pointed out.

Minerva took a deep breath. 'I'd like an interview with Meggie.'

'Excuse me?'

'I'd like an interview with Meggie, for my newspaper,' Minerva repeated. 'Can you arrange it for me?'

I stared at her. 'Are you drunk or what? I'm not going to ask Meggie to let you interview her. What d'you take me for?'

'Sephy, I need this interview. If Meggie does

307

this, my future on the *Daily Shouter* is secure.'

'No way!'

'Sephy, I need this job.'

'That's not my problem,' I told her. 'And I don't intend to make it Meggie's either. Didn't you hear a word of what I just said? Meggie is going through hell—again. How can you even ask me something like that?'

'I'll make sure she has a sympathetic hearing in my article.'

'Minerva, which part of NO are you having trouble with? The "N" or the "O"?'

'If you could just ask her,' Minerva persisted. 'Let Meggie make the decision.'

I began to shake my head.

'Please, Sephy. For me. Just ask her—that's all I want.'

I studied my sister, not attempting to keep the disdain off my face.

'It's my job, Sephy,' Minerva said. 'And it means a lot to me. Please.'

'No, I can't . . .'

'I got shot for you,' Minerva said quietly. 'Do this for me and we'll be even.'

My head and my heart went very still at her words. It was as if something inside of me took a step back from her and just curled up into a ball to hide.

I got shot for you . . .

'I see,' I said at last.

'Look, forget what I just said.' Minerva shook her head. 'I don't even know where that came from. I didn't mean it.'

308

I said nothing.

'Sephy, I'm really sorry I said that. Forgive me?'

I shrugged. 'It's OK, Minerva. I'll do what you want. I'll ask Meggie—but that's all I can do. The decision is hers.'

'That's great. Thank you so much,' Minerva beamed.

'I can tell you now—Meggie will say no,' I warned.

'You'll swing it for me—I know you can.' Minerva was all smiles.

I didn't bother to reply. There was no point. Minerva was convinced that given time and a little pressure from me she'd get her exclusive interview with Meggie. A few choice words on her part and she had me where she wanted me. Her job meant more than the world to her. Which was fair enough. Besides, I had no doubt that once Minerva found out what I intended to do with the information she'd just given me about Jude, she'd change her mind about asking me for anything ever again.

Using people was a two-way street.

fifty-three. Jude

'Mr McGregor, I'm on your side—you have to believe that,' said Mr Clooney.

'I don't have to believe a damn thing you tell me,' I said icily. God knows where they dug up

309

the fossil in front of me. He must've been pushing sixty-odd and marking time until retirement. And the man didn't have a clue. He was a doddering old fart of a Cross with short-cut, white- silver hair and a thin salt-and-pepper moustache. We were in one of the three private visitors' rooms in the prison, strictly reserved for prisoners' interviews with their lawyers, conjugal visits and imparting bad news.

'I'm trying to give you the benefit of my experience,' the dagger said as he struggled for patience. 'This is a serious charge.'

'Don't patronize me,' I said. 'I know it's a serious charge. I'm the one with my head in a noose, not you.'

'Then will you let me advise you?'

'Let's hear your advice first.' I sat back in my chair, not expecting much. And that was exactly what I got.

'I think you should plead guilty and throw yourself on the mercy of the court,' said the bloody idiot before me.

'And that's the best you can do?' I said with contempt.

'It's your only chance to escape the death penalty. If you plead innocent and you're found guilty, you'll automatically receive the death penalty,' said Mr Clooney.

Like I didn't already know that.

'And if I plead guilty?'

'You'll get out in twenty-five to thirty years but you'll still be able to have some kind of life.'

Twenty-five to thirty years? Could he hear himself? He might as well have said twenty-five to thirty centuries. I wasn't going to grow old that way, rotting away slowly but surely like some of them I'd seen in this prison. I'd rather hang—and that was the truth.

'And if I say yes?'

Clooney's face lit up like a Crossmas tree. 'I can submit your new plea for the court's inspection and we could have the whole matter sorted out inside of a fortnight.'

'And if I say no?'

Clooney's smile faded. 'Then the trial will probably drag on for months and you'll more than likely be found guilty anyway.'

'Your faith in me just moves me to tears,' I said with disdain. 'I'm all moist!'

Jude's law number two was ringing in my head, with a bit of Jude's law number nine—*The only person you can ever rely on is yourself*—chucked in for good measure.

'I'm trying to be realistic,' Clooney told me.

'You're trying my patience is what you're doing,' I replied. 'And if you're the best I've got in my corner, then I'm in deep crap.'

'I am on your side,' Clooney began.

'Not any more. You're fired.'

'Pardon?'

'Turn up your hearing aid, granddad. You're fired. Your services will no longer be required. You can take a hike.'

'You need someone to defend you,' said

311

Clooney.

'I'll do it myself,' I informed him.

'I really wouldn't advise that.'

'I don't give a rat's fart about your advice,' I said. 'Hit the road.'

Clooney got to his feet and gathered up his papers, putting them in his briefcase.

'You're making a serious mistake,' he said.

'Maybe, but at least it's *my* mistake not yours,' I replied.

Clooney looked down at me and shook his head. I stood up.

'You know what I'm looking at?' Clooney asked quietly.

'No. What?'

'A dead man walking.'

And if the guard hadn't stepped forward at that point, I'd've smacked Clooney down for sure. Pompous arse. One thing was certain. Defending myself, I couldn't do any worse.

fifty-four. Sephy

Sephy, think long and hard about what you're proposing to do. You know only too well what Jude McGregor is. If you were dangling over a cliff and your hand was glued to his, he'd rather chop off his own arm at the elbow than haul you up to safety. And he shot your sister. He would've shot you too if he hadn't thought of a much better way to get back at you. Don't do it, Sephy.

Don't do it.

But what about Meggie? I owe it to her.

Get off the Cross, Sephy. Someone else needs the wood. You don't owe Meggie or anyone else anything. Stop taking the problems of the world onto your own shoulders.

If it wasn't for me, Callum would still be alive. Jude got that bit right at least. And I have to help Meggie. She's been through so much.

Even if it means helping your worst enemy?

It'd be for Meggie . . .

Are you sure about that? Wouldn't it be more for your own benefit . . .

Of course not. How would it help me, for heaven's sake?

Maybe it's your way of trying to feel better about yourself.

I feel just fine, thank you.

Look in the mirror and tell yourself that . . .

You're forgetting one important thing in all this. Jude might actually be innocent.

Look in the mirror and tell yourself that too. When are you going to forgive yourself, Sephy? When're you going to give yourself a break?

Stop it! Just stop . . .

*   *   *

I groaned and rolled over, unable to get to sleep. The darkness, which was supposed to be my friend, didn't bring me the comfort it usually did. I always felt safe in the dark. Free.

313

I was anonymous. No eyes watching. No one judging. But now the darkness just seemed to be mocking me. I groaned again. If anyone could hear my thoughts at that precise moment, I'd be instantly committed to a mental institution. Here I was, mentally arguing with myself over what I planned to do. How far gone was I!

But who could I talk to?

Who could I turn to?

One way or another, I was about to do something incredibly stupid, not to mention dangerous, but deep down I knew that that wouldn't stop me. I was at the start of my journey to hell.

And there was no turning back.

fifty-five. Jude

'You have a visitor,' the dagger guard told me.

'I don't want to see anyone,' I hissed back.

I didn't even bother looking at him. I lay on my bed in my prison cell, counting the flecks of paint still left on the ceiling. In a few days' time, my court case was due to start. They'd pulled out all the stops to get this trial scheduled and on the move. I was going to try again to be let out on bail but the chances of that happening were minuscule. It was far more likely that I'd be remanded in custody until my trial was over. That's what they did to noughts like me. This prison would be my home until the day I died—which wouldn't be long now. I turned my head. The guard was still watching me.

'Yes?' I snapped.

'Your visitor said to tell you that your brother sent her,' said the dagger.

My head snapped up at that one. Mum . . . I didn't want to talk to her again—not after what happened the last time. I didn't want to watch the hurt on her face as she looked at me. I already had one foot in the grave. It'd be best for everyone if she just left. But even as I opened my mouth to say I wouldn't see her, the words refused to leave my mouth. I tried a second time. The same thing happened. So much for Jude's law number four—*Caring equals vulnerability. Never show either.* I sighed inwardly.

'OK, I'll meet her,' I said reluctantly, swinging round to sit up on my bed. Instinct told me that I was making a huge mistake but she was the only family I had left—and that counted for something. I stood up and headed for the cell door. The door lock clicked and clunked as the lock was undone.

'Do I need to handcuff you again?' asked the dagger.

I shook my head. I didn't want Mum to see me in handcuffs.

'Are you going to behave yourself?'

'I said so, didn't I?' I snarled.

If this dagger didn't get out of my face, he'd

be sorry. I might be going down but I could still take some of the bastards with me.

Another dagger guard arrived from nowhere and they flanked me as we walked down the corridor. They led the way to the visitors' room. For hardened criminals like me, there were no face to face meetings. Instead, a toughened-glass partition which reached from floor to ceiling separated each visitor from the inmates. The glass partition was sectioned off into semi cubicles so there was the illusion of privacy, but the guards walked up and down constantly, listening and watching. I walked past a few other prisoners before one of the guards pointed at my chair. I'd half sat in it before I fully took in who was my visitor. It wasn't Mum.

It was Persephone Hadley.

What the hell was she doing here? Shock made me sit down slowly, though I never took my eyes off her. For a moment, I wondered if my eyes were playing bizarre tricks. We both sat, regarding each other. Anger began to swell inside me. Now that I was going to die, I was so sorry I hadn't shot Sephy dead when I had the chance. The only thing I regretted was that it was Cara who'd been in front of me when I had flipped and not Sephy. Now that I would've enjoyed.

'Hello, Jude,' Sephy said quietly.

'Come to gloat, have you?'

'No. I've come to save your life.'

Whatever else I'd been expecting, that wasn't

it. Sephy wasn't laughing, but I sure as hell did.

'That's a good one!' I told her at last when my chortling began to fade. 'Thanks for giving me a good laugh if nothing else.'

'I mean it,' Sephy told me seriously.

'You're going to save my life? How're you going to do that?' I asked.

She leaned forward and I could only just hear her whisper, 'By giving you an alibi.'

And all at once this wasn't funny any more. I frowned at Sephy, trying to figure out if she really meant it, then mentally kicked myself for believing that she might, even for a second.

'Did you . . . kill Cara Imega?' Sephy asked. But then she added, so quickly and softly that I could hardly pick up the words, 'No, never mind. Don't answer that. I don't want to know.'

I stayed silent. Sephy glanced to either side. To her left, a female nought visitor was trying to comfort a screaming baby; to her right, both prisoner and visitor were lost in their own private conversation and leaning so close together that if it hadn't been for the screen in their cubicle, they would've been touching.

'How long were you in Cara's house?' Sephy asked in a low voice.

I studied Sephy, still trying to gauge from her expression, from her body language, from the clothes she wore to the long, dangly silver earrings that stood out against her dark skin, whether or not she was serious. Sephy sat in silence waiting for my answer to her question.

317

Well, OK. I'd play along—for now.

'Where is all of this leading?' I asked.

Sephy didn't speak for a moment, pausing as one of the guards walked past. As he reached the end of the line, she leaned forward again and said, 'If I give you an alibi, are you going to back me up or would you rather hang calling me a liar?'

I didn't answer.

'I need to know,' Sephy told me.

'Why're you doing this?'

'Meggie.'

'What about her?' I said sharply.

'If you die, you'll take her with you.' Sephy shook her head. 'I can't let that happen.'

'Why not? She means nothing to you,' I dismissed. 'And I mean nothing to her.'

'You're never willing to admit that you might be wrong about anyone or anything, are you?' Sephy said. 'You closed your mind and threw away the key a long time ago and you couldn't open it now even if you wanted to. How sad for you.'

'I don't want your pity. Sod your pity. Did you come here to lecture me? 'Cause if you did . . .'

'Calm down,' Sephy said quietly.

I scowled at her, but my rage was directed at myself. How had I let her get to me? I wouldn't let her do that, not again.

'Tell me,' I began. 'D'you still dream about my brother?'

Sephy didn't answer, but her body became

318

still and her eyes grew watchful.

'He was your bit of erotica-exotica, wasn't he?' I smiled. 'Taken up with any more of us blankers since Callum's death? Once you've had white, you've seen the light.'

'The saying is, "Once you've had black, there's no turning back,"' Sephy told me. 'If we're trading ignorant sayings.'

'You didn't answer my question. D'you still dream about Callum?'

'We're not here to talk about your brother,' Sephy said evenly. Her eyes flicked from side to side, checking that the guard was still too far away to hear her. 'I think what we should do is this. You can't deny that you were at Cara's house because your fingerprints were everywhere, so we say that you were there, but then I arrived and you left with me. That way I can testify that Cara was alive when we left her. The cheques are easy—they can't prove that she didn't give them to you.'

'And you'd get on the witness stand and perjure yourself for me? You'd risk going to prison if you get caught for me?' I didn't believe it for a second.

'It won't go to trial,' Sephy told me. 'We have to stir up enough reasonable doubt before the trial to make sure that it never happens.'

'They'll never believe we left Cara's house together,' I told her. 'Everyone knows we hate each other. I shot your sister for God's sake.'

'No one knows about the shooting except you, me and Minerva. And she won't say anything, or everyone will wonder why on earth she didn't speak out before. And as for hating each other, we can tell everyone that that's why we agreed to meet up that night.' Sephy leaned forward and started to talk faster. 'We'll tell them we wanted to put aside our differences and work together to clear your brother's name. We could say that we'd both agreed I should meet you at Cara's. You introduced us but you and I both left almost immediately after that.'

'The police aren't going to be keen to let me off the hook if they can't put someone else on it,' I told her.

'Yes, but—'

And then I had an idea. I sat back in my chair. Could Sephy be trusted? For my idea to work, I'd have to rely on her to do her part— and that was the one thing in the world I really didn't want to do.

But I had no choice.

'So how would this work?' I began carefully. 'Would you go to the police with this so-called alibi of yours?'

'No. The police can suppress evidence. I'd go to the newspapers. Then when you're taken to your hearing, they'll have TV cameras and reporters all around you asking for your side of the story. You can talk about your alibi then and back up what I've said.' Sephy seemed to have it all figured out.

But I had a plan or two up my own sleeve.

'Well? Are you going to let me help you?' she

320

asked.

'How do I know I can trust you?' I said.

'You don't,' came her immediate reply. 'But you have no choice. And like I said, I'm not doing this for you. I do hate you, Jude—you got that bit right at least. You make me more sick than undercooked chicken. So get any idea out of your head that I want to help you. I'm doing this for Meggie.'

'I see.'

'I hope you do. Because if I do this for you, I want your word that you'll leave me and my daughter alone.'

'Ah! So it's not so much my mum's welfare you're concerned with, as your own.' I allowed myself a small smile. Sephy didn't hold all the cards. Most of them, but not all.

'You must believe what you want to believe.'

'And am I supposed to be in your debt when this is all over—if it works?' I leaned forward. 'D'you know what I think?'

'I really don't care what's in your nasty little brain,' Sephy interrupted. 'Promise you'll leave Rose alone and hopefully after this I'll never have to see you, hear you or even think about you again.'

'Is that how you feel about my brother now? I notice you haven't said his name since you got here,' I said.

'What're you talking about?' Sephy frowned. 'Your brother has nothing to do with this.'

'He has everything to do with this. If it wasn't for Callum, you wouldn't be here now.'

'Do we have a deal or not?' Sephy asked impatiently. Visiting time was coming to an end and the guards were beginning to move along the line, reminding everyone that they'd have to leave in a minute.

'And what d'you get out of it?' I asked.

'Peace of mind.'

I couldn't let that happen. I leaned forward and whispered softly, 'Even knowing that I killed the dagger bitch?'

For the first time, Sephy looked away, unable to hold my gaze. I smiled. I was back in control.

'The peace of mind isn't for me,' Sephy said softly.

'It's a deal then.' My smile broadened.

Live or die, one way or another, I'll still have my revenge on you, Sephy Hadley. Even if I have to return from hell itself to get you. That's a promise.

fifty-six. Sephy

The doorbell rang. A short, sharp ring followed by another.

'I'll get it,' I called upstairs.

There was no danger of anything else happening. Meggie was in her room and she didn't answer the door any more. Too many photographers flashing too many cameras in her face had put paid to that. I took a deep breath, then opened the door.

It was Minerva.

'What're you doing here?' I frowned.

'Hello to you too!' Minerva raised her eyebrows. 'Can I come in?'

I stepped to one side. Minerva swanned past and waited for me to shut the front door.

'Sephy, who is it?' Meggie called from upstairs.

'Minerva, my sister.'

'Oh.' Meggie appeared at the top of the stairs, looking old and, oh, so tired. 'Hello, Minerva.'

'Hello, Meggie.' Minerva smiled up at her. 'How're you?'

'OK.' Meggie nodded. 'Can I get you a cup of tea or coffee or maybe some orange juice?'

'Meggie, I'm quite capable of getting my sister a drink. You should go and get some rest.'

'I'll have a coffee, please—if it's no trouble,' Minerva said directly to Meggie.

'Sephy, would you like a drink too?'

'No thanks, Meggie.'

I frowned at Minerva, an unpleasant thought creeping into my head. Whilst Meggie trudged into the kitchen to make the drinks, I ushered Minerva into the living room, shutting the door behind me.

'Minerva, I swear if you've come here for an interview with Meggie, I'm going to kick your arse so hard you'll be wearing your bum cheeks as ear muffs,' I told her furiously.

'Charming!' Minerva sniffed. 'You've obviously been living around noughts for too long.'

'Sod you, Minerva. What d'you want?'

The door handle began to turn. I moved forward to open the door. Meggie came in carrying a tray with three mugs on it, plus a bowl of sugar and a small jug filled with milk.

'Sephy, I thought you might like a cup of jasmine green tea.' Meggie smiled at me.

'That's very kind of you,' I said, taking the tray from her hands. I held the tray out to Minerva, glaring at her all the while. For anyone else, Meggie would've asked them up front if they took milk and sugar and would've put it in their cup for them accordingly.

Not for a Hadley.

'The coffee is in the yellow mug,' said Meggie.

Minerva poured some milk into her coffee before she took her cup and sat down in the armchair. 'Won't you join us, Meggie?'

Meggie took the blue mug off the tray and sat down on the sofa. I took the last cup off the tray before sitting down next to Meggie. Minerva looked from Meggie to me and back again.

'I was in the area so I thought I'd pop in and see how my niece was doing,' smiled Minerva.

'She's upstairs, asleep,' I told her.

'Shame,' said Minerva.

Yeah, right. No appeals to just take a quick peek at her. No requests for more information about her height, weight, general appearance. Nothing. We sat in silence for several awkward moments. I wasn't going to speak first.

'Meggie, I was so sorry to hear about . . . what's happening with Jude,' said Minerva with beautifully faked sincerity.

'Thank you,' said Meggie, taking a sip of her coffee, even though it was still too hot to drink.

'Is he . . . is Jude managing to stay positive?'

'I think so. I hope so,' said Meggie. 'He has right on his side.'

'Minerva—' I warned, but she completely ignored me.

'It must be hard though. Have your neighbours been supportive?' my sister asked.

'Are you kidding?' Meggie scoffed.

The neighbours didn't even say hello to either of us any more, including Mrs Straczynski. As I learned when Callum was arrested, so-called friends consider bad luck and notoriety to be contagious.

'So what're you hoping for, Meggie?' asked Minerva.

'That justice is done.'

Enough was already too much. Time to spike Minerva's guns. She was nothing if not doggedly persistent—but then so was I.

'I hope it gets sorted out the way you want soon,' smiled Minerva.

'I hope so too,' said Meggie. 'And at least I've got Sephy fighting in my corner. I don't know what I'd do without your sister.'

'Oh yes?' Minerva said sharply. 'And how're

you helping, Sephy?'

'In any way I can,' I told my sister evenly.

Minerva cast me a speculative look. 'So you're convinced Jude is innocent?'

'He told me he didn't do it,' Meggie said. 'And my boy wouldn't lie to me.'

But Meggie had made a mistake. Minerva's question was directed at me, not her.

'Have you been to see Jude then?' Minerva asked Meggie eagerly.

'Yes, we went last week when he was still in a police cell,' Meggie replied.

'Both of you?' said Minerva sharply.

'Sephy was there to lend me moral support.' Meggie smiled at me. 'But Sephy went to see Jude in prison on her own a couple of days ago. She's been so wonderful . . .'

'Sephy—'

'So, Minerva, how's your job at the *Daily Shouter*?' I interrupted. 'It must be tough working as a junior reporter, trying to fight your way up to the top of the journalistic dung heap.'

Meggie's mouth closed like a steel trap—at last. Minerva's lips tightened slightly as she considered me.

'You don't have a very high opinion of my profession, do you?' said Minerva.

'Can't say I do. You forget, I've seen you lot in action. I've been on the business end of too many stories full of distorted half-truths and vitriol to dance for joy around journalists,' I said. 'But I wish you luck with it, if that's what

326

you really want to do.'

'Minerva, I didn't know you were a journalist at the *Daily Shouter*,' Meggie said quietly.

'Yes, she got the job a few months ago,' I told Meggie.

'You didn't tell me that,' said Meggie, giving me a curiously speculative look.

And it took me a few moments to decipher her expression. She was wondering *why* I hadn't told her. She was actually wondering.

Take another step back, Sephy.

Step back from them all.

'I'm sure you have to go now,' I said to my sister.

'Oh I—' Minerva began. And then she saw my face. 'Yes. Yes, I do have another appointment.'

'I'll tell Rose you were asking for her,' I said standing up.

Meggie went to rise also.

'No, Meggie. Don't get up,' I told her. 'I'll see Minerva to the door.'

Meggie sat back down again. I led the way to the front door, not even bothering to turn and check that Minerva was following me. I just knew she would be. She'd finally got the hint.

'Thanks for nothing, Sephy,' Minerva hissed at me as I opened the door.

'I told you that you couldn't interview Meggie. You had no business coming here if that was your only reason,' I said unrepentantly.

'You could've let me ask a few more

questions,' said Minerva. 'And you didn't have to tell Meggie I was a journalist.'

'You don't need statements from us,' I told my sister. 'Do what all you lot do and make it up.'

'I thought blood was supposed to be thicker than water,' Minerva said with bitterness.

'So did I,' I replied. 'But you showed me I was wrong when you tried to blackmail me into getting Meggie to give you an interview.'

'I said I was sorry for that. You always did bear grudges.'

And as I looked at Minerva, I realized I was just wasting my breath. She just couldn't see that she'd done anything wrong. I could talk until my voice box exploded and she still wouldn't see it. So what was the point?

'Bye, Minerva,' I said. 'Don't let the door hit you on your way out.'

Minerva strode past me without another word. I slammed the door behind her. And that—as they say—was that. I turned round, and there was Meggie standing in the living-room doorway. I wondered how long she'd been standing there.

Not that it mattered.

Upstairs, Rose started to cry.

'I'll see to her if you'd like,' Meggie offered.

'No, thank you,' I said, already moving past her and up the stairs. I turned when I was halfway up them. Meggie was still watching me.

'Meggie, do you trust me?' I couldn't help

asking.

She waited just a tad too long to reply. 'Yes, I do.'

But she didn't. I nodded and turned to carry on up the stairs.

Maybe Meggie was like me, always waiting to be let down. Always hoping for the best, but expecting the worst. Maybe she was just like me—too bruised and battered to believe in anyone or anything.

fifty-seven. Jude

What's she doing? Is she talking to the papers? The TV stations? Why haven't I heard anything? Maybe she's changed her mind? What I have in mind won't work if she denies everything. I'm just going to have to go for it. Ironic really. My life, my future, lies on a knife edge—in the hands of a Cross—Persephone Hadley of all people. All she has to do is call me a liar and that's my neck stretched.

But I've got two things working for me.

Her guilt.

And her fear.

Cara was worth a hundred of Sephy. But I don't really think of Cara that much any more. I've buried her image deep down. I've forgotten her smile, the way she used to look at me, the way she spoke, her laugh—I've forgotten it all. Except when it's late at night

329

and I finally manage to fall asleep. Then every dream has something of her in it. And I wake up sweating. And I stay awake, shivering.

But I sweat because it's too hot in my cell.

And I shiver because it's too cold.

What do they call that again? When two opposites happen at the same time and place and space. I can't remember. So I force myself to laugh.

Because in my dreams, I'm always standing over Cara—and crying.

So I laugh and laugh—until the crying stops.

fifty-eight. Sephy

Sorry, Minerva. I kept saying the words over and over again in my head. Sorry, Minerva. I broke my word. I used you. But what choice did I have? I owed it to Meggie.

I didn't have any choice.

But thinking that one phrase over and over wasn't doing any good. Because of me, Jude might go free. Because of me . . .

Stop it! Don't think about it. Think of something else.

What else could I do? A sob broke from my lips. I tried to smother it even though I was alone, but I felt so heartsick at what I'd done. The enormity of what I was trying to do was only just beginning to sink in. And if I'd felt alone before, it was nothing to the way I felt now. I'd already contacted three different newspapers—not the *Daily Shouter* though—but two had refused to see me and although I'd been interviewed by the third, the story hadn't appeared. I'd phoned the local radio station. I'd had an interview over the phone but that hadn't been broadcast.

For which a major part of me was so grateful. With each passing hour, the reality of what I'd attempted to do pressed down on me harder and faster. Now I just wanted to forget the whole thing, turn the clock back. What on earth had I thought I was doing? All I could do was pray fervently that Jude would keep his mouth shut, that he wouldn't talk to the press about his so-called alibi. If he did say we were together on the night Cara Imega died, then what would I do? Back him up, knowing I was helping a stone-cold killer get away with murder? Or deny his story and crucify Meggie in the process? I couldn't do that to her, I just couldn't. Not when I'd been responsible for the death of one of her sons already. The rock and the hard place I stood between were crushing me to death.

I sat in the living room with my notebook and pen on my lap, whilst the TV played in the background. Rose was up in our room, fast asleep. How I envied her. Just to sleep without all the dreams I'd been having recently would've been bliss. I was so tired, I knew I wasn't thinking straight. How could I be thinking straight to provide Jude with a 'Get

331

out of jail free' card. Jude had me right where he wanted me. And telling me he'd committed Cara Imega's murder had been a masterstroke.

Stop it! Think of something else.

But I couldn't. Jude and his words were poison, seeping into every part of me. Something else Jude said kept spinning in my head like a hated song I couldn't get out of my mind.

Erotica-exotica.

Is that why Callum turned against me and ended up hating me? Because he reckoned that's how I thought of him? Surely he knew better? Is that how everyone else regarded me and him though? Erotica-exotica.

I wrote it down all over the first clean page that I came to in my notebook. Erotica-exotica. I wrote the words upside down, sideways on, slanted writing, underlined, capitals—over and over.

Erotica-exotica . . .

And then the words started to drip from my pen without me even thinking about it.

I close my eyes, you kiss me,
Your touch brings me no shame.
I hold on tight, you move within
As I call out your name.
I breathe you in, you hold me
Like you'll never let me go.
I look into your burning eyes
And feel our loving grow.

But it's just a fantasy,
A trick of the light.
Can you hear what I'm saying?
We take these dreams,
Pretend they're real
And give no name to the game we're playing.

I'm the lover in your hand,
Trickling through like so much sand.
You're forbidden fruit,
I watch you fall,
You're two words that describe it all –
Erotica-exotica.

But whatever else I'd been about to write went straight out of my head when something on the TV captured my attention. Jude was being led through the gate out of prison to be surrounded immediately by a mob of journalists. I shivered. I turned up the TV volume, waiting to hear what Jude would say. There were so many journalists around him that it was difficult for the security guards on either side of him to lead him forward to the security van which was supposed to take him to court. Even now I couldn't help shaking as I watched Jude being jostled by the riot of reporters around him. Jude's face was the face of true evil, and just seeing it on the TV made me shudder. After all the things he'd told me in the prison, I felt like I'd never be clean again. He scared me. No, he petrified me.

'Jude, how're you feeling?'

'Jude, are you guilty?'

'Would you like to make a statement, Jude?'

He pulled away from the prison guard, who was trying to get him to move forward, and turned to face the horde of journalists pushing TV cameras and microphones in his face.

'Is this going out live?' he asked.

'Yes.'

My heart began to thump painfully in my chest. This was it. What would Jude do now?

'I'd just like to say one thing,' Jude began. 'I didn't kill Cara Imega. As God is my witness, I'm completely innocent. Yes, I did know her— she was a good friend—but Persephone Hadley, the daughter of Kamal Hadley, knows I didn't kill Cara. Yes, I was at Cara's house on the night in question, but then Sephy and a friend of hers came to call for me and Cara was alive when Sephy and I left Cara's house. Me and Sephy were together until well into the early hours of the morning—so I couldn't've done it.' Jude turned from the journalists before him to look directly into the TV camera. It was like he was looking directly at me with only the glass of the TV screen separating us. 'Sephy, why won't you come forward and tell the authorities the truth? I can't believe you'd let me hang for something I didn't do.'

I felt sick, gut-wrenchingly sick. What acting. Jude lied so convincingly, with just the right amount of angry bewilderment as to persuade anyone watching that he was telling the

334

absolute truth. And who was this fictitious friend I was supposed to have turned up with? Why invent someone else to complicate matters?

'What did you and Sephy do when you left Cara Imega's house?'

Jude sighed. 'We walked and talked—mostly about my brother, Callum. We'd both decided to put the past behind us and fight to have his name cleared posthumously. He shouldn't've been hanged. You Crosses seem determined to wipe out my entire family.'

'Is Persephone Hadley your alibi, Jude?'

'Yes, I guess she is.' Jude spoke into the bank of microphones around him as he was pulled forward by one of the guards, 'I wish she wasn't because she hasn't come forward. But Sephy knows I didn't do this. I couldn't kill anyone.'

'Why d'you think she hasn't come forward?'

Jude sighed deeply again. He had the sighing act down pat. 'I honestly don't know. The only thing I can think of is that she's covering up for her friend, who we left behind at Cara's house. But I can't believe she'd let me swing for something she knows I didn't do.'

It was like my mind was closing in on itself, shutting down. I could see, hear and breathe—all the basics—but that was it. Jude's guard started pulling him forward, more urgently this time.

'Jude, d'you know who *did* kill Cara?'

Jude pulled away from his guard to turn and

face the journalists again. 'Yes, I do. It was the man Sephy brought to Cara's house. His name's Andrew Dorn. He was left in Cara's house after me and Sephy left. He asked Cara if he could make a phone call because the battery in his mobile was dead. Cara was more than happy to let him use her phone, so Sephy and I left him to it. Andrew Dorn is the one who should be behind bars, not me.'

'You're convinced it was him?'

'I know it was him. Sephy already told me that Andrew Dorn works undercover for her father Kamal Hadley, but I've only just learned that Andrew Dorn is not just a member of the Liberation Militia but also one of its leaders. He's obviously some kind of double agent but I have no idea why he killed Cara. Maybe she overheard something she shouldn't whilst he was on the phone? All I know is, he did it, not me.'

I gasped—and I wasn't the only one. Camera flashes were going off so fast they looked like fireworks. I felt like a juggernaut had just flattened me. How had Jude learned about Andrew Dorn working for my father? I groaned as I realized. I'd told Callum after . . . after I escaped from him and the others in the L.M. when they kidnapped me. Callum must've told his brother before he died. And in one deft move, Jude had signed Andrew Dorn's death warrant. Andrew would have nowhere left to hide after this. He was as good as dead already. He'd be of no further use to the

336

Secret Services, in fact he could be a major embarrassment. And the Liberation Militia would execute him for sure for betraying them. Jude had not only managed to wriggle off the hook and put Andrew on it, but he'd handled it so I looked like a coward and a betrayer myself. Jude was slicker than olive oil on ice. He'd set up both Andrew and me without even breaking a sweat.

'Whichever way you look at it, Andrew Dorn is a traitor and a murderer,' Jude continued. 'I don't know whether he's working for the L.M. and betraying the government, or vice versa. But I do know he's the one who killed Cara. The authorities must know he's the one who did it, so they must be covering up for him because he's their spy in the L.M. But I won't let them hang me for something I didn't do. Not without a fight—'

Jude was bundled into a security van and the doors slammed firmly behind him. The TV journalist turned to face the camera, still looking stunned, her microphone in her hand.

'There you have it,' she began. 'Jude McGregor's sensational statement about the death of Cara Imega. He categorically denies murder and has protested his innocence by giving us the name of the alleged real murderer. No doubt the police will be trying to find this man Andrew Dorn just as quickly as possible. This has been an astonishing—'

I pressed the button on the remote control to switch off the TV. I sat in the roaring silence

337

as my heart thundered inside me. The sound of my fear was deafening. My mouth began to fill with cool, thin bile. I jumped up and rushed to the toilet, only just in time to vomit up what felt like everything I'd eaten in the last week. As I washed my mouth and hands, myriad thoughts crashed and smashed their way through my head. I'd deny it. I'd deny everything. But then I thought of the three newspapers and the radio station I'd contacted. I'd been recorded and taped saying pretty much what Jude had just said, even if none of them had used the story.

But I had no doubt that that was all about to change.

With my help, Cara Imega's murder was going to go unpunished.

With my help, Cara Imega's murderer was going to get away with it.

With my help, Meggie McGregor wasn't going to lose her son.

With my help, Andrew Dorn was a marked man. He'd be looking over his shoulder for the rest of his life.

My debt to Meggie was repaid in full. Because of me, Callum had died. Because of me, Jude was going to live.

I looked down at my hands, palms up, fingers splayed. But it wasn't water dripping down into them. My hands were awash with blood.

BLUE

Waiting

Watching

Secrets

Cold Blood, Old Blood

Tasteless

Peaceful Seas

Cold Fish

Ice

Tasteless

Whispers

Foetal Position

Fire

Blue Aquamarine Purple Navy

Icy

Dying

THE DAILY SHOUTER

www.dailyshouter.news.id   Friday 10th September

ANDREW DORN IS DEAD

BY MINERVA HADLEY

Andrew Dorn, the man accused by Jude McGregor of the murder of Cara Imega, was found dead yesterday afternoon. In an ironic twist he was found with a single bullet wound to the back of his head in Turncoat Street off A404 in Archwell.

A police spokesman said, 'This is a classic style of execution as carried out by the Liberation Militia. We in the police will leave no stone unturned in our efforts to track down the killer of Andrew Dorn and bring him or her to justice.'

In an excusive interview, Kamal Hadley told me, 'Jude McGregor may not have pulled the trigger, he's the one responsible for Andrew Dorn's death. The man never stood a chance once Jude denounced him as working for the government. And the worst thing of all is, Jude will get away with it. We can't touch him for this.'

Jude McGregor, who was originally arrested for the murder of Cara Imega, had the murder charge against him dropped due to 'lack of evidence.' The case against him fell apart when Persephone Hadley sensationally provided Jude with an alibi for the night of Cara Imega's death. Persephone Hadley is currently residing with Jude's mother in Meadowview. Jude was not given his freedom, however, as he is still being held on the charge of belonging to the Liberation Militia, which carries a maximum penalty of two years in prison. A police spokesman said *(continued on page 4)*

fifty-nine. Jude

Happy days are here again! I'm no longer charged with murdering . . . that Cross woman. The case against me has fallen apart like a snot-filled tissue. Crossmas has come early this year. And Luke, a fellow Liberation Militia inmate, has told me that I'm being welcomed back into the open arms of the L.M.

I feel like I've been invited back home. And it's great.

They're not letting me out of prison though. They couldn't dig up enough evidence to get me on the charge of kidnapping Sephy, either, but they didn't give up. They've now got me for belonging to the L.M. which carries an automatic sentence of two years in jail. I have no doubt that I'll be found guilty of that one. They're desperate to get me for something. But with good behaviour, I'll be out in six to eight months. Even the prospect of spending the next few months in prison can't stop me smiling. I bought the *Daily Shouter* this morning and the headline has had me grinning so hard all day that my lips are beginning to ache.

Andrew Dorn is dead.

Things couldn't've worked out better. One down, only Sephy and her daughter to go. And the only dead fly in my potato and leek soup is the fact that Sephy is living with my mum. I

343

still can't believe that. I didn't know till I saw Sephy and my mum on the TV. Still, all this publicity should guarantee that she has to move on. She'll have no friends after this—on either side. Her fellow Crosses will blame her for giving an alibi to a nought accused of the murder of a Cross. They'll say she's betrayed one of her own. And noughts will hate her for not coming forward as my alibi sooner, when she had the chance. In fact, if she hadn't given a newspaper and a radio interview before I told the press my story, I doubt if she'd've said another word about it. I think she'd've denied it all if she could've—but she was too late. Thank God. I watched on the TV in prison as the newspapers and TV cameras camped on my mum's doorstep, desperate for an interview after my revelations, but Sephy never said a word. She didn't corroborate or deny my story. But then she didn't have to. Her previous interviews had done the job for her. And although she never actually mentioned Andrew Dorn in any of the interviews she gave before my heartbreaking tale of injustice was broadcast, it didn't matter. The press kept asking her about Andrew Dorn. As far as they and everyone else was concerned, Sephy knew him, had left him at Cara's house and had then kept quiet after Cara's death to cover it up. She was guilty by association. Not that any of the reporters got very far with Sephy. Every question thrown at her was met with a stony silence. A telling, damning silence.

A silence which brought a grin to my lips and joy to my heart. I've got you, Sephy. And this is just the start. I've got you.

I hope you're proud of me, Callum.

I did it all for you.

Andrew Dorn has paid for betraying us. And no matter where Sephy goes now, she'll be alone and despised by everyone she meets. And best of all, I'll still have my vengeance against her when I come out. I couldn't've asked for a better outcome.

And although it's not enough, it sure is close.

sixty. Sephy

'D'you like this one, Rose?'

'Yyang yyang!' Rose told me.

'I quite agree,' I smiled, putting the orange sleepsuit back on the rack. Orange was not Rose's colour. It didn't suit her, but it was the only colour that didn't.

We were out shopping for new clothes for Rose because she was putting on weight like nobody's business. It was the first time in a long time that Rose and I had been out together with nothing to do but enjoy each other's company. And after everything that'd happened recently, I didn't want to be around anyone else. I didn't have that right. I'd re-enter the world when the photo of Cara Imega that'd been in the papers stopped dancing

345

before my eyes. When the memory of how I'd helped her murderer get away with it stopped slashing at my mind and haunting my dreams, then and only then would I be ready to rejoin the human race. But in the meantime I had to carry on for Rose's sake. I didn't have that much money but I had enough to buy a couple of things. When I used to have money, I never noticed the price of anything. Now I studied the price of everything. And I couldn't remember the last time I'd bought myself any clothes. Not that I was ever into that kind of stuff, but it would've been lovely to have had the choice financially. I kissed Rose's forehead before placing her back in the baby carrier I had strapped around my body. I put her facing forwards so she could give me her opinion of the clothes I was selecting for her. Ensuring the straps around us both were secure and that Rose was comfy, I picked up another sleepsuit set which caught my eye. I kissed Rose on the top of her head. I couldn't help it. Maybe I'd get the hang of this motherhood lark yet. Maybe. When I stopped feeling so wretched and worthless.

'How about these, Rose? They're lovely, don't you think?' This set was so pretty. There was a vivid red sleepsuit with blue flowers, a yellow one with red flowers and a dark-blue one with yellow flowers.

'Yyangga!' Rose gurgled.

'You've got good taste, sweet-pea,' I told her.

'You're Persephone Hadley, aren't you?'

346

At the sound of my name, I spun round—and then instantly wished I hadn't.

'It *is* you, isn't it?' said the middle-aged woman behind me.

And if looks could kill, I'd've been cold on the floor with a chalk outline around my body.

'Thanks to you, that murderer Jude McGregor is going to get away with killing one of us,' the woman hissed at me. 'Not that you care—blanker-lover.'

I put the sleepsuit back on the rack and tried to walk away, but she grabbed my arm and swung me round. Others were beginning to gather round now. My face had been all over the newspapers over the last few days, but I really hadn't expected to be identified. Out of the corner of my eyes I could see that others were beginning to recognize me. One hand stole protectively around Rose. I didn't say a word. What was there to say?

'That's her . . .'

'That's the one . . .'

'Kamal Hadley's daughter . . .'

'Is that Callum McGregor's baby? You know, the terrorist they hanged . . .'

And more. And worse. And on and on.

'My husband is a policeman,' the woman who'd started all this told me. 'He says everyone knows Jude McGregor killed that girl. But thanks to your lies muddying the waters, no way could they get a conviction now.'

The evidence was all circumstantial,

otherwise both Jude and I would be in court by now. The police had no conclusive evidence, no blood, no DNA, just fingerprints. But I only thought that. I didn't say it.

'D'you really hate your own kind so much?' a Cross man with his Cross girlfriend asked me.

'I feel sorry for that child,' said another, pointing at Rose. 'With a mother like you, she doesn't stand a chance.'

And more. And worse. And on and on.

I started to walk but there was no safe, clear direction. They were all around me.

'Excuse me, please.' I tried to move past the police officer's wife but she wouldn't move.

If I hadn't had my daughter with me, I'd've made her move. But then, if I hadn't had my daughter with me, they would've aimed more than barbed words at my body. I pushed past her, and this time, reluctantly, she let me pass.

'Blanker-lover!'

'Scum . . .'

'Slag . . .'

'Skank . . .'

Rose started to cry.

'It's OK, baby,' I whispered in her ear. 'It's OK.'

But it wasn't. And my tears falling on her forehead probably told her that more clearly than anything else I could've said or done. They were right. I wasn't any kind of mother. Rose would be better off without me. Rose deserved to be happy. And with me, she wouldn't be. How could she be with me?

I had to make sure she was happy.
I'd failed miserably in everything else.
In that one thing at least, I had to succeed.

INDIGO

Anticipation

Revenge, retribution

Contemplation

False divisions

Nighttimes

Darkness

Absence of light

Illusions

Delusions

Tricks in the Dark

Blazing

Buried

Stillness

Purple

Sacrifice

Nought Education 'a flop'

The long-awaited report into the educational achievements of both nought and Cross children was published yesterday after a two-month delay. For those who have always supported the idea of noughts and Crosses being educated together, it made disappointing reading. The report showed that nought children do worse at school than their Cross counterparts, with nought boys doing worst of all.

Sofia Taylforth, Minister of Education, stated, 'Noughts have enjoyed the same educational opportunities as Crosses for only a few years. It's unrealistic to expect great strides in educational achievement after such a short space of time. Yes, it is disturbing that nought children do less well in integrated schools than in nought-only schools and it's especially regrettable that nought boys in particular seem to fare less well, but it is simplistic to conclude that nought children are less able than Cross children because of it. Teacher expectations, teaching methods, parental support, home environment, peer group pressure and a host of other factors all have to be taken into account. We in the government will be studying this report in far greater depth before we reach any conclusions.'

Cedric Hardacre, backbench MP, told the *Daily Shouter*, 'This report just proves what I've said all along. The integration of our schools just doesn't work. It's time for an honest debate on the subject without the knee-jerk reaction of those who speak out against integration being called racists and segregationists.'

Cedric Hardacre has also spoken out against inter-racial marriage and spoken for the repatriation of noughts back to their country of origin.

sixty-one. Jasmine

'Sephy, listen to me. You mustn't let all this get you down. I know it's easier said than done, but you've got to ease up on yourself.'

'Yes, Mother.'

There it was again, that flat, dead tone to her voice. It matched the look in her eyes. I wanted to grab her and shake her or hug her— anything to bring back my original Sephy. Not this sorrowful, hurting girl before me.

'How's Callie?' I asked.

'She's fine. I'm sorry I haven't been to see you this week . . .'

'Sephy, I know you've had other things on your plate. And although I appreciate you coming to see me every week, it doesn't mean that I can't ever come and see you.'

Sephy shrugged. 'I didn't think you'd be comfortable travelling around here.'

I shook my head. Sephy had a strange idea about me. Did she really think I was some delicate flower who only had to step out of my house to wither? Didn't she understand that I would travel to anywhere on the planet to be with her if she needed me?

'Sephy, would you like to come home with me for a while?'

When Sephy began to shake her head, I rushed on. 'I don't mean to live. I know you'd rather stay with Meggie. But just for a while. I can shield you from the reporters and the TV cameras. They won't get past my security.'

'But you can't shield me from how people think and feel about me, Mother,' said Sephy sadly. 'Most people think he did it, and thanks to me, he got away with it. And the ones who truly believe he's innocent despise me for not stepping up and telling the police he was with me on the night Cara Imega died.'

'I don't give a damn about other people,' I told her. 'My only concern is you and Callie Rose.'

Sephy looked at me, the merest trace of a smile playing across her lips. 'Thanks.'

'I mean it, Persephone. My home is open to you, any time, day or night. You don't even have to ask.'

Sephy nodded, her head bent. Then she looked up and asked, 'D'you think Jude did it?'

'I don't know enough about the case to make an informed judgement, one way or another,' I told her   carefully. I'd learned from my mistakes on that score at least.

Sephy nodded again, but didn't reply.

'Sephy, love, I'm worried about you. Are you all right?'

Sephy shook her head. 'No, but I will be.'

I looked at her, and I wasn't so sure. Sephy was always so ready to face life and come out fighting, but now she just looked totally worn down and worn out. The spark inside her had been extinguished.

'How's Minerva?'

My glance fell away from Sephy's. I realized at once that I shouldn't've done that. I should've looked her in the eye.

'Does she hate me?'

'She's a bit upset,' I said carefully. 'But she'll get over it.'

'I doubt it,' sighed Sephy. 'Did she tell you why she's mad at me?'

'Not really,' I admitted. 'She said she told you something in confidence and you used it. Against her?'

'I didn't use it against her,' Sephy denied. 'I used it against myself maybe, but not against her. Did I get her into trouble?'

'She's still got her job—just—if that's what you mean,' I said. 'She reckons no one but her knows for sure where you got your information from. But her boss did ask some searching questions. Minnie's afraid she might not get another front page for some time.'

'I wouldn't blame her if she did hate me,' said Sephy.

And what could I say to that? Nothing.

'Can I tell you something?' Sephy said after a long pause.

'I'm listening.'

'I . . . I love you, Mother. You know that, don't you?' Sephy said unexpectedly.

My eyes immediately began to water. I looked away and pinched the bridge of my nose the way I always did when I had the beginnings of a headache, but it did no good.

The tears still threatened. I took out a tissue and blew my nose. 'The pollen's driving me mad,' I muttered.

When my eyes cleared of tears, Sephy was smiling at me.

She looked at me like she was drinking me in for the first and last time. I don't know how else to explain it. She had a look on her face like she was saying goodbye.

'Sephy, darling, please let me help you,' I pleaded.

'No, Mother. You can't do anything for me now,' said Sephy softly. 'No one can.'

sixty-two. Meggie

I'm so worried about Sephy. Since that business in the shopping centre, she's hardly said a word. She just sits in her room or in the living room, holding Callie in her arms like she's afraid to let her go. And the look on her face scares me. So sad it breaks my heart. So set, it turns me to stone as I look at her.

The sorrow inside her is locked in with no way out. And each setback, each word just pushes her down further to where it's harder to reach her. I phoned my doctor and he came to see Sephy at my request. Sephy didn't say a word to me about it. She let the doctor examine her and answered his questions, but she didn't shout at me for interfering the way I thought she would. She didn't storm at me for not minding my own business. She didn't rant and rage like I wanted her to, like I hoped she would.

Sephy didn't say a word.

Doctor Mossop told Sephy and me that Sephy was suffering from post-natal depression and he prescribed fresh air, exercise, mother and baby clubs and some mild tranquillizers. Sephy hasn't had any of them. She nodded and said, 'Yes, Doctor,' as appropriate but the moment he left, his prescription went straight in the bin. I fished it out and filled it out at the local chemist, then I put the tranquillizers on Sephy's bed where she couldn't fail to see them. An hour later I found the unopened bottle in the bin. That's when I gave up. I can't force the things down her throat and, to be honest, I'm not convinced they're what she needs anyway. Tranquillizers and sedatives get a lot of people through the day when there's nothing else on the menu, but Sephy has a beautiful daughter and everything to live for. I just wish I knew what to do to make her see that.

Jaxon came round yesterday afternoon with Sonny and Rhino. The moment I opened the door, I knew it wasn't good news.

'Is Sephy in?' Jaxon asked.

As Sephy was coming down the stairs behind me holding Callie, the question was unnecessary.

'Sephy, can we talk to you?' asked Sonny.

Sephy indicated the living room before following after them. I dithered for a few moments, wondering whether I should leave them to it or be nosy and go into the living room as well. After everything that'd happened, I decided on the latter.

As I entered the room, Sephy had moved to stand by the window. She still held Callie in her arms and the afternoon sunlight streaming through my windows made it seem like Sephy and Callie had some kind of golden halo around them. Just at that moment, Sephy looked stunningly beautiful—like one of those Madonna and child pictures painted by a Renaissance artist. Sonny, Jaxon and Rhino stood in my living room, looking at each other. Rhino, who I understood from Sephy scarcely ever said a word, walked over to Sephy and put a hand on her shoulder. She turned round, surprised.

'Sephy, I want you to know this isn't my idea,' he said softly.

Sephy turned round to face Jaxon and Sonny then. I stood forgotten by the door.

'D'you have something you want to say, Jaxon?' Sephy asked.

'Sephy, we can't have you in the band any more—at least not for a little while. No one will hire us whilst you're our singer.'

Sephy didn't say a word.

'It's not a permanent thing,' said Sonny. 'It's just until the fuss dies down.'

Rhino looked at Jaxon and Sonny with

disgust before turning to Sephy. 'They're afraid we'll all get lynched if you get up on stage with us. They think you're in no man's land and they're afraid of being dragged there with you.'

'And what d'you think, Rhino?' asked Sephy.

'I think they're full of crap, but I've been outvoted.'

Sephy stroked Rhino's cheek, her fingertips light on his skin. 'Thanks,' she said, smiling as a deep red spread over his face.

I thought Sephy had said Rhino was the one who resented her the most in the band. I'm sure she told me he'd said barely five sentences to her since she joined them. I must've got that wrong.

'Sonny, d'you agree with Jaxon?' Sephy asked, looking directly at him.

To my surprise, Sonny's face instantly flamed red. His gaze skittered away from Sephy's as he searched for the right thing to say.

'It's only for a little while,' he mumbled. 'Maybe you could still rehearse with us . . .'

'I see,' was all Sephy said.

'There's no reason why we couldn't still see each other,' Sonny appealed. 'All of us. We still . . . I still want you . . . with us.'

'But not enough to stand by me,' said Sephy evenly.

'It's nothing personal,' Jaxon tried.

'It never is.' Sephy shrugged. 'But don't worry, I understand.'

'When the whole thing has blown over then

361

we'd gladly have you back,' Jaxon said, a trace of desperation in his voice.

'Could you all leave now, please?' said Sephy. 'I'm very tired.'

Sephy turned to carry on looking out of the window. I immediately moved forward to show the gutless wonders out of my house.

'If she'd just let us explain,' Jaxon said to me in the hall.

'Me and Sephy understand perfectly,' I told him as they all headed out of the door. 'At least Sephy knows who her friends are.'

'You have to see it from our side,' said Sonny.

'No, I don't. You didn't even have the courtesy to ask Sephy if she did the things she's accused of,' I told them with disgust.

At least Sonny had the grace to look ashamed. Jaxon pursed his lips and got a set to his jaw like a sulky school kid. Here was a boy who needed an attitude adjustment clap and no mistake and my hand itched to give it to him.

I turned to the other man. 'You're Sonny, aren't you?' I asked, before I offloaded onto the wrong person.

The guy before me nodded.

'I thought you and Sephy were the closest in this so-called group of yours,' I said.

'We are. We were—' Sonny began.

'And this is how you show it? When the going gets tough, the weak run for the hills, is that it?'

'You're not being fair. It's just until this all blows over . . .' Sonny's weak protest trailed off into nothing.

'One day someone's going to stab you through the heart the same way you're doing to Sephy,' I told him straight. 'Although in your case it'll be easy, you not having any backbone to get in the way.'

Jaxon glared at me. Rhino scowled at Jaxon and Sonny. Sonny looked me straight in the eye, with not a hint of an excuse on his face. I'll say one thing for him, he took what I dished out.

'You can all get out now. And don't bother coming back.'

They trooped out in silence. I slammed the door on the lot of them. Newspaper reports and magazine articles have all blasted poor Sephy. Her mother's been round and told Sephy to hold her head high no matter what. I think Sephy heard that, at least. But she won't discuss what she thinks or how she feels. And she washes her hands a lot. Before and after meals. Even before picking up Rose.

This morning, I asked, 'Sephy, when are we going to sit down and talk about Jude?'

'Your son isn't going to hang for Cara Imega's murder. What else is there to say?' Sephy asked.

And after that she didn't say a word. She looked down at Callie in her arms, that strange, blank, unblinking look on her face.

I'm worried.

363

I'm more than worried.
I'm scared.

sixty-three. Jasmine

I feel like such a failure. Sephy is hurting so much and I don't know what to say to her. I don't know how to reach her. And I'm afraid. Minerva's always been the strong one, the one who lands on her feet no matter what. But Sephy . . . Sephy lives by her heart, not her head. I let her go to Chivers boarding school because I thought some time away from home would help her to toughen up. She'd have to rely on herself and no one else. I thought she'd learn something about people and life away from the narrow circle of her friends at Heathcroft High. And it did work.

Until that boy showed up again. Until he tricked Sephy into meeting him just so he could kidnap her with his other Liberation Militia friends. I still don't understand how Callum could've done it. He was supposed to love my daughter and yet he could do that to her. He kidnapped her and victimized her and had sex with her. Sephy insisted that Callum didn't force her but that's not the point. She was vulnerable and he knew that and yet he still took advantage.

That's supposed to be love?

Now look at her.

Vilified and ridiculed and unable to set foot outside her house without some idiot or other making her life a misery. And it's all thanks to that boy Callum. I love my granddaughter very much, she's very precious to me—but so is my daughter. And I watch Sephy's eyes permanently shrouded in pain as I speak to her and I see her shoulders drooping and her head bowed and I can't do a single thing to change it. I'd give my life if it'd help Sephy to find some kind of peace but it doesn't work that way. Sephy is heading for some kind of breakdown—Meggie and I are both agreed on that at least. But Sephy won't get help and she's so notorious now, she's afraid to set foot outside Meggie's front door.

I'd like to take Jude McGregor and wring his scrawny neck for what he's done to Sephy and his niece. I know everything he said about Sephy was a lie. What I don't understand is why she won't come right out and say so? Why won't she defend herself? What hold does he have over her?

I've tried phoning Kamal about Sephy but he's too busy to be interested. He has his new wife and family now. We're yesterday's news. I don't care about that so much—I'm getting over him. But I do mind for my daughter's sake. And Sephy was so close to her father. How could he just abandon her like this? Sephy is like a ship without a rudder. She's trying to do everything alone, by herself, and it's too much.

If she doesn't get help soon, I'm afraid of what will happen to her. All I can do is make sure that she knows I'm here for her.

I just wish I'd let her know that sooner.

VIOLET

Death

Sounds like Violence

Sounds like Violates

Sounds like Music

Sombre

Coldness

Emptiness

Promises

Flowers in the Rain

Acceptance of Pain

Silence

Peace

THE DAILY SHOUTER

www.dailyshouter.news.id   **Thursday 23rd September**

Cedric Hardacre, MP,

caught with nought prostitute

BY JON GRESHAM

The career of Cedric Hardacre, MP, was thought to be all but over when it was revealed by his estranged wife that he had been regularly visiting a nought prostitute for almost a year. Mrs Hardacre called a press conference where she revealed her husband's lover to be Edwina Hewitt of Granada Street, Hackton Palace.

'I know a lot of people will think I'm revealing this to be vindictive,' Mrs Hardacre went on to say. 'But that's not the case. Cedric is a Member of Parliament who won his seat on the back of advocating racial intolerance against the noughts. His hypocrisy is astounding. He speaks out against inter-racial marriage and integration on our schools but he's still for inter-racial bedroom antics. Well, it's not on.'

Cedric Hardacre had no comment to make when we caught up with him in his town flat yesterday evening. But Edwina Hewitt told a close friend, 'Both Cedric and I saw this as strictly business. I can't see what all the fuss is about. He's just another punter as far as I'm concerned.'

sixty-four. Sephy

Rose, you're so lovely. Too lovely for all this violet around you. You deserve better. You deserve more. I've put you in my favourite of all your dresses. It's the cream-coloured satin one with silk ribbons across the bodice and the long, puffed sleeves. Nana Jasmine bought you that dress. My mother always did have good taste. The dress looks so beautiful against your beige skin. You're so beautiful. I look at you, drowning in your blue-brown eyes, and even now I can't believe I made something so precious. Meggie has gone shopping and we're all alone in the house. And I'm grateful for the solitude. I smile as I watch you chew on your fist with toothless gums. You're dribbling all over your hand and all over me. I can't help but smile.

'I love you, Rose. I want you to be happy,' I whisper. 'It's what you deserve.'

And you could be happy, we could both be happy if people would just leave us alone. But that's never going to happen.

I know that now.

This world was never meant for someone as beautiful as my baby. I gather you into my arms and take you downstairs to the living room. You begin to grizzle. I kiss your forehead and your nose and your lips.

'Hush, my darling. Mummy loves you very

much. More than life itself,' I whisper in your ear. 'It's my birthday today, Rose. And I want to make it a special day. A day just for you.'

In the background, on the radio, as if on cue, *Rainbow Child* begins to play. I smile at you, you smile at me. I hold you to me, hug you to me so that your face is against me, as close to my heart as I can get you. You begin to whimper. I'm holding you too tight. I'm sorry, darling. But I can't let you go. I don't know how. I start to sing along to the radio, very softly.

You bring a sweet embrace
And with the smile upon your face
You bring me grace, my rainbow child.
You bring me autumn days,
Turn my face to golden rays,
You bring me bliss, my rainbow child.

And what was life before you?
And do you know how I adore you?
And it scares me how I feel,
All my past scars fade and heal
When I hold my rainbow child.

You bring a quiet time,
Life has meaning, thoughts have rhyme,
You bring me peace, my rainbow child.
You bring down all my fences,
You invade my heart and senses,
You bring me hope, my rainbow child.

And what was life before you?
And do you know how I adore you?
And it scares me how I feel,
All my past scars fade and heal
When I hold my rainbow child.

Take a look,
Stop and stare,
Love is shining,
Everywhere.
There is nothing
Left to fear,
I am with you
Always near
And if this world should make me bleed
I'll remember you're all I need.

You bring the blinding light,
You bring the stars at night,
You bring me love, my rainbow child.
You're all the colours that I see,
You mean everything to me.
Yes, you will always be, my rainbow child.

And what was life before you?
And do you know how I adore you?
And it scares me how I feel,
All my past scars fade and heal
When I hold my rainbow child.

By the time I stop singing, you've stopped whimpering. You're so quiet, Rose. So very quiet. Meggie steps into the room, a carrier bag full of shopping in each hand. I can hardly see her through the tears in my eyes. I try to get up but my legs won't work. I look down at you. You're so very quiet. So peaceful. The very thing I want for you.

Peace.

'Meggie,' I whisper. 'What should I do? Rose isn't breathing . . .'

sixty-five. Meggie

I run over to Callie and snatch her out of Sephy's unresisting hands. Callie's warm but as limp as a rag doll.

Oh my God . . . I can't speak. Words have fled, threatening to take my reason with them. Shock is numbing every part of me. But only for a moment—a moment that lasts as long as a life time. Now terror is threatening to overwhelm me. Callie . . . I force myself to think. Think. Think. I've got to get Callie breathing again.

Please, God,
I know you can hear me.
I hope you can hear me.
If you're even up there . . .

I place my mouth over Callie's nose and open mouth and exhale—forcing myself to be gentle and not do it too hard. She has only baby lungs. I could do more harm than good. I don't know what to do. Panic rises up like vomit. I force it back down. But it won't stay down. I'm shaking. Quaking. I move my face to suck air into my mouth, then I cover Callie's mouth and nose again. Exhale. Slowly, gently.

I place two fingers down on her chest and press with a slow, steady rhythm. Press for three. Breathe for three. Press for three. Breathe for three. Is this right? Am I doing this right? I don't even know. Should I press for four? Breathe for five? I don't know. I should know. After three kids of my own, I should know. But I don't.

Call an ambulance . . .

No time.

Callie's run out of time. We all have.

Please, God . . .

Come on, Callie darling, you can do it. Breathe, darling. Please breathe.

'Is she going to be all right?' Sephy whispers.

I turn to her, screaming, 'Sephy, what've you *done*? WHAT'VE YOU DONE?'

Sephy looks at me and her face crumples. But I don't care about that. I don't care about her. I turn away from her face, awash with tears. If I look at her, I'll kill her. Right this minute. Right this moment.

'Is she going to be all right?' Sephy cries out. 'Is my baby going to be all right?'

I carry on exhaling, trying to force air, trying to force life back into Callie.

Callie Rose, breathe for me, darling.

Beside me, Sephy makes a strange sound—a harsh, gurgling gasp. And there's such a odd note to it, almost like a crack. I glance at her. She looks down at her daughter with the saddest expression I've ever seen. Was the noise she made the sound of her heart breaking? I hope so.

'Go and phone for an ambulance,' I tell Sephy.

But she doesn't hear me. She looks at Callie without a word, without even blinking. But the silent tears spill over onto her cheeks and keep coming.

Come on, Callie. Take a breath. Don't give in.

Callum, if you're watching over us, if you ever loved Sephy, if you love your daughter, bring her back to us.

Bring her back.

Please bring her back.

'Sephy, what've you done?'

Callie Rose, breathe for me, darling.

Breathe.

BREATHE.

Breathe . . .